T0340614

RETHINKING
WORK

GLOBAL HISTORICAL

AND SOCIOLOGICAL

PERSPECTIVES

RETHINKING
WORK

GLOBAL HISTORICAL
AND SOCIOLOGICAL
PERSPECTIVES

Edited by
RANA BEHAL
ALICE MAH
BABACAR FALL

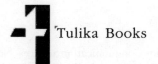 Tulika Books

Published by

Tulika Books
35 A/1 Shahpur Jat, New Delhi 110 049, India
in association with
International Research Centre
'Work and Human Lifecycle in Global History'
Humboldt University, Berlin, Germany

First published in India in 2011

© IGK Arbeit und Lebenslauf in globalgeschichtlicher
Perspektive, Humboldt-Universitat zu Berlin

ISBN: 978-81-89487-85-0

Typeset at Tulika Print Communication Services, New Delhi;
printed at Chaman Enterprises, Delhi 110 002

Contents

Acknowledgements

The editors acknowledge the generous support of the International Research Centre 'Work and Human Lifecycle in Global History' at Humboldt University, Berlin, in the organization of the international workshop on the 'Global History and Sociology of Work' in Berlin, and in the publication of this volume. We would like to extend particular thanks to Andreas Eckert, Felicitas Hentschke, Maïté Kersaint, Jutta Hägele,Constanze Röderstein, Stephanie Lämmert and Sebastian Marggraff at the International Research Centre in Berlin. We are grateful for the insightful comments and feedback on this collaborative project from Ravi Ahuja, Ineke Phaf-Rheinberger, Jan-Patrick Heiss, Paulette Reed Anderson, Aditya Sarkar, Michael Mann, Nitin Sinha, Vincent Houben, Patrick Harris and Therese Garstenauer. Thanks are also due to Tulika Books for their hard work and enthusiasm in publishing this volume.

Foreword

It is with much pleasure that I am writing the Foreword to this volume. The first versions of the papers collected in this book were presented at an international and interdisciplinary workshop held at the International Research Centre 'Work and Human Lifecycle in Global History', Humboldt University, Berlin. This Centre came into existence in 2009, within the framework of a grant format designed by the German Federal Ministry of Education and Research, both to promote internationalization of the humanities and to assure the necessary scope for innovative research. Among other things, the International Institutes for Humanities Research aim at enabling a learning community that questions its own assumptions by testing them through systematic confrontation with other cultures of knowledge. These institutes award one-year scholarships to internationally renowned scholars, enabling them to do their research work at German universities. The Institute in Berlin attempts to rethink the subject of 'work' from a global perspective and emphasizes the 'life course' aspect.

Actually, work defines an individual's status in many societies. The supposed clarity of the concept should not obscure the fact that 'work' encompasses an enormous spectrum of activities and concepts that are allied with various horizons of experience in time and space. However, the European discussion generally puts forward the use of a very limited definition of work: gainful employment which is more or less clearly distinguished from the sphere of the household. This definition is still used even though the separation between work and home no longer corresponds to what many individuals experience today, in contrast to the time when the modern work society used to be the incontestable model. Just consider, for example, the home–office debates or the monetization of educational work, to challenge this approach. Moreover, a historical and global perspective relativizes notions of life-long 'normal working conditions', which would seem to be increasingly threatened in industrial societies. Historically speaking, the 'normal' career for life is an exceptional situation that was a reality for only a small (predominantly male) minority of the gainfully employed. Research on work is ultimately strongly influenced by dichotomous conceptual binaries: industrial versus non-industrial, capitalist versus non-capitalist, liberal versus illiberal, natural versus artificial, nuanced versus primitive, the workaday world versus the everyday world. Still, concrete case studies from many parts of the world show variegated mixtures of these categories.

The Berlin Institute's focus on 'Work and Human Lifecycle in Global History' attempts a new approach that may lead to innovative, and perhaps even surprising, insights to the notion of work. Recently, the relation between 'life course' and 'work' has become increasingly popular in Germany in both the academic and journalistic fields, with respect to our concern with the opportunities and problems of ageing societies. On the one hand, the rapidly changing demographic situation has led to discussions of whether or not one's working life – which, until just a few years ago, was becoming shorter and shorter – can be expanded once again. Indeed, the manner and point at which one exits one's working life have become controversial topics. It is perfectly clear that the relationship between ageing and being active should be renegotiated; and the need for a new definition of the concept of work beyond 'gainful employment' has taken on renewed urgency. At the same time, the demand for an 'equalization' of particularly challenging phases of life against the backdrop of much-discussed demographic problems (low fertility, the multiple burdens shouldered by young families due to the intensive professional work of both partners, the raising of children, and care of the elderly), as well as the findings of behavioral scientific research in the last few years, have led to proposals to open up and make more flexible the traditionally firmly established and sharply delineated divisions of average working life into three phases: childhood/youth/education, working life, retirement.

It is in view of these facts that the Institute is undertaking a comparative investigation of precisely how the relationship between work and life course has been – and still is – linked in a variety of historical constellations ever since the rise of capitalism in the eighteenth century. Research and discussions at the Centre have the overarching goal to pursue the interrelationship between work and life course in order to arrive at a certain typology, and to determine the main trends as well as zero in on the present historical situation from a comparative and historical perspective. With the focus on work, age and social/generational justice, our Centre takes up a range of themes that at the moment are being discussed very intensively – particularly in increasingly ageing industrial societies. Indeed, little systematic work has been done on this topic from a comparative global and profoundly historical angle. The research carried out at the Institute is based on the structural hypothesis that the emergence of capitalism, industrialization and the social state, at least in the west, essentially changed the relationship between work and life course. Comparisons with non-European societies are obviously necessary to test and verify this hypothesis. New post-industrial models are currently looming in the transition towards a knowledge-based society, and in the face of new technical possibilities in bridging space and time. These models are clear and capable of interpretation only through a historical comparison that reaches back centuries. Among others, we are particularly interested in the following sets of questions.

- Are certain specific forms of work, or specific nexuses of work, non-work and other life expressions, typical for various ages in life – or at least believed to be so? Is the current disposition of life course normatively and practically defined through participation in various forms of work? How strongly is the apportionment of opportunities in life determined by work?
- Inter-generational relations are nodal points for the reproduction of societies, the placement of individuals in society, and the definition, realization or abuse of principles of social justice. What role does work play here, considering its various forms, allocations and results?
- Are the historically variable ideas and practices of work connoted in ways specific to certain ages in an individual's life? And if so, how does this change in the course of demographic, economic and cultural transformation? How gender-specific are these constellations?
- Does non-work always and everywhere define childhood and youth?
- How do work–biographical models develop between ongoing, continuous occupational processes, on the one hand, and, on the other hand, frequent shifts with many interruptions (patchwork)?

The central research focus is the overlapping sphere of life courses and households/families. Such a methodological approach enables sharply defined processing of the aforementioned sets of questions and thematic fields. Central to this is the question of the degree and kind of differentiation of 'work' from other life expressions considered from a conceptual and practical standpoint, and both these from a historical perspective. What was perceived as work, and what not?

I am very thankful to Alice Mah, Rana Behal and Babacar Fall – all three belonging to our first Fellow year – for having organized the conference that this publication has emanated from, and for having selected the papers to be included in this volume. This volume not only discusses some of our Centre's central research concerns in truly innovative ways; it also offers an excellent example of a fruitful cooperation between scholars of different generations as well as academic and regional backgrounds.

ANDREAS ECKERT
Director, International Research Centre
'Work and Human Lifecycle in Global History'
Humboldt University, Berlin

Contributors

Author of the Foreword

ANDREAS ECKERT is Director of the International Research Centre 'Work and Human Lifecycle in Global History' at Humboldt University, Berlin, and Professor of African History.

Editors

RANA BEHAL is Associate Professor at the Department of History, Deshbandhu College, University of Delhi, where he teaches Indian colonial history. He was Visiting Professor at Oberlin College, Syracuse and Cornell Universities (USA) in 2005, and a Fellow at Cambridge University (UK) and the International Research Centre 'Work and Human Lifecycle in Global History', Humboldt University, Berlin, in 2009–10. The focus of his research is the history of work in modern India, and his most recent book (forthcoming 2012) is on the history of tea plantations in colonial Assam.

ALICE MAH is Assistant Professor in Sociology at the University of Warwick, UK. She completed her Ph.D. at the London School of Economics, and has held post-doctoral research positions at Southampton University, the International Research Centre 'Work and Human Lifecycle in Global History' at Humboldt University in Berlin, and the University of Warwick. She is the author of *Industrial Ruination, Community and Place: Landscapes and Legacies of Urban Decline* (forthcoming 2012). Her research interests include the sociology of work, urban sociology, place memory and identity, socioeconomic change, and historical sociology.

BABACAR FALL is Head of the History and Geography Didactic Department at Cheikh Anta Diop University in Dakar, Senegal. He was a guest researcher at the Wissenschaftszentrum Berlin für Sozialforschung (Social Science Research Centre, Berlin) at Stanford University, and at the International Research Centre 'Work and Human Lifecycle in Global History' at Humboldt University, Berlin. He has recently completed a book project, titled *Senegal: The Labour Question in the Twentieth Century*. In 2008 he was awarded an honorary doctorate by the University of Le Havre.

Contributors

HEIKE DOERING is a researcher at the Wales Institute for Social and Economic Research Data and Methods (WISERD) at Cardiff University, UK. She studied British Cultural Studies, Law, Economics and History at the Technische Universitaet Dresden and Nottingham University, and completed a Ph.D. in Sociology at Cardiff University. She is currently involved in researching processes of socio-economic transformation in old and new industrial regions (UK and Brazil).

DENNIS GALVAN is Professor of International Studies and Political Science, and Co-Director of the Global Oregon Initiative, at the University of Oregon, USA. He was Fulbright Professor at Cheikh Anta Diop University in Dakar, Senegal, in 2009–10. Central to all of his work is a concern for how ordinary people adaptively transform the nation-state, markets, law, local government and natural resource management systems, to suit their changing and mutable notions of morality, heritage and identity.

STEVEN GASCOIGNE is based at the Sociology Department at the University of Warwick, UK, where he recently completed his Ph.D. on 'Managing Redundancy: a capability approach to a Swedish case study' (2010). His research interests are in social policy and the labour market.

OMAR GUEYE is Associate Professor at the History Department of the Faculty of Humanities, Cheikh Anta Diop University, Dakar, Senegal. His research work is devoted to an exploration of questions of labour and social conflicts in Senegal and former French West Africa, and their political implications in colonial and post-colonial states.

ABDOULAYE KANE is Assistant Professor of Anthropology and African Studies at the University of Florida, USA. He completed his Ph.D. in Sociology at the Amsterdam School for Social Science Research, University of Amsterdam. His research interests cover a variety of themes including African transnational migration, African diasporas in the west, gender and migration, migration and development, and transnational religious organization. He has published a number of articles and contributed book chapters on African migrants' social networks and their role in promoting local development.

MILENA KREMAKOVA is a Ph.D. student at Warwick University, UK. Her current research focuses on the social effects of post-socialist marketization of labour, and uses qualitative methods. Her academic background is in European Studies and Sociology.

SANTOSH KUMAR RAI is Assistant Professor in Modern Indian History and Early Modern European History at Sri Guru Tegh Bahadur Khalsa College, University of Delhi. He has also worked as a Research Associate in Modern Indian History at the Department of History, University of Delhi. His doctoral work is on the *julaha* (weavers) community of eastern Uttar Pradesh, India. His research interests include the social history of modern India and popular culture.

NICOLE MAYER-AHUJA is Director of the Sociological Research Institute (SOFI) at University of Goettingen, Germany. As a labour sociologist, her research interests include work, the utilization and reproduction of labour power, as well as social and labour market policy from a historical and transnational perspective.

JÜRGEN SCHMIDT studied History, Political Science and German language in Heidelberg, Innsbruck/Austria and Berlin, where he completed his Ph.D. He has worked in several exhibition and archival projects, as a researcher at the Social Science Research Centre, Berlin, and as postdoctoral fellow since 2009 at the International Research Centre 'Work and Human Lifecycle in Global History' at Humboldt University, Berlin. His research areas include the relationship between middle classes and working classes, civil society, food, and the history of medicine.

SHASHI B. UPADHYAY is Associate Professor at the Indira Gandhi National Open University, New Delhi. His publications include *Existence, Identity and Mobilization: The Cotton Millworkers of Bombay, 1890–1919* and a co-edited (with Imtiaz Ahmad) volume, *Dalit Assertion: Society, Literature and History*. He has also published several articles in the fields of labour history, Dalit studies and literary studies.

Introduction

Rana Behal, Alice Mah, Babacar Fall

Understanding 'Work'

Work is something that people across all cultures, nations and geographies experience and conceptualize, albeit in very different ways – as play, as economic necessity, as exploitation, as pride, as vocation. The subject of work in its diverse manifestations has been widely studied within different regional and national contexts, and within different traditions in western scholarship and South Asian and African studies including labour history, the sociology of work, the anthropology of work, the study of work and organizations, labour geography and gender studies. Some scholars prefer the term 'labour' to 'work', to emphasize the politics of productive work within the labour process, whereas others prefer to use the term 'employment' to separate paid from unpaid work.

In framing this book, we use the term 'work' to encapsulate a broader range of human activities across the globe as part of an attempt to break down binaries of waged and unwaged, formal and informal, and highly skilled and unskilled/low-skilled work. Our aim in focusing on 'work' is to generate rather than conclude discussions: while we have been careful not to depoliticize or obfuscate debates through language, contributors to this volume have used whichever term – work, labour, employment, occupation – suits their argument and their discipline.

The German scholar Jürgen Kocka argues that while the history of workers and the labour process have received much scholarly attention, the history of work, broadly defined, has been relatively neglected in modern history (Kocka 2010: 1). He claims that 'by dealing with the history of work in a general way, historians can relate to ongoing debates of the present time . . . [such as] . . . mass unemployment and the changing nature of work under the impact of globalization and computerization' (ibid). The present book takes up this challenge of addressing the broad subject of work both historically and in contemporary times. Engagement with history and sociology encourages us to break down both disciplinary and temporal dimensions, and to identify processes and trajectories of social and economic continuity and change. As Calhoun (2003: 383) argues, the 'most compelling reason for the existence of historical sociology . . . is the importance of studying social change'.

In this book, wide-ranging themes such as work transformations, working life cycles and trajectories, informalization of work, labour migration, precariousness of work and labour relations are studied with the aid of historical as well as contemporary case studies. Recent sociological enquiry has focused on the rise of 'flexible' or 'precarious' work under 'new capitalism', characterized by reduced job security, growth of the 'knowledge' and service economy, atypical work contracts and ever-changing working conditions (cf. Beck 2000; Gill and Pratt 2008; Sennett 1998). These transformations in the world of work have spatial implications as well, with the uneven clustering of different types of labour (irregular, manual, high skill, manufacturing, high technology *et al.*) in particular geographies (Harvey 1996; Hudson 2001; Massey 1995).

There is also a gendered dimension to work transformation: feminization of labour and the rising precariousness of labour tend to be interlinked within the literature on the advent of flexible employment practices in the 'knowledge' economy (Leadbetter 1998). The connections between feminization and precariousness, however, have often been assumed rather than studied, leading to misconceptions about both male and female employment (cf. Vosko 2000). Moreover, many sociological studies focus on precarious, irregular or informal employment as new trends in western industrialized countries and as 'typical' within the global South, rather than as a form of employment with a long, uneven and complex history around the globe.

Labour historians, particularly scholars working within the vibrant labour history tradition of South Asia and Africa (cf. Burawoy 2009; Freund 1984; van der Linden 2007), have traced similar issues – work transformations, patterns of labour migration, informalization, precarious work, labour conflict and deindustrialization – across different time-periods and geographies. *Labour Matters: Towards Global Histories* (van der Linden and Mohapatra 2009) makes the case for broadening the scope of labour history beyond the conventional binaries of space–time and the employer–employee relationship, as well as beyond the confines of the nation-state, in order to seek global comparisons. Similarly, this book addresses themes and issues of work and labour across time and space. This analytical move towards the global represents an attempt to break down the differences between relatively isolated discourses of work in western scholarship and industrialized societies on the one hand, and studies which focus on the global South, including South Asia and Africa, on the other. The book cannot claim to be truly global in the sense of speaking for all or even many voices and regions, but it aims to bring together different voices and distinctive perspectives from parts of Europe, Africa and Asia which hitherto have had little dialogue on the general theme of work.

The inspiration for this book was a two-day workshop held at the International Research Centre 'Work and Human Life Cycle in Global History', Humboldt University, Berlin, during the first year of the Centre's work. The workshop brought together interdisciplinary perspectives from different regions of the world including Europe, Africa and Asia, and provided a unique opportunity for researchers from diverse disciplines and regions to debate and discuss distinctive and common issues around work, life cycle, labour relations and work transformation from global historical and sociological perspectives. The book includes a selection of ten papers presented at the workshop, and is organized in three parts corresponding to three interrelated themes: (i) work and life cycle; (ii) work transformation, precarious work and labour migration; and (iii) labour conflict and relations.

Organization of the Book

The first part of the book consists of three essays on the theme of work and life cycle. These essays address different kinds of work (highly skilled information technology [IT] work in Germany and India; manual work in the shipbuilding industry in Sweden; and lowly/symbolically shameful manual work, often involving waste, undertaken by the Dalit castes in India), and are anchored in different socio-economic conditions (high-technology clusters of international companies in Germany and India, caste divisions in modern India and deindustrialization in Sweden). They set the stage for a consideration throughout the book of both individual and collective dimensions of work and life cycle, demonstrating how working people shape their own lives, and also how individual working lives are shaped and constrained by specific socio-economic, political and cultural contexts.

Nicole Mayer-Ahuja explicitly takes up the theme of work, life cycle and global comparison in her essay through an examination of the relationship between organization of work and the human life cycle in transnational collaborations in the software industry. Drawing upon intensive sociological case studies which focus on Indo-German teams employed by a German producer of standard software and an Indian provider of software services, her essay explores three interrelations: between global value chains and human life cycles; between work biographies and the transnational division of labour; and between life cycles and spatial/temporal rhythms of work. Mayer-Ahuja argues that in transnationally operating companies life cycles play a decisive role in shaping the terms and conditions of recruitment and employment strategies, transnational division of labour, and team cooperation.

A more individual and intimate perspective on life cycle is offered by Shashi Bhushan Upadhyay in his essay, focusing on experiences of work recorded in Dalit biographies and autobiographies. Poverty and low social status characterize a large part of the Dalit work force in both rural and urban areas. Work has always been an important component in the life of Dalits, as a majority of them have been involved in some form of manual work (often considered shameful and degrading) over the centuries. Yet the role of work in defining the experience of being Dalit has mostly been neglected. Upadhyay's essay attempts to fill this gap. It also explores the phenomenon of inter-generational changes among Dalits with respect to the kind of work they do, particularly brought about by mobility and modern education.

Steven Gascoigne looks at the impact of labour market policies on individual and collective lives in a case study of 'workfare' policies and discourses, in the context of deindustrialization in the Gothenburg shipyards in 1970s Sweden. He analyses an early example of a 'workfare' scheme in the country, and highlights the crucial role of officials and experts whose role it is to assess clients and design tailormade solutions for their re-entry into the labour market. Gascoigne demonstrates how this evaluative process can dictate what direction a client will take within a given policy, and also what options are and are not available in a wide range of auxiliary services in shaping the route back to work.

The second set of articles examines the processes of work transformation in the context of precarious work and informalization, both historically and in the present day. The first two papers on this theme examine the impact of socio-economic and political changes on working lives through the examples of post-socialist marketization in Bulgaria and industrial restructuring in late nineteenth- and early twentieth-century India. Milena Kremakova's essay explores the dramatic social effects of marketization, globalization and 'new managerialist' practices in the post-1989 Bulgarian maritime shipping industry. It focuses on issues of deskilling/deprofessionalization, broken career trajectories and the withering of work-based communities. She argues that the post-socialist marketization of labour in the European Union's (EU's) newest member-state has carried a high social price, creating precarious labour markets with ever-reducing social and economic security.

Santosh Kumar Rai offers a historical perspective on work transformation through an analysis of handloom weaving in a micro-region of India at the turn of the twentieth century. His essay argues that the work process in the handloom sector was produced by, and was a product of, changes in life cycle and social differentiation among local weavers' communities in the course of the nineteenth and twentieth centuries. The transformation of work was evident in the rapid internal differentiation among handloom weavers, with the emergence of the merchant artisan capitalist, on the one hand, and the loomless weaver, on the other.

The next two essays on the theme of work transformation explore the relationship between labour migration, precarious work, socio-economic change and individual life cycle. Dennis Galvin's essay explores labour, migration, family, community and crisis in Senegal. At one level his narrative is macroeconomic, set in the broad sweep of historical change, and rooted in large-scale movements of culture and society. At the same time, it is also centrally about individual lives, hopes and experiences. The article by Abdoulaye Kane also investigates the related themes of labour migration, precarious work and life course, drawing on both historical and contemporary trends. It examines how Haalpulaar labour migrants negotiated their socio-economic insertion in three different American cities, and the extent to which their previous experiences of intra-African migration were instrumental in their ability to successfully adapt in the United States.

The third and final theme of this book revolves around labour conflict and labour relations, drawing on historical and contemporary examples: militancy in British coalfields, late nineteenth- and early twentieth-century trade unions in Erfurt (Prussia/Germany), and the Inspection du Travail as an instrument of labour control in French West Africa. These themes, in some sense, are the traditional domain of labour history and study, with a focus on trade unions, workers' organizations, workers' voices and conflict; in other words, the politics of labour. With the cultural and postmodern turn, the rejection or avoidance of Marxian political economy by many social scientists and labour historians (but cf. Harvey 1996; Hudson 2001; Peck 2001), and the decline of manufacturing and trade unionism in many European countries, the landscape of labour politics has changed significantly. The case of labour militancy in British coalfields shows that labour politics along the lines of unions and communities have endured nonetheless, and the historical cases in Germany and West Africa show common themes of voice and visibility of labour as key issues in labour conflicts and relations.

The first essay on the theme of labour conflict and relations by Heike Doring analyses militant responses to deindustrialization in two British coalfields of Leicestershire and Kent. It examines changing labour identities in the context of resource mobilization for socioe-conomic transformation. Deindustrialization and responses to it have been understood as having various causes, consequences and time-scales. The question of place and local embeddedness of economic, social and cultural responses, however, has rarely been the focus of attention. Doring's paper deals with the locally specific trajectories of those involved in restructuring the social topography of places in transition.

The next two essays explore issues of institutional mediation, communication and organization, using the examples of trade unions in Erfurt (Germany/Prussia) and the Inspection du Travail in French West Africa. Juergen Schmidt analyses the possibilities and constraints of trade union organizations, using the local context of the Prussian town of Erfurt at the turn of the twentieth century as a starting point for developing global perspectives on labour relations. The essay argues that social contacts and communication – on the shop floor and outside the factory/enterprise – are decisive for engagement in unions. This analytical framework not only tells the 'success story' of European/German labour movements, but also dicusses the facet of exclusion (for instance, with respect to unskilled and female workers) which accompanied the rise of unions in the nineteenth century.

Omar Gueye examines the key role of the institution of Inspection du Travail in controlling, mediating and solving difficult labour conflicts in French West Africa. In the context of the tumultuous post-war period, African workers were involved in general strikes that mobilized African populations and threatened colonial power. The main aim of the Inspection du Travail during this period was to find solutions to social conflicts and to prevent disagreements.

A number of common themes and ideas emerged in the process of rethinking work through multiple lenses and frameworks. First, we identified a broader perspective on the relationship between work and life course – one that includes individual working lives, as well as larger embedded social and economic structures. Second, we highlighted the importance of values, discourses, judgements and categories of work. Third, we critically examined changing forms of work organization and employment relations both historically and in the present day, and the socio-political consequences of these changes. Fourth, we reflected upon ideas of entanglement evident in migrant labour patterns and working practices in different countries. Finally, we addressed the changing conceptualizations of labour history, the politics of labour, and the relationship between research and activism, over the course of the nineteenth, twentieth and twenty-first centuries. What emerged from the latter discussion was the notion of invisibility of labour as an enduring theme in labour history. This theme of visibility or invisibility – or the voice or voicelessness – of labour connects with the themes of how individual and collective working lives are shaped by socio-economic and political changes, and what is fought for or what is lost in changing definitions, experiences and imaginings of work.

References

Beck, U. (2000), *The Brave New World of Work*, Cambridge University, Cambridge.

Burawoy, M. (2009), 'The Global Turn: Lessons from southern labor scholars and their labor movements', *Work and Occupations*, vol. 36, no. 2, pp. 87–95.

Calhoun, C. (2003), 'Afterword: Why historical sociology?', in G. Delanty and E.F. Isin, eds., *Handbook of Historical Sociology*, Sage, London.

Freund, B. (1984), 'Labor and Labor History in Africa: A review of the literature', *African Studies Review*, vol. 27, no. 2, pp. 1–58.

Gill, R. and A. Pratt (2008), 'In the Social Factory? Immaterial labour, precariousness and cultural work', *Theory, Culture & Society*, vol. 25, nos. 7–8, pp. 1–30.

Harvey, D. (1996), *Justice, Nature, and the Geography of Difference*, Blackwell, Oxford.

Hudson, R. (2001), *Producing Places*, Guilford Press, New York.

Kocka, J. (2010), 'Work as a Problem in European History', in J. Kocka, ed., *Work in a Modern Society: The German historical experience in comparative perspective*, Berghahn, Oxford.

Leadbetter, C. (1998), 'Who Will Own the Knowledge Economy?', *The Political Quarterly*, vol. 69, no. 4, pp. 375–85.

Massey, D. (1995), *Spatial Divisions of Labour*, Routledge, New York.

Peck, J. (2001), *Workfare States*, Guilford Press, New York.

Perrons, D. (2005), *The New Economy and Earnings Inequalities*, Gender Institute, London.

Sennett, R. (1998), *The Corrosion of Character: The Personal Consequences of Work in the New Capitalism*, W.W. Norton, New York.

van der Linden, Marcel (2007), 'Labour History: The old, the new and the global', *African Studies*, vol. 66, nos. 2–3, pp. 169–80.

van der Linden, Marcel and Prabhu P. Mohapatra, eds. (2009), *Labour Matters: Towards global histories*, Tulika Books, New Delhi.

Vosko, L.F. (2000), *Temporary Work: The gendered rise of a precarious employment relationship*, University of Toronto Press, Toronto.

Work and Life Cycle

'I felt like a kid in front of them'
Work Organization and Human Life Cycle in Indo–German Software Programming

Nicole Mayer-Ahuja

In spring 2007, a 25-year-old Indian software engineer in Bangalore was asked if and how the German developers she cooperated with differed from her Indian colleagues. She said:

> They are actually all . . . old people. I think, they're all . . . they were no young crowd. All those were like 30 plus, 40 plus. And . . . whatever I spoke to them I got the impression that they study for some . . . till 27, 28 they study well. And then they start working. And they all were, like, working in the same things for some ten, twelve years. So they had all become experts in that. In one module itself, they're like working since some twelve, thirteen, fourteen years. So they were experts, and I felt like a kid in front of them.

Statements like this abound in the interview material gathered for a sociological study on Indo–German project work in the software industry.[1] Although the human life cycle was not originally the focus of our study, it soon became obvious that both Indian and German developers perceived the striking age difference between the information technology (IT) work forces in both countries as one of the most important factors influencing the terms and conditions of transnational cooperation at the team level. Thus this cooperation involves people not just from two different countries, but also from two distinct age groups. Consequently, it highlights the complex interrelations between the organization of work and the human life cycle which shape transnational work in the present period of increasing economic integration across world regions. Three aspects of this dynamic may be of specific interest, i.e. the interrelation betweens:

- global value chains and human life cycles;
- work biographies and the transnational division of labour; and
- life cycles and spatial and temporal rhythms of work.

---

[1] This project, funded by the German Research Foundation (DFG) between 2006 and 2009, was headed by V. Wittke and carried out by the author and P. Feuerstein. Empirical research was concentrated on four workshops where we conducted 68 interviews with workers and managers (of one-and-a-half to two hours duration each). Additionally, we talked to roughly thirty experts about the IT industry, and economic, social and labour market developments in India and Germany.

In this essay, each of these aspects will be briefly sketched out in order to enhance the discussion on transnational work from a life cycle perspective.

Age of the Sector – Age of the Work Force

When new regions are integrated into global value chains, transnational project teams often display a marked 'age gap'. Managers tend to explain this phenomenon with reference to structural differences between 'ageing societies' (in Europe or the US) versus 'growing societies' (in India or China), whose exploding 'young talent pool' many western companies wish to tap. A closer look, however, reveals that the overall age composition of a society does not have to be evenly reflected across the economy; instead, older workers may well be concentrated in some economic sectors and younger workers in others.

Among transnationally operating companies in the software industry, the average age of the work force is much higher in Germany than in India. One reason for this difference may lie in the history of regional software industries, since the average age of the work force in any economic sector seems to be influenced by the age of the sector itself in the region under concern. This argument obviously requires further empirical substantiation, but there is reason to believe that the average age of German software workers is higher because the software industry has built up (relatively stable) jobs in this country since the 1970s (Boes and Baukrowitz 2002; Boes and Trinks 2006); in India, on the other hand, the average age of the software sector work force is lower since most software companies have expanded only from the second half of the 1990s (Lakha 1994; Heeks 1996; Aspray, Mayadas and Vardi 2006; Upadhya and Vasavi 2006). In the process of corporate transnationalization, then, 'old' and 'young' industrial settings in different regions of the world get connected. This results in a characteristic 'age gap' between the respective work forces, even though different varieties of transnationalization have to be discerned (for an outline of the 'global shift' in software production, see Dicken 2007).

During the last decades, most transnationally operating companies were based in centres of capitalist production (especially in the United States, but also in Europe). Moreover, the big and well-established corporations, especially, experimented with far-reaching disintegration of value chains, splitting up production processes and distributing the tasks to subsidiaries or business partners often based in distant regions of the world (Lema and Hesbjerg 2003). At the home-base of such companies, the work force typically comprises different age groups since the staff has often been recruited over decades, and at least parts of the work force stay long-term. This is especially true of companies in Germany. The (West) German model of employment and professional qualification that was established after World War II implied that workers were recruited as apprentices, or after completing their university education, and stayed with a company for long, often until retirement (for Germany's 'productive model', see, for instance, Boyer *et al.* 1998). Over the years, such workers would broaden and especially deepen their knowledge, and slowly proceed along certain career tracks within corporate boundaries. This model of long-term employment in the same company can be traced back to the 1950s, a period of scarcity of labour and qualifications. However, since the German social security system with its strong emphasis on social insurance provisions favours permanent, full-time jobs, and since labour regulation (whether in the shape of labour law or collective agreements) connects many entitlements to the duration of employment (seniority), life-long 'standard employment' and permanent company affiliation are still widely considered as the norms of a proper, desirable working life, although these standards were never universal in a statistical sense and have been losing practical importance since the 1970s (Mückenberger 1985; Mayer-Ahuja 2003).

In the software industry, this model of transnationalization (i.e. corporate expansion from a home-base in capitalist centres to countries of the semiperiphery) was most prominent among producers of software packages such as Microsoft, SAP or Adobe (Boes and Schwemmle 2005). Many of these companies were established in the 1970s, when software was turned into a commodity in its own right; instead of being provided free as attachments to a hardware system designed for a specific customer, standard software packages could now be sold independently of hardware components and used on any personal computer.

The German producer of standard software labelled G-Pro (which was part of our sample), for instance, expanded its staff in Germany almost continually during the 1970s, 80s and 90s.[2] Employment was relatively stable until a new insecurity began to spread among German software companies around the turn of the millennium (Kämpf 2008). Consequently, G-Pro's work force today comprises almost all age groups up to the retirement level. There is one exception, however: in reaction to the worldwide IT industry crisis around the turn of the millennium, this software company (like many others) reduced recruitment in Germany. Instead, growing emphasis was put on establishing centres of research, development and production in 'low-cost' countries like India, where the software industry gained importance from the mid-1990s and experienced an enormous expansion in the following decade. Hence it can be argued that the disintegration of value chains not only resulted in the establishment of transnational work forces, but also promoted a disintegration of these work forces along the dividing line of age.

In the case of G-Pro, most of the German employees fall within the midthirties to late fifties age group. The lack of younger German workers can be attributed to two main reasons. First, G-Pro only recruits holders of a Diploma or a Ph.D., and both university degrees were typically not obtained before the age of twenty-five or thirty (at least until the restructuring of the German university system), as the Indian interviewee quoted at the beginning of this essay remarks correctly. Secondly, even the hiring of these rather mature 'fresh' university grad-

---

[2] In order to ensure anonymity, existing literature on the sample companies is not quoted here, although the information contained therein has been used for the analysis of our empirical data.

uates has been massively reduced during the last few years. Hence, the lower strata of the age spectre among G-Pro's work force are occupied not by German workers but by their new colleagues in countries such as India. After establishing a subsidiary in Bangalore around the year 2000, G-Pro expanded its Indian staff from roughly one hundred to several thousand employees. Most of them are not fresh college graduates, since the company prefers applicants with a few years of job experience. Nonetheless, the transnational age gap is clearly discernible:

Most Indian software engineers leave university around the age of twenty-two. By the time they have acquired sufficient experience to join a western product company they are twenty-five or twenty-six, which still renders them at least ten years younger than most of their German colleagues. This pattern seems to be fairly common in western companies with subsidiaries in India, and also in other countries which have attracted the bulk of foreign direct investment (FDI) during the last two decades, like Eastern Europe or China.

This prominent model of transnationalization (from the centre to the semi-periphery) is increasingly complemented by a reverse development, with many companies from countries like India starting to establish subsidiaries in the west. In the software industry, Indian providers of software services (like Infosys, Wipro or Tata Consultancy Ltd. [TCS]) have expanded massively since the 1990s, and found the bulk of their corporate customers in the US and, increasingly, in Europe (Huws and Flecker 2004; Upadhya and Vasavi 2008). Yet, despite differences in the country of origin and the business model (see below), the age spectre in the Indian company of our sample (labelled I-Serve) displays a similar level of disintegration as described for G-Pro.

In India, I-Serve has recruited an ever-increasing number of 'fresh' university graduates since the 1990s, but this has not resulted in an equal distribution of age groups among the staff. Although the management tried hard to stabilize employment, the scarcity of skilled Indian software labour and growing corporate 'competition for talent' resulted in notoriously high rates of attrition, at least until 2007 when we conducted our empirical research (Mayer-Ahuja and Feuerstein 2008). Consequently, the vast majority of I-Serve's Indian employees are in their early or mid-twenties, and since the number of managers in their late thirties or even forties is relatively small, the average age in this company was only twenty-six in 2007). (For similar results about Indian service companies, see Ilavarasan 2005.)

In Germany, this company has to struggle hard to acquire projects, since many German clients are reluctant to cooperate with an Indian service provider. In order to overcome such resentment, I-Serve has started recruiting experienced German IT consultants as customer advisors, many of whom are in their late thirties or forties. Moreover, the 'offshoring model' of Indian service companies implies that Indian teams are performing so-called onsite work at client locations (Upadhya 2006) – and again, their German cooperation partners in the clients' IT-departments typically belong to the same age group which dominates the German work force of G-Pro. Hence, the young Indian software engineer's statement that her German colleagues are 'old people' or 'no young crowd' appears realistic. It refers to the typical disintegration of age spectres in transnationally operating companies, which create direct links within their corporate structures between the relatively permanent work force of 'established sectors' in centres of capitalist production, and the massively expanding and fluctuating work force of 'new sectors' in semi-peripheral countries.

Work Biographies and the Transnational Division of Labour

Older Work Force in Germany – Younger Work Force in India. It may appear self-explanatory that this constellation has repercussions for the organization of work, but interrelations between work biographies and the transnational division of labour are more ambiguous than might be expected. After all, the age gap between the Indian and German software work force cannot simply be equated with a gap in qualifications.

Most Indian employees have indeed had a shorter period of formal (university) education than their German colleagues. In India, a Bachelor of Engineering degree is obtained in four years, whereas most German students of informatics or natural sciences stayed at university considerably longer before receiving a Diploma or Ph.D. during the 1980s and 1990s (Aspray, Mayadas and Vardi 2006). After graduation, however, Indian engineers join the labour force and acquire practical job experience at an earlier age than their German counterparts, which renders the comparison between Indian and German qualification profiles difficult (Mayer-Ahuja 2011). This may be one reason why corporate perceptions of the Indian talent pool vary considerably, and why software companies experiment with different forms of work organization in India. Thus, young Indian software workers are confronted with a wide range of (partly conflicting) work requirements and career prospects, and work organization as well as the transnational division of labour take different shapes.

The 'offshoring model' of Indian service companies, for instance, may strengthen the assumption that the age gap favours a radically unequal division of labour between German and Indian work forces. Since competition for customers and projects is fierce in the field of software services, the central objective of management is price reduction. In the case of I-Serve, then, the vast majority of workers are employed in India, where labour costs are low. This huge Indian work force performs the bulk of relatively low-skill, standardized and easily controllable programming tasks. In order to be able to react to rapidly changing workloads and customer requirements, I-Serve aims at a far-reaching standardization of work processes, qualification profiles and measurable performance (per time-unit), and human resources are continually reshuffled to different tasks, projects and customers – a scenario which inspired Prasad (1998), and later Upadhya and Vasavi (2006), to talk about a 'Taylorisation' of software work.

In this business model, a successful career for Indian employees implies collecting as many experiences with different customers, tasks and projects as possible, even if this requires frequent changing of jobs. In the German subsidiary of I-Serve, on the other hand, the small number of locally recruited customer advisors work under completely different conditions. They have higher formal qualifications and far more job experience than their colleagues in India, since these are essential to be at par with the representatives of demanding German customers. Moreover, they are required to work independently and react flexibly to changing customer demands, which renders standardization of work processes, qualification profiles, or performance per time-unit and close surveillance by superior managers, impossible. As far as I-Serve is concerned, then, the Indian and German work forces not only belong to different age groups, but also differ with regard to qualification profiles, working tasks, and levels of standardization and management control, which are in accordance with the necessities of labour utilization in the offshoring model.

G-Pro, on the other hand, practises the 'distributed development' of standard software packages. In this model, work processes are spatially distributed to different locations, but have to be closely integrated as far as the speed and quality of work are concerned, since all team members pursue their tasks 'hand-in-hand' and contribute to the same software modules (Lema and Hesbjerg 2003). Marked differences in formal qualification, job experience or work efficiency are hardly compatible with this particular transnational division of labour, which reflects the management objective to shift the complete ownership of (i.e. formal responsibility for) certain software packages to India in the long run. In order to pave the way for such an organizational upgrading of the Indian subsidiary, even though G-Pro cannot abolish the age gap between German and Indian employees, the management does make discernible efforts to render it irrelevant. For instance, the company recruits only older Indian software professionals with some years of job experience, assigns relatively complex tasks to Indian team members, and encourages them to increase their level of specialization as well as their capacity and willingness to work independently of superiors. Consequently, the most promising career prospects offered to Indian employees at G-Pro are long-term company affiliation and deep professional specialization. Broadly speaking, this corporate strategy aims at an increasingly equal division of labour between the German and Indian work forces.

Thus the age gap between German and Indian work forces can have very different repercussions for corporate strategies of labour utilization, depending primarily on the business model of the company concerned. For the German product company G-Pro, the age gap is a major challenge which has to be tackled actively; for the Indian service company I-Serve, it helps to legitimize an unequal division of labour between German and Indian workers, which constitutes a precondition for the offshoring model.

It would be too easy, however, to equate corporate strategies of labour utilization with actual practices of work organization. Despite all the differences between the business models of western product companies and Indian service companies, empirical research on the shopfloor reveals an unequal division of labour between Indian and German workers in both sample companies. German workers typically play the role of 'experts', while Indian workers may well feel 'like kids' in these structures of cooperation, as the Indian interviewee quoted at the beginning of this essay put it.

In the case of I-Serve, this constellation may be argued to be a logical consequence of its business model. As far as G-Pro is concerned, however, 'distributed product development' does in fact require upgrading the Indian subsidiary and assigning more responsibility to Indian teams. But despite all efforts by its management, German employees with their longer academic education, higher levels of professional specialization and greater in-house work experience were still the team leaders, were assigned more complex tasks and granted more freedom to work independently of interference from superiors during the period of our research, whereas the Indian employees of G-Pro tended to be 'stuck' with less qualified tasks and were controlled in a far more elaborate manner. Corporate efforts to equalize standards of work organization had obviously not yet succeeded.

Interestingly, however, in some instances G-Pro managers attempted to exploit this constellation, which they otherwise struggled to overcome, in order to undermine standards of work organization at the German home-base. A few years back, for example, G-Pro started to experiment with a standardization of work processes in the name of 'quality management'. These initiatives were first deployed in the Indian subsidiary, but were supposed to be extended to the German headquarters as well. According to an Indian team member in charge, however, German colleagues openly refused to accept the new regulations and guidelines, or simply ignored them. Hence G-Pro not only faced problems in 'upgrading' the performance of the Indian work force, but also failed to 'downgrade' the performance of the German work force, since many German employees regarded themselves as experts in their specific fields of work and would not be pressed into any pre-defined process description. When the Indian representative of the quality management team tried to explain to us the failure of these initiatives, he not only pointed to the important role of individual expertise at G-Pro, but also mentioned the stubbornness of German colleagues who had developed their own methods of software development over many years. He described their attitude as: 'We know what is right!' In his point of view, German G-Pro employees were too inflexible to adapt to new management methods. In other words, they were simply too old for change. If this attitude collided with corporate strategies of labour utilization, it could well render organizational reforms impossible.

Life Cycles, and Spatial and Temporal Rhythms of Work

In order to tackle the complex interrelation between human life cycles and transnational work organization, another question needs to be raised: how far does a specific 'age' allow for conclusions with regard to biographical constellations at all? Or, to put it differently: is there a typical 'IT life cycle', in the sense that software workers at the age of, say, thirty years, would display similar characteristics with regard to their educational, employment or familial status? Our interviews with employees of G-Pro and I-Serve again suggest considerable differences between Indian and German workers. Hence it may not be coincidental that D'Mello and Sundeep (2008), for instance, describe 'the life cycle of the IT person' with reference to Indian workers, while this concept is never used in the German context.

After all, the biographical passage of 'family foundation' seems to follow a much more standardized pattern in India: Indian employees have to take care of spouse and child(ren) after reaching a certain age, and this age is clearly defined by social norms (for similar perceptions, see Upadhya and Vasavi 2006). Among German employees (but by no means all German employees), instead, no clear pattern emerges. This is not surprising, since German household structures have undergone a process of increasing differentiation over many years – the share of households occupied by single persons, single parents or childless couples has increased significantly since the 1980s, whereas the share of couples with children is in continuous decline (SOFI *et al.* 2005). In India, the spectre of socially accepted ways of life seems to be much more narrowly defined, at least among the middle classes, whose members mainly staff the IT industry (Fuller and Narasimhan 2007, 2008; Upadhya 2008). Our sample cannot be regarded as representative in a statistical sense, but if it is not completely misleading, it may well strengthen the assumptions that: Indian women tend to get married between the ages of twenty-four and twenty-six; Indian men get married in their late twenties; and the first child is born roughly one to two years after marriage. Taking into account this pattern, the fact that cooperation in Indo–German software teams usually involves twenty-five-year-old Indians and Germans who are forty plus does not allow for any general conclusions about the precise 'biographical position' of the employees concerned. It may be argued with some reason, however, that most Indian employees (who are predominantly male) would probably be unmarried, and many women would be newly married and childless, at the age of twenty-five. German employees (who seem to be even more predominantly male than their Indian colleagues), on the other hand, might or might not be single at the age of forty, and might or might not have children.

This striking difference between 'standardized' Indian and considerably 'less standardized' German life cycles (rather than merely the age gap between Indian and German employees), then, can be argued to have important repercussions for the spatial and temporal rhythms of work in both countries. Two examples may provide a first impression of how these rhythms influence the organization of work on the shopfloor.

The first example refers to standards of transnational mobility as a specific expression of spatial rhythms of work. Surprisingly, our empirical research reveals that neither the German company G-Pro nor the Indian company I-Serve encourage the physical movement of employees between the two countries; rather, they aim at an immobilization of labour. In the case of I-Serve, however, at least members of the onsite teams are transnationally mobile since they are delegated to the sites of US or European clients for several weeks or even months. Considering that preparedness to be posted abroad is especially strong among employees without family obligations, the need to staff a growing number of onsite teams may well pose a strong incentive for I-Serve to keep recruiting young and single graduates.. After all, female Indian IT workers seem to refrain from international postings as soon as they get married, and Indian men tend to 'take their wives along' if they are posted abroad, but return to India as soon as their children reach schooling age (Arun and Arun 2002; Devi 2002; Parikh and Sukhatme 2004; Fuller and Narasimhan 2008). For this reason, Raghuram (2004) considers migration and gender in the IT sector as giving rise to 'intersecting debates'. The standardized patterns of family structures in India thus simultaneously enable and impede corporate strategies of labour utilization with respect to transnational mobility. On the one hand, software companies can more or less rely on Indian workers in their early and mid-twenties to be interested in transnational mobility; on the other hand, their onsite teams have to do without more experienced Indian workers beyond the age of thirty, since they are likely to be parents of schoolgoing children. In Germany, on the other hand, the willingness of employees to accept transnational mobility does not seem to be linked to any specific biographical constellation. Among German G-Pro managers in India, who were all around forty, we met single men, married men without children who had taken their wives to India, and married men with children who had relocated with their whole family. For male German IT employees who are married, however, a transfer to India seems to present more difficulties than for their Indian peers. This is because it is more difficult for German men to 'take their wives along', due to the substitution of the sole breadwinner model, which gained importance in Germany around 1960, by a 'modernized main breadwinner model' in which male full-time and female part-time employment are combined (Auth 2002). Since married women tend to keep up paid employment despite marriage and motherhood in this arrangement, they face professional and economic risks if they accompany their husbands abroad, for instance, to India. This may well contribute to 'spatial rootedness', which is much more widely spread among German employees than among Indian employees. For G-Pro this is not problematic, since 'distributed development' implies keeping all workers in their own location. If this company were to opt for more transnational mobility, however, it would probably face resistance from many of its German employees. Hence, the fact that G-Pro does not employ single workers in their early twenties, and cannot rely on any standardized 'IT life cycle' with regard to older age groups in Germany, arguably exerts a direct influence on spatial rhythms of work, which may well restrict corporate options of transnational labour utilization.

Secondly, the fact that Indian software professionals typically do not have any family obligations at the age of twenty-five has repercussions for the temporal rhythms of software work, with regard to both its duration and intensity. As far as working hours are concerned, the young and single men who dominate the Indian software work force often lead rather isolated lives in IT hubs like Bangalore (Upadhya and Vasavi 2006). Away from their family and region of origin, they tend to stay in office for long hours since 'there is nothing to do at home', as one interviewee put it. Office is where these youngsters meet friends, write emails, surf the internet, etc. Moreover, they are eager to prove their high levels of motivation to superiors by performing excessive overtime work. Hence, the low average age of the Indian software work force, but especially the fact that family foundation typically occurs at a later point of an Indian IT biography, arguably favours corporate strategies of labour utilization which are based on an extension of working hours, rather than on an intensification of the work process. In fact, many Indian interviewees describe their working day as being interspersed with coffee-breaks, long team lunches, frequent birthday celebrations, etc., and they wonder about the absence of such activities among their German colleagues. Even collegial consultation seems to take strikingly different forms in the two countries. In India, a group of developers would spontaneously gather around the desk of a colleague who calls out a work-related question; if other tasks get delayed thus, especially the young men among the developers would willingly stay back late to complete them. In Germany, instead, as reported by many Indian interviewees, German colleagues would fix a formal appointment if an urgent problem occurs and would terminate the meeting as soon as the stipulated time was over. Spontaneous night-shifts were rare among German employees, Indian colleagues would emphasize, but their concentration and productivity from 9 to 5 was much higher than that of their Indian counterparts.

Once again, these reports point to the close interrelation between life cycle and work organization. The fact that the Indian IT work force is dominated by young men in their early and mid-twenties, and that (conforming to the typical Indian 'IT life cycle') most of these employees do not have family obligations, is arguably central in determining corporate options of work organization. Many managers, for instance, told us that it is much easier to extend working hours than to persuade young and single men to intensify their work process in India – this pattern is substantiated by studies on European labour which argue that generally not single men but young mothers on part-time jobs pioneer a combination of highly intensive work and regular working hours (see, for instance, Oertzen 1999; Raehlmann 2004).

For I-Serve, this is not a problem. The provision of software services does not permit high levels of concentration anyway, but regularly requires the extension of working hours – the latter is essential, for instance, in order to respond at short notice if software problems occur during western office hours and have to be solved during late evenings or nights in India. For G-Pro, instead, the fact that newly recruited Indian employees are typically in their mid- to late twenties and thus at a stage in their life cycle which makes them prone to prefer working overtime rather than to a highly concentrated labour process, poses considerable management problems. The company's preference for highly intensive, specialized and independent work, which is impossible without a continuously high level of concentration, conflicts with the working style of most Indian employees. G-Pro managers may leave the office at 5 in the evening telling their teams to do the same, but young (Indian) developers would still stay on. In the long run, some interviewees complain, this working style might well lower the intensity of work to an extent that would undermine corporate strategies aimed at allotting more complex tasks to Indian teams and at upgrading the Indian subsidiary.

Conclusion

In conclusion, three aspects of the complex interrelation between transnational work organization and human life cycle deserve particular attention.

First, the 'disintegration of the age spectre' in many transnationally operating companies is closely interrelated with corporate investment, recruitment and employment strategies. On the one hand, companies have to adapt to local labour market conditions – they can hardly recruit mature and experienced employees if the economic sector is just emerging (as was the case with the software industry in India during the 1990s). On the other hand, the management of transnationally operating companies has considerable room for manoeuvre with respect to the choice of investment locations, the recruitment of workers (in Germany and/or India) and the terms offered to potential employees. The latter have boosted job-hopping in India during the last few years, but may well enhance permanent employment, thus overcoming the divide between young workers in India and old workers in Germany in the long run.

Secondly, the age gap between the German and Indian work forces favours, but by no means determines, specific forms of work organization or (more precisely) an unequal transnational division of labour. As argued previously, corporate strategies of transnational labour utilization can vary markedly, for instance, due to the requirements of different business models. Moreover, corporate strategies of labour utilization cannot be equated with actual work organization. While I-Serve was quite successful in realizing its strategy of employing workers in Germany on completely different terms than in India, G-Pro failed to realize the more equal division of labour its management was aiming at – attempts to strengthen the position of Indian workers and to weaken the position of German workers, both proved unsuccessful.

Thirdly, the difference between corporate strategies of transnational labour utilization and actual work organization is at least partly due to the fact that their implementation on the shopfloor requires adaptation to localized standards of labour reproduction. Among these are spatial and temporal rhythms of work, which take different forms in Germany and India. These rhythms are closely related to the age composition of the respective work force, especially in India, where the 'IT life cycle' seems to follow a remarkably standardized pattern, for example, with regard to family foundation. The interrelation between work organization and life cycle, however, is ambiguous. On the one hand, software companies do have to adapt to localized standards (like the division of labour between the sexes or levels of spatial mobility) to some extent. If German workers refuse to accept transnational postings or Indian workers cannot be made to intensify their work (for structural and/or personal reasons), certain corporate strategies of labour utilization are hard to realize. On the other hand, localized standards of reproduction and preferences of employees may not always be central criteria for organizing work from a corporate perspective.

Labour utilization on the shopfloor is influenced by a complex scenario of political, economic and social regulation, in which the strategies of both companies and employees are of critical importance – but their respective weightage can vary considerably. Whether and to what extent the age composition of the work force, the positioning of employees in standardized or de-standardized life cycles, and workers' preferences resulting from specific biographical constellations, can actually influence modalities of work organization, then, is mainly a question of (changing) power relations. In our interviews, for instance, many managers discussed the 'young age' of Indian workers and their favoured styles of working or living – these issues were important since companies wished to offer attractive jobs under the conditions of labour scarcity and high fluctuation which shaped the Indian software industry around 2007. With respect to German employees, however, age and biographical constellations were rarely mentioned as criteria for management decisions. Since both managers and employees were convinced that German workers (especially at G-Pro) lacked attractive job alternatives due to a combination of high average age and narrow specialization, standards of reproduction or worker preferences, while not meaningless for corporate decisions, were of far less importance. Interestingly, categories relating to human life cycles (like age, expertise, job experience, family constellations, etc.) were mainly discussed as determinants of workers' negotiating power vis-à-vis the management in our interviews. This renders developments in the software sector of interest for a more general, conceptual approach towards transnational work organization from a life cycle perspective.

References

Arun, Shoba and Thankom Arun (2002), 'ICTs, Gender and Development: Women in software production in Kerala', *Journal of International Development*, vol. 14, no. 1, pp. 39–50.

Aspray, William, Frank Mayadas and Moshe Y. Vardi, eds. (2006), *Globalization and Offshoring of Software: A Report of the ACM Job Migration Task Force*, Association of Computing Machinery, New York.

Auth, Diana (2002), *Wandel im Schneckentempo: Arbeitszeitpolitik und Geschlechtergleichheit im Deutschen Wohlfahrtsstaat*, Opladen.

Boes, Andreas and Andrea Baukrowitz (2002), *Arbeitsbeziehungen in der IT-Industrie: Erosion oder Innovation der Mitbestimmung?*, Sigma, Berlin.

Boes, Andreas and Katrin Trinks (2006), *'Theoretisch bin ich frei!' Interessenhandeln und Mitbestimmung in der IT-Industrie*, Sigma, Berlin.

Boes, Andreas and Michael Schwemmle, eds. (2005), *Bangalore statt Böblingen? Offshoring und Internationalisierung im IT-sektor*, VSA, Hamburg.

Boyer, Robert, Elsie Charron, Ulrich Jürgens and Steven Tolliday, eds. (1998), *Between Imita-*

tion and Innovation: The transfer and hybridization of productive models in the international automobile industry, Oxford University Press, Oxford.

Devi, S. Uma (2002), 'Globalization, Information Technology and Asian/Indian Women in the US', *Economic and Political Weekly*, vol. 37, no. 43, pp. 4421–28.

Dicken, Peter (2007), *Global Shift: Mapping the changing contours of the world economy*, Sage, Thousand Oaks/London/New Delhi.

D'Mello, Marisa and Sundeep Sahay (2008), 'Betwixt and Between? Exploring mobilities in a global workplace in India', in Carol Upadhya and A.R. Vasavi, eds., *In an Outpost of the Global Economy: Work and workers in India's information technology industry*, Routledge, London/New Delhi/New York.

Fuller, Chris and Haripriya Narasimhan (2007), 'Information Technology Professionals and the New-Rich Middle Class in Chennai', *Modern Asian Studies*, vol. 41, pp. 121–50.

—— (2008), 'Empowerment and Constraint: Women, work and the family in Chennai's software industry', in Carol Upadhya and A.R. Vasavi, eds., *In an Outpost of the Global Economy: Work and workers in India's information technology industry*, Routledge, London/New Delhi/New York.

Heeks, Richard (1996), *India's Software Industry: State policy, liberalization and industrial development*, Sage, Thousand Oaks/London/New Delhi.

Huws, Ursula and Jörg Flecker, eds. (2004), *Asian Emergence: The world's back office?*, IES Report 409, Institute for Employment Studies, Brighton.

Ilavarasan, P. Vigneswara (2005), 'Indian Software Workforce: A critical analysis', paper presented at International Conference on 'New Global Workforces and Virtual Workplaces: Connections, Culture, and Control', National Institute of Advanced Studies, Bangalore, 20–22 August.

Kämpf, Tobias (2008), *Die neue Unsicherheit: Folgen der Globalisierung für hochqualifizierte Arbeitnehmer*, Campus, Frankfurt/New York.

Lakha, Salim (1994), 'The New International Division of Labour and the Indian Computer Software Industry', *Modern Asian Studies*, vol. 28, no. 2, pp. 381–408.

Lema, Rasmus and Bjarke Hesbjerg (2003), *The Virtual Extension: A search for collective efficiency in the software cluster in Bangalore*, Roskilde University, Denmark.

Mayer-Ahuja, Nicole (2003), *Wieder dienen lernen? Vom westdeutschen 'Normalarbeitsverhältnis' zu prekärer Beschäftigung (1973–1998)*, Sigma, Berlin.

Mayer-Ahuja, Nicole (2011), *Grenzen der Homogenisierung: IT-Arbeit zwischen ortsgebundener Regulierung und transnationaler Unternehmensstrategie*, Campus, Frankfurt/New York.

Mayer-Ahuja, Nicole and Patrick Feuerstein (2008), 'Everywhere is Becoming the Same? Labour utilization, regulation and the inherent tensions in transnational IT-production', *Work Organization, Labour and Globalization*, vol. 2, no. 2, Autumn, pp. 162–78.

Mückenberger, Ulrich (1985), 'Die Krise des Normalarbeitsverhältnisses: Hat das Arbeitsrecht noch Zukunft?', *Zeitschrift für Sozialreform*, vol. 7, pp. 415–34, 457–75.

Oertzen, Christine von (1999), *Teilzeitarbeit und die Lust am Zuverdienen: Geschlechterpolitik und gesellschaftlicher Wandel in Westdeutschland, 1948–1969*, Vandenhoeck and Ruprecht, Göttingen.

Parikh, P.P. and S.P. Sukhatme (2004), 'Women Engineers in India', *Economic and Political Weekly*, vol. 39, no. 2, pp. 193–201.

Prasad, Monica (1998), 'International Capital on Silicon Plateau: Work and control in India's computer industry', *Social Forces*, vol. 77, no. 2, December, pp. 429–52.

Raehlmann, Irene (2004), *Zeit und Arbeit: Eine Einführung*, VS, Wiesbaden.

Raghuram, Parvati (2004), 'Migration, Gender, and the IT Sector: Intersecting debates', *Women's Studies International Forum*, vol. 27, pp. 163–76.

SOFI/IAB/ISF/INIFES (2005), *Berichterstattung zur sozioökonomischen Entwicklung in Deutschland: Arbeit und Lebensweisen*, Erster Bericht, Wiesbaden.

Upadhya, Carol (2006), 'The Global Indian Software Labour Force: IT professionals in Europe', Working Paper Series No. 1, Indo-Dutch Programme on Alternatives in Development.

—— (2008), 'Rewriting the Code: Software professionals and the reconstitution of Indian middle class identity', in Christophe Jaffrelot and Peter von der Veer, eds., *Patterns of Middle Class Consumption in India and China*, Sage, New Delhi.

Upadhya, Carol and A.R. Vasavi (2006), *Work, Culture, and Sociality in the Indian IT Industry: A sociological study*, Final Report submitted to the Indo-Dutch Programme for Alternatives in Development, August.

Upadhya, Carol and A.R. Vasavi, eds. (2008), *In an Outpost of the Global Economy: Work and workers in India's information technology industry*, Routledge, London / New York / New Delhi.

Work and Untouchability
Experiences of Work in Dalit Autobiographies

Shashi B. Upadhyay

The term 'Dalit' is generally linked to experiences of untouchability. This association, which has discursively evolved over decades, has become the core of the Dalit identity. The role of work in the constitution of the Dalit identity has been neglected, despite the fact that it is an inseparable attribute of untouchability. Historically, an increasing number of castes have joined the ranks of the untouchables due to their association with certain types of work (see, for example, Jha 1975, 2004; Gurukkal 1997; Hanumanthan 2004). Many of these jobs possess ritually loaded meanings. However, the majority of the Dalit population is involved in what may be called non-ritual/secular work, like agrarian labour. They have worked for centuries as attached or bonded labourers, and now are mostly employed as low-paid wage workers. Due to their poverty and low social status, they form a major part of underpaid labour, both in rural and urban areas. Thus, it is not possible to ignore work as a central lived experience of the Dalits.

Dalit people, who are also known as Scheduled Castes or ex-untouchables, form about 16 per cent of the total Indian population and number around 166 million; about 16 per cent of them live in urban areas while 84 per cent live in rural areas (Shah *et al.* 2006: 37).

This essay examines how experiences of work in various contexts as well as across generations are narrated in Dalit autobiographies. It further explores the perception of work in general in these texts, as well as the context of what has been traditionally associated with the notion of lowly/degrading work. Dalit autobiographies are a part of the Dalit movement against discrimination and oppression, and constitute the vanguard of the Dalit literary movement. The protagonists/authors of the texts discussed here have all been involved in some form of manual work, particularly in their early lives, even as some of them occupy high offices now. The texts provide us insights into their experience of various kinds of work over a relatively long period.

It has been pointed out that in Indian, as indeed in most colonial/postcolonial contexts, the idea of personhood is collective and culture-specific (Arnold and Blackburn 2004; Moore-Gilbert 2009). This applies to Dalit autobiographies to an even greater degree. These texts transcend the individual/collective binary by constantly, and consciously, transgressing the boundaries between the two. Thus we find innumerable instances where the particularities of experiences are immediately generalized, while generalization is brought in to elucidate the specific. This is not due to an absence of selfhood, but a result of a deliberate desire to combine the two realms. Dalit writers have never hidden the positioned nature of their writings. In fact, the process of the positioning itself reveals the nature of their experiences as labourers, as untouchables and as organic intellectuals. These autobiographies, therefore, reveal various levels of reactions and responses on the part of these ex-labourers: as social inferiors and economic dependants, as those involved in instinctual and primary rebellion against unjust practices and exploitation, and, finally, as activists and intellectuals.

This essay focuses on eight Dalit life-stories – three in Hindi, three in Marathi, and two in English. In six of these, the author, the narrator and the main protagonist are the same. In the text by Jadhav (2003), the author is different from the main characters, but he shares some of the experiences which are narrated as an offspring. The authors of *Viramma* (1997) are different from the narrator-protagonist, whose version they have recorded over a long period of time. Out of the eight life-stories, two are by women and the rest are by men. Besides these, autobiographical extracts from *Poisoned Bread* (1992), edited by Arjun Dangle, have also been used to illustrate certain points.

Village Work

Dalits perform two types of work: socially demeaning work with ritual connotations connected with organic waste or death; and secular work, difficult or hazardous work that is mostly avoided by the non-Dalit poor. The associated experiences may be placed on several grids that are linked, yet different.

Exploitation

Being exploited in terms of low payment, sometimes non-payment, for doing even those jobs which nobody else is prepared to do, is a predominant feeling that runs through all these texts. The exploitation consists in payment of low wages or no wages for work. It also involves regular assignment of the toughest jobs to particular groups of people, not allowing free choice of work to individuals or groups. Thus, various forms of both economic and extra-economic coercion are involved in this process. While exploitation may be an objective economic fact that economists may try to measure, its extent and intensity on the human psyche varies according to individual experience as well as rising consciousness. Some of the texts reveal this awareness more poignantly than others. Valmiki's narrative is particularly forthright in this regard, whereas Viramma's life-story is relatively quiet on this issue.

Most rural Dalit families cannot survive without work. Valmiki, who belongs to a Bhangi (scavenger) caste, describes the position of his family thus:

Everyone in the family did some or other work. Even then we did not manage to get two decent meals a day. We did all sorts of work for the Tagas,[1] including cleaning, agricultural work and general labour. We would often have to work without pay. Nobody dared to refuse this unpaid work for which we got neither money nor grain. (Valmiki 2003: 2)

The Dalits face exploitation while performing the traditional work associated with their particular castes as well as in doing secular work. In Narendra Jadhav's life-story, his father, one of the narrators, was forced to watch over a corpse in the well for a long period of time without being allowed to take any food. After that he was abusively asked to take the bloated corpse out of the well, which he refused to do despite receiving a beating (Jadhav 2003). In Shankarrao Kharat's earlier-written account there is a harrowing description of what the Mahar's[2] village duty involved. Someone had committed suicide by jumping into a well and the bloated corpse was discovered floating there a few days later. The police were informed in the morning. The village servant, the author's father, had guarded the corpse the whole night without eating anything. The next afternoon, he was ordered by the police constable to remove the corpse from the well. It was an abandoned well in a dilapidated condition. 'The upper part of the well had collapsed in ruins and its big long stones were scattered around. Green moss floated on the unused water of the well, and foliage from the trees near the edge had fallen into it and rotted. The well was quite deep' (in Dangle 1992: 75). Thus it was quite dangerous to climb down. Moreover, it was not part of a Mahar's village duty to remove corpses. Yet he was abused, beaten and forced to do the job. 'His only crime was being the Mahar of the village' (ibid.: 76).

In Valmiki's autobiography, there is a particularly detailed description of what was expected of the Dalits as agricultural workers:

At harvest time, all the people in our neighbourhood used to go to the field of the Tagas to reap the crop. Cutting the sheaves of wheat in the midday sun is a very hard and painful task. The sun pouring on your head. Fiery hot ground underneath. The roots of the cropped wheat plants pricked your feet like spikes. The roots of mustard and gram lentils hurt even more. The harvesting of these lentils presented an extra difficulty. The leaves are sour and stick all over the body during harvesting. Even bathing does not get rid of them completely. Most of the reapers were from untouchable castes of the Chuhras[3] or Chamars[4]. They had clothes on their bodies in name only. There was no question of shoes on their feet. Their bare feet got badly injured by the time the crop was brought in.

The harvesting would often lead to arguments in the fields. Most of the

---

[1] Locally used term for Tyagis, a dominant caste group in west Uttar Pradesh and the main landowners in some areas.

[2] Mahar is a Dalit caste predominantly found in the state of Maharashtra. Mahars are substantial in number and form the largest proportion of the Dalits in that province.

[3] The caste traditionally associated with sweeping and cleaning.

[4] A caste group traditionally associated with leather work, although the majority of them have been working as agricultural labourers for a long time.

Tagas were miserly when it came to paying wages. The reapers were helpless. Whatever they got, they took over after protesting a bit. They kept fretting after coming back home, cursing the Tagas. But their protests died when confronted with hunger. Every year there would be a meeting in the neighbourhood at harvest time. People swore to demand one sheaf out of sixteen as wages. But all the resolutions passed at the meetings evaporated in thin air the moment harvesting began. They got one sheaf for cutting twenty-one as wages. One sheaf had less than a kilo of grain. Even the heaviest sheaf did not yield a kilo of wheat. That is, a day's wage wasn't worth even a kilo of wheat. After the harvesting, the grain had to be loaded on bullock or buffalo carts and unloaded. Neither money nor grain was given for that work. Sooner or later all of us had to drive the bullocks on the threshing floor, again without payment. In those days there were no threshes for cleaning up the wheat. The bullocks would be taken round and round to break down the sheaves into straw. Then the grain would be separated from the chaff by blowing it in a winnow. It was a very long and tiring work, performed mostly by Chamars or Chuhras. (Valmiki 2003: 7–8)

Daya Pawar's narrative is relatively neutral as far as non-traditional work is concerned. He describes it as consisting of collecting and chopping wood, performing agricultural work, and other stray jobs (Pawar 1980: 34–35). Very few Mahar families owned any land and they were generally poor. On the other hand, he is particularly bitter about the Mahars' traditional work, which was

> to carry all the taxes collected in the village to the *taluqa* headquarters, to run behind the carriages of officials visiting villages, to look after their horses, to make announcements by beating drums, to spread the news of a death in the village to other villages, to remove the carcass of dead cattle, to chop wood, to play musical instruments during a village festival . . .

and all they received in return was '*baluta*', a fixed payment in the form of a small plot of land as well as some regular payment in kind from the whole village, which has been described by many Dalit activists, including Ambedkar, as a form of begging. Even Kausalya Baisantry,[5] who otherwise writes very little about work, describes the work her grandmother had to do as a child as very hard: 'Untouchability was observed very rigorously, so they did not get the inside jobs in an upper-caste household. Only chopping wood and carrying certain heavy loads were the jobs they got. Often only the toughest work came to them' (Baisantry 2009: 16). Thus, the Dalit autobiographies generally view the work done by them in the villages as exploitative, although the intensity of exploitation may vary according to personal experience.

In Viramma's narrative,[6] however, the descriptions of the experience of

---

[5] Baisantry was born and brought up in Nagpur, Maharashtra. Her mothertongue is Marathi, but she chose to write her autobiography in Hindi.

[6] Viramma, belonging to a Tamil Dalit Paraiyar family, is not an activist; she lives in rural areas and works as an agricultural labour. Her story, narrated by Josiane and

rural work are quite mixed. The complexity probably derives from the fact that her life-experience as a rural worker is the longest of all the persons discussed here, and she continues to be village-based. It is not that she is unaware of her subordinate position in the rural social hierarchy. Her story starts with the statement, 'My paternal grandfather Samikkannu was a serf of Swara Reddi' (Viramma 1997: 1); and soon afterwards she says, 'My grandparents had slaved away in the fields until their dying day to feed the family' (ibid.: 4). Her parents, her husband's parents, her husband and she worked as labourers attached to Reddi landlords. And she possesses enough experience of the tough nature of her work:

> It's so much work, the paddy field! We used to sing to while away the hours and forget the tiredness and the pain in our backs:
> Our legs stuck in the mud make us suffer
> Ellamba élan!
> Have pity on us, executioner!
> Ellamba élan!
> …
> Pain in our knees, drawn faces,
> Ellamba élan!

Yet for her it is good to 'learn agricultural work and housework from a young age: that was work and it paid immediately!' (ibid.: 12). She also praises her landlord for being generous: 'Thanks to the Reddiar, thanks to his fortune . . . we have enough to eat without worrying. . . . The serfs who work at the Reddiar's have their rice guaranteed!' (ibid.: 156). She has adjusted to her work and feels bad when, due to a conflict with the landlords over payment, their 'traditional' work, such as playing music during a festival, is taken away from them (ibid.: 121–25). In this respect, her views are quite conservative and opposed to the winds of change blowing in her settlement. Such an attitude in modern times may also derive from the fact that she is a poor woman who has no other avenue for survival. At the same time, however, she occasionally expresses resentment against her condition. What is important to note here is the mediated feeling of exploitation which makes it relatively tolerable.

Humiliation

More than exploitation, it is humiliation that forms the core of the Dalit life-stories. In their contexts, exploitation is inextricably linked to humiliation. In fact, the rural work as such is experienced as unending degradation that causes an upheaval in the minds of even those who are relatively less sensitive. This is the most important emotion associated with rural work that informs most of the autobiographies discussed here. The feeling of humiliation indeed encompasses almost all areas of a Dalit's existence, and it is depicted as such in these life-

---

Jean-Luc Racine from taped conversations, was published originally in French in 1995. It was translated into English in 1997.

narratives. Here, however, I shall focus on work-related feelings of humiliation. As mentioned earlier, Dalits' work in villages may be broadly categorized as traditional work or work with ritual meaning, and secular work. Although even the secular sphere of work brings humiliation, the most intense feelings of humiliation inflicted on the Dalit psyche are in the sphere of traditional work, even when such work is not heavy or burdensome.

In an important collection on this theme, humiliation in the Dalit context is defined as a modern phenomenon that exists in the inner, psychological realm. The editor of the volume argues that 'the reorganization of society on modern lines also creates the condition for the production of humiliation' (Guru 2009: 5). Ashis Nandy, one of the contributors, states: 'Unless the humiliated collaborates by feeling humiliated, you cannot humiliate him' (ibid.: 42).

It is arguable that the feeling of humiliation is specific to the modern era and that pre-modern conditions did not generate it. There are several references to such feelings in Bhakti (devotional) and other literature. Moreover, placing it entirely in the realm of the subjective by claiming the collaboration of the victim tends to divest humiliation of any moorings in reality and consign it to the psychological zone, which, in some senses, denies specificities of experiences that are both personal and common to particular communities. Nevertheless, it is true that these conditions have become more generalized in modern and contemporary times, and the feelings generated thereby are more widely and more intensely reflected in literary and other writings. These writings structure such feelings within the context of generalized experiences specific to the Dalit communities, and help in the construction and consolidation of the latter in the process.

Thus, when Kharat gave vent to this feeling in one of the earliest personal narratives in this genre, he straddled the realms of both the individual and the community, even though the community was still only broad enough to encompass the Mahars: 'I knew clearly the dangers of village duty. It was a perpetual noose around the neck of a Mahar! My father was crushed flat by this duty' (in Dangle 1992: 73). The work of removing a corpse from the well was not part of his village duty, but he was abused, threatened and compelled to do it. This could happen only because he was a Mahar. The experience of such humiliation leads Daya Pawar to compare village duty to slavery: 'The Mahar-dom I saw as a child is imprinted on my heart. This part is hard to erase. It will go only when I die. The helplessness you see besmeared on my face is from that time. Scratch it – draw blood even – but it will not be wiped away' (in Dangle 1992: 86).

Valmiki relates an incident when he had to dispose of a dead bullock, which was part of the traditional responsibility of his caste group. In his words:

> In those days it was Chuhras' responsibility to dispose of dead cattle in the villages. Wherever one worked, the disposal of the employer's dead cattle was a part of the job. No wages were paid for doing his work. . . . The person whose animal had died . . . would come into the basti [settlement] and shout. He would start swearing if there was a delay. (Valmiki 2003: 33)

The author-narrator was called from school to accompany his uncle for lifting and skinning a dead bullock. When he started assisting his uncle to skin the bullock, 'something broke inside me . . . I felt I was drowning in a swamp. I was being drawn into the very quagmire that I had tried to escape from. The wounds of the torment that I suffered with chacha [uncle] on that hot afternoon are still fresh on my skin' (ibid.: 35).

This was work which, besides being hard and poorly paid, was also ritually tainted and hence extremely humiliating. While carrying the load of hide on his head towards the bus-stand he experienced mortal fear: 'What if someone saw me! What if I bumped into a fellow student! If someone started to ask me, what would I say?' (ibid.: 35). Exploitation and humiliation combined to produce a miserable experience. Another source of humiliation (which is also reflected in the title of the text) that has left a bitter memory in the narrator's mind, is being given '*joothan*' (leftover, unclean food) as partial payment for household jobs: 'What sort of a life was that? After working hard day and night, the price of our sweat was just joothan. And yet no one had any grudges. Or shame. Or repentance. . . . When I think of those days today, I feel nauseated' (ibid.: 10)

One of the regular sources of such experience was the *begaar* (forced, unpaid labour) expected by government servants. Once, in Valmiki's village, a land survey was going on. As usual,

> a government employee came to the Bhangi basti. Some people were required for clean-up work, for which they would not be paid. As always, it would be unpaid labour. For days on end, hungry and thirsty people would work to clean the Kothi. In return they would be sworn at. (Ibid.: 37)

This time round, the labourers refused to work without pay; they were caught by policemen and thrashed:

> Those who had been captured from the basti were being made to stand like a rooster, a very painful crouched up position. Moreover they were being beaten with batons. The policeman who was beating them was getting tired. The one being beaten would scream after every blow. This festival of valour was being celebrated openly. People watched quietly, without a word. (Ibid.: 38).

Such experiences make the author ask: 'Why is it a crime to ask for the price of one's labour? Those who keep singing the glories of democracy use the government machinery to quell the blood flowing in our veins. As though we are not citizens of this country' (ibid.: 39).

Alienation

Such experiences also give rise to a feeling of alienation vis-a-vis the village and village work. The association of the village with social subordination is very strong. Laxman Gaikwad narrates the painful experiences of a partially untouchable community in Maharashtra, some of whose members had to steal to remain alive because they could not find work in the village. The entire community, as a consequence, was termed a criminal tribe during the colonial period. And even when they were legally freed from the bondage of this nomenclature after the country's independence, the attitude of the state and the dominant classes in the villages towards them remained much the same. The author, therefore, has only negative memories about his village:

> This was my village just because I was born there! Otherwise what other relationship I had with this village? This village had kept me hungry and helpless. Even the smallest child from Maratha caste used to insult me. . . . This village had forced me to live a life of slavery. I had no other memories than these about this village. (Gaikwad 2000: 84)

Similarly, Omprakash Valmiki writes about his feeling of alienation:

> The poem by Sumitranandan Pant that we had been taught at school, 'Ah, how wonderful is this village life' . . . each word of the poem had proved to be artificial and a lie. . . .
>   . . . One after the other they took off for the city where a new brightness was beckoning. When the earth of the village becomes barren, one no longer has the desire to irrigate and fertilize it. When one's village is no longer one's own, there is nothing to lose in leaving. (Valmiki 2003: 39)

He laments: 'What a cruel society we live in where hard labour has no value' (ibid.: 34). And his solution is to avoid such work altogether: 'All I knew was that I did not want to go into the line of work that my ancestors had been doing for thousands of years' (ibid.: 77).

In Narendra Jadhav's narrative, there is a clear separation between caste work in the village and class work in the city. The former symbolizes indignity, slavery, darkness and inhumanity, while the latter denotes dignity, freedom, a new dawn and humanity, despite the fact that both involve manual labour and that there was sometimes greater security in village work (Jadhav 2003). Even Daya Pawar, in whose writings one can discern occasional nostalgia for the village, says that he has 'no desire to waste my life in the village. And the village – it was like millions of scorpion bites' (Pawar 1980: 136). Shankarrao Kharat's father, who is forced to perform the traditional village duty of the Mahar caste, vehemently tells his son: 'No! No village duty for you. It's bad enough that we have to endure it. Once you are saddled with the village duty, you'll be stuck with it for life! That's the tradition! That's our doom!' (in Dangle 1992: 74). Alienation from the village and the work there is also reflected, though differently, in *Viramma*: '. . . one day they decide to go and look for work in town, leaving behind their parents who've suffered to bring them up. That's the fate of our Pariah caste' (Viramma 1997: 12).

Thus, the feeling of alienation from villages is almost universal among these writers. The narratives evince a feeling of estrangement, of hatred towards villages where the protagonists, and Dalits in general, face the worst forms of discrimination and often the worst poverty. It is clear that, given an opportunity, a large number of Dalits would be ready to forego whatever security their commitment to traditional work provides in favour of even insecure secular jobs. The objection is not to a particular task being hazardous or repulsive to the senses, but to its ritually polluting nature. Thus, beating the drums or announcing deaths is considered no better than cleaning dry latrines or carrying nightsoil (Shah *et al.* 2006: 106–07). This alienation is produced by the socio-cultural conditions of work and not necessarily by the economic processes whereby the labourer progressively loses control over the labour process.

Protest

In these texts, the resentment of the Dalits is mostly expressed in the form of escape from the village, but it is also articulated in the form of opposition to humiliation. Valmiki's autobiography relates how his mother sharply reacted against the insult heaped on them at the time of a wedding in the landlord's house as they waited to collect the leftover food from guests' plates. When his mother asked for some clean food for her children, the landlord abused her for daring to demand any clean food after she had already collected the leftover food. It was extremely humiliating, but

> [T]hat night the Mother Goddess Durga entered my mother's eyes. It was the first time I saw my mother get so angry. She emptied the basket right there. She said to Sukhdev Singh, 'Pick it up and put it inside your house. Feed it to the baratis [guests from the groom's side] tomorrow morning.' She gathered me and my sister and left like an arrow. . . . After that day Ma never went back to his door. And after this she had also stopped taking their joothan. (Valmiki 2003: 11)

On another occasion his father was compelled to raise his voice against the gross injustice faced by Valmiki in school, where he was forced to provide free labour as a sweeper rather than be a normal student like the non-Dalit boys:

> Pitaji snatched the broom from my hand and threw it away. His eyes were blazing. Pitaji who was always taut as a bowstring in front of others was so angry that his dense moustache was fluttering. He began to scream, 'Who is that teacher, that progeny of Dronacharya[7], who forces my son to sweep?' (Ibid.: 6)

In Jadhav's story, the narrator (the author's father) resists the order by the police constable to draw a dead body out of the well on the ground that it is not part of a Mahar's duty. Even when the policemen assault him, he does not

---

[7] Dronacharya was the legendary teacher in the Indian epic *Mahabharata* who taught the princes martial arts. Ekalavya, a tribal youth, proclaimed himself as his student without ever meeting him. As the youth was extremely skilled in archery, even better than his favourite pupil Arjuna, Dronacharya asked him to give his thumb as *gurudak-shina* (gift to the teacher), thereby effectively eliminating any competition from him.

yield: 'With all his might, Damu cried out, "I will die but I will not bow down before you. Come on, beat me all you can and kill me. Let the world know that a helpless Mahar was killed doing his duty"' (Jadhav 2003: 9). He later refuses to accept the traditional work imposed on him, and dares both the dominant villagers and his own kinsmen to punish him for it:

> 'What kind of a tradition is this that treats Mahars worse than cats and dogs?' Damu yelled. 'I spit on these inhuman traditions. I am not going to abide by such traditions. I am a man of dignity and I will not go from house to house begging for *Baluta*. What are all of you going to do? Kill me?' (Ibid. 10)

Viramma, the Tamil Dalit woman, is quite fatalistic and tries to rationalize landlord exploitation by saying: 'God gave the land to the rich high castes and he gave the poor low castes the duty of cultivating the land' (Viramma 1997: 160). At the same time, however, she shows occasional flashes of intense resentment against her condition: 'We only eat if we've got work, otherwise our stomach stays empty. . . . This is the reign of the rich and they don't worry about the poor'; 'they don't want their workers to be respectable and civilized here in the country'. The tone becomes angry when she is denied adequate help for her son's marriage: 'We work like that all our life for a Reddiar and then, when we need money for a very important matter, to light a lamp in a new household, he goes and gives us [only] two hundred rupees and a sack of rice. How are you meant to manage with that?' The work they do is hard and demanding: 'When you sweat, it's water. When we sweat, it's blood! Standing under an umbrella making us work isn't tiring.' And yet the landlord has 'got the right to rest' whereas constant work is demanded from the labourers because 'we're not just poor, but on top of that, we've suffered the great wrong of being born Pariahs' (ibid.: 265–67).

Work in Urban Areas

Work and life in urban areas have distinct advantages as compared to their rural counterparts. The stigma attached to the traditional work of the Dalits, and the exploitation and humiliation involved even in a secular work regime in rural areas are unbearable for the more conscious and sensitive individuals among them. Cities fare much better in their assessment as even similar work here is relatively less stigmatized. Moreover, despite a certain level of caste-wise segmentation of the labour market, Dalits find more opportunities for upward mobility in urban areas. The public sphere is less discriminating and the anonymity of urban existence whereby they can become part of the crowds inhabiting public spaces is also a boon for the Dalits.

Some Dalits may take up similar jobs in the urban areas, but payments are higher and they are not marked quite in the same way as in the villages. It is true that given a choice, they would prefer not to do such work even in the urban situation, but their loathing for such work is not so strong there. This is but natural because dignity of labour is difficult to achieve in situations where such work is considered ritually impure, socially degrading and economically unrewarding. The situation in urban areas, particularly in the big cities, may even prove to be quite rewarding for some Dalits. There is a Dalit woman in Daya Pawar's *Baluta* who is very assertive, owns quite a lot of property in Mumbai and maintains a caste Hindu man as her keep, which would be impossible in a rural setting. Similarly, there are instances of even illiterate Dalit individuals finding good jobs owing to their hard work and proximity to employers, as is the case with the protagonist in Jadhav's account. Although the protagonist, his wife and his mother find the city quite dirty and congested as compared to the village, the one thing that sets it apart and makes it desirable is that it does not enforce untouchability: 'In our village I could not have entered a tea shop without being identified as a Mahar, and would surely have been driven out instantly' (Jadhav 2003: 89). It is this that makes him equate the city with freedom.

Mohandas Naimishray, a Dalit writer in Hindi, delineates the differences between the city and his town as follows: 'In Bombay there was hunger, poverty and unemployment, but there were no walls separating man and man. Nobody here ever asked me about my caste' (Naimishray 1996: 136). Daya Pawar expresses a similar sentiment: 'It was impossible to forget Bombay. It appeared to me as a city of freedom' (Pawar 1980: 112). Even in relatively smaller urban centres, the feeling of humiliation is not so intense. In Naimishray's account, there is depiction of the life of a Chamar boy living in a Chamar *mohalla* in Meerut city. His family is involved in making leather footwear, a profession often considered polluting. But there is no taint attached to it in his account; he describes it naturally (Naimishray 1996: 15). As he lived in a predominantly Chamar *basti* in an urban locale, the brutal forms of behaviour experienced in the rural areas were not evidenced. Similarly, despite hard work in a mill and, later, a life of uncertain work and poverty, Laxman Gaikwad is better adjusted to the city than he ever was in the village.

However, the feeling of freedom is not always lasting because urban areas are not immune to similar socially restrictive influences. The stigma of untouchability is not fully removed by moving from jobs that were considered low and ritually impure. There is discrimination in the urban areas also. Caste continues to be related to birth, even though the restrictions related to commensality are not so strong. When he is told by a friend that the 'Maharashtrian Brahmins, that too, from Poona . . . don't allow Mahars to touch their dishes', Valmiki feels shocked that such things happen even in a city like Bombay:

> My village was divided along lines of touchability and untouchability. The situation was very bad in Dehradun and in Uttar Pradesh in general at this time. When I saw well-educated people in a metropolitan city like Bombay indulging in such behaviour, I felt a fountain of hot lava erupting within me. (Valmiki 2003: 95).

Even though public spaces do not discriminate any longer, private spaces still do. It is difficult for the Dalits to find rented accommodation or own property in caste Hindu localities. They have to hide their caste names and lie about their caste. When they visit public offices they do not reveal their identity for the fear of putting off the officers there. Once their identity is known, it hinders their efforts to find jobs or to get work done. But hiding one's identity is not a fool-proof guarantee. In fact the reaction is even stronger once the identity is revealed. Friends become enemies and houses erect invisible barriers to bar their entry. There is an ever-present danger of being exposed, and, as a consequence, of being insulted, even assaulted and thrown out. This theme is present in almost all the narratives. The protagonist of Valmiki's autobiography encounters a particularly tormenting situation when an emotional relationship gets shattered because of this.

Still, urban places are preferable because the villages only arouse feelings of intense discrimination and deep hatred. For a large number of the Dalits, urbanization has proved to be a very potent factor for mobility. Although the majority of them still live in the villages, a sizeable number has moved to towns and cities. This has influenced Dalit villagers also, making them more conscious of their rights. The consciousness of and opposition to discrimination is rising and getting more widespread. This has led to a growth in tensions between the Dalits and caste Hindu villagers, who resent the new-found confidence among them and their demand for civic rights. Thus the push factors behind the mobility to urban areas are poverty and social discrimination. And although poverty is also prevalent in the urban areas, the most important pull factor is a sense of relative freedom from caste rules.

Mobility

The mobility depicted in the Dalit autobiographies is both horizontal and vertical. These two types are not necessarily exclusive and sometimes feed into each other. Horizontal mobility occurs between villages or from villages to small urban centres and back. Vertical mobility is of two types: upwards and downwards. Some forms of horizontal mobility take place in a sort of transitional zone. As shown in the narratives by Laxman Mane and Dadasaheb More, they have been occurring since pre-colonial times. These are forms of circular mobility which certain nomadic and semi-nomadic communities undertake for survival. They specialize in particular jobs, like basket-weaving, fortune-telling, sugarcane-cutting, etc., and move from place to place in search of markets for their products and services. The income from this kind of work has to be supplemented by forms of 'non-specialized work' like begging and stealing. The impact of the capitalist economy might have had certain negative effects on the modes of their current livelihood, but it has also created alternate avenues. The modern society and economy, by providing them more opportunities, have greatly increased the scope of their mobility and enhanced the possibility of finding relatively free avenues of livelihood. Although social discrimination is not always apparent as the motivating force for initial mobility, it remains a strong subterranean motive. The shift to urban and semi-urban areas brings a sense of liberation from the caste codes of rural society.

In this way, horizontal mobility to urban centres, even if the earnings are not higher initially and the jobs are insecure, also acts as a lever for vertical mobility. The movement to urban areas occurs for both economic and socio-cultural reasons. Reverse mobility is restricted due to the widening social space in urban areas. Poverty, sometimes extreme, and accompanied by squalor and congestion, does affect them, but the feeling of not being looked down upon socially provides the Dalits great relief. Moreover, there is always the likelihood of upward mobility for individuals if there is an opportunity and if they work hard. The social restriction on upward mobility for individuals and groups is much less than in the villages. Thus the pattern of mobility is often determined as much by socio-cultural factors as by economic ones.

It was education, however, that was, and still remains, one of the most important factors inducing upward mobility. The period of British colonial rule in India had provided this opportunity to the Dalits, though to a very limited extent. In the post-independence period, this space was significantly expanded through reservations in educational institutions and jobs, facilitating a small section of the Dalits to move upwards both economically and socially. The government's policy of affirmative action, help and encouragement from caste Hindu teachers and others, and a lot of self-effort by the concerned persons themselves and their families, have all contributed in some measure towards this goal. However, the road to education has not been an easy one for the Dalits. As Mane's and More's autobiographies portray, for the semi-nomadic communities, getting educated was like working a miracle. These are occupationally mobile groups, staying in one place only for two to four weeks at a time. Sometimes their stay could be as short as two to three days. Thus aspiring children get can get education too only in a 'mobile' manner. For example, Laxman Mane does not remember the name of the village where he first went to school, without books, a slate, pencils or even clothes to wear; More also depicts similar problems. Apart from that, they have to do several odd jobs alongside studying, such as collecting firewood, bringing bamboo from the forest for basket-weaving, begging and so on. Getting an education in such a situation is nothing short of miraculous. It is of course out of the question for girls. Even boys with a modicum of education is a rarity in such communities, for most of their members continue to eke a living by wandering from place to place as in the past, which acts as a deterrent to opportunities for sustained education. In settled Dalit communities, the effects of education are a little more widespread. Moreover, a few success stories encourage many more in that direction. But these communities continue to be bogged down by poverty, hunger, the necessity to work and social discrimination.

There is also a less emphasized theme of downward mobility in these life-narratives. The growth in population, the withdrawal of land allocated to the Dalits by the landholders, the mechanization of agricultural operations, the slow disappearance of community land due to land grab by powerful groups in the villages, and the disappearance of forests or growing restrictions on their use have deprived the disprivileged groups of their traditional means of livelihood. This process has increased the economic dependence of the Dalits on the land-holders in the villages. The nomadic communities also suffer due to the disappearance of public lands where they could pitch their tents, or get raw material for their work or fodder for their animals. All this has led to a deterioration in the condition of Dalits in the rural areas. If there are urban centres nearby, they offset these negative impacts by occasionally providing alternative jobs. Otherwise, the Dalits have to either migrate – individually or in groups – or suffer increasing poverty.

Inter-Generational Changes

From the evidence provided in these life-stories, it may be said that there have been drastic changes in the lives of the characters depicted, in the course of a single generation. All the narrators, except one, have seen within their life-time a transformation in the nature of their work as well as their position. Some of them have gained prestige, power and wealth. Valmiki's parents used to work as agricultural labourers and cleaners in the houses of the landlords. His brothers later did odd manual work in a small city, while he himself became a government officer. Naimishray's father was a leather worker; Naimishray became a journalist and writer. Narendra Jadhav's father earlier did village service and then shifted to Mumbai to become a semi-skilled worker in the railways, while he himself rose to a very high government job.

Although this may apply only to a very small number of people from the Dalit communities, it does point towards things to come. Even Viramma, who remains an agricultural worker till the end of the narrative, has witnessed many changes since her childhood. For one, the attached and servile nature of her work has given way to better employment conditions. Moreover, her son Anban is quite assertive vis-à-vis the landlords, unlike the earlier generation:

> They insist on the old rules: I should always be half naked in front of them, I should speak to them with my arms crossed, I shouldn't wear my *soman* hanging down to the ground, I shouldn't walk in front of them or dress like them! And why should it be like that? They don't feed me, they don't dress me. I don't owe them a thing. I work and they pay for my work, that's all! (Viramma 1997: 192)

It is this change in occupation and attitude that is more commonly seen among the Dalits. In the rural areas, the incidence of attached labour has gone down, and even where it is still seen, it is now renegotiated on an entirely new basis, with the supplicatory attitude replaced by a somewhat assertive tone.

However, the upward mobility does not involve entire families or the kin-network. It is mostly individual, affecting only a few members of the family or relatives. It creates a sort of intra-familial disparity, both at the economic level as well as the mental, behavioural and social levels.

Conclusion

Covering a wide range of time and space – from 1980 to 2009 and from Tamil Nadu to Uttar Pradesh – these life-stories narrate the personal and community experiences of the Dalit writers. Thematically, they reflect upon and generalize multiple dimensions of Dalit existence in rural and urban locales. The depth of experience contained therein and the narrative intensity are quite moving. In these texts, experiences of exploitation and humiliation have been generalized into ontological conditions that have served as the basis for creating a broader identity. However, work has no role in the paradigmatic concerns of the Dalit identity. Since the very beginning, the emerging Dalit movement sought to assert the otherness of Dalits in terms of their putative indigenous roots. The Ad Dharm movement (literally, 'original religion' movement) in Punjab, the Adi Dravida movement in Tamil Nadu, the Adi Karnataka and Adi Andhra movements, and the Adi Hindu movement in Uttar Pradesh were some of the important movements of the early twentieth century which were socially based on the urban Dalits, and derived their sustenance from the resentment and anger generated by their experiences (Juergensmeyer 1982; Lynch 1969; Gooptu 1993; Omvedt 1994). These Dalit movements attacked the notion of a caste-based division of labour and desired freedom in the choice of jobs. However, although they emphasized hard work as in the case of Ad Dharm, they did not question the notion of purity and pollution related to work, nor did they question the idea of work or occupations as inherited. Their assertion, instead, was that they were not the ones who inherited these jobs as they had earlier been the rulers of the land, and were later forced to undertake such low and polluting work by the victorious Aryans. As Jagjivan Ram, a Congress leader and the Labour Minister of newly independent India, emphasized, some Dalits 'did not take up their present callings out of a consideration that all work was noble but because society forced them to menial jobs' (Prashad 2000: 45).

B.R. Ambedkar, the most respected leader of the Dalits, did not much believe in racial differences between Dalits and non-Dalits. He emphasized that the division between them should be viewed in social and religious terms. Moreover, he condemned the village as the most oppressive place for untouchables, and the entire structure of work in rural areas as forced, demeaning and unremunerative for the Dalits. Ambedkar advised his followers, and indeed all untouchables, to move out of the village whenever they found an opportunity. He argued that the association of work with caste and the characterization of some types of work as degrading produces an aversion among those who are engaged in such work. He believed that it was better for the Dalits doing such jobs to move away from them (see Ambedkar 1987–89, Vol. 1: 47–48, Vol. 3: 67–68). Thus, even Ambedkar did not press for a rationalist solution to the problem by detaching work from its ritual meanings and connotations. The lived experience of untouchability proved to be so powerful and painful that it emptied the work and occupations associated with it of all secular meaning.

In these autobiographies also, the village and work in the village are the negative other in any assumption of identity. This remains so in a situation where the great majority of the Dalits have to live and earn their livelihood, and struggle for justice and dignity, in the rural areas.

References

Ambedkar, Babasaheb (1987–89), *Writings and Speeches*, vols. 1 and 3, compiled by Vasant Moon), Education Department, Government of Maharashtra.

Arnold, David and Stuart Blackburn, eds. (2004), *Telling Lives in India: Biography, Autobiography, and Life History*, Permanent Black, Delhi.

Baisantry, Kausalya (2009), *Dohra Abhishap (Dual Curse)* (in Hindi), Parameshwari Prakashan, New Delhi.

Dangle, Arjun, ed. (1992), *Poisoned Bread: Translations from Modern Marathi Literature*, Orient Longman, Bombay.

Gaikwad, Laxman (1987), *Uchalya (The Thief)* (in Marathi); *Uthaigir* (in Hindi), Sahitya Akademi, New Delhi, 2000.

Gooptu, Nandini (1993), 'Caste and Labour: Untouchable Social Movements in Urban Uttar Pradesh in the Early Twentieth Century', in Peter Robb, ed., *Dalit Movements and the Meaning of Labour in India*, Oxford University Press, Delhi.

Guru, Gopal, ed. (2009), *Humiliation: Claims and Context*, Oxford University Press, Delhi.

Gurukkal, Rajan (1997), 'From Clan and Lineage to Hereditary Occupations and Caste in Early South India', in Dev Nathan, ed., *From Tribe to Caste*, Indian Institute of Advanced Studies, Shimla.

Hanumanthan, K.R. (2004), 'Evolution of Untouchability in Tamil Nadu up to AD 1600', in Aloka Parasher-Sen, ed., *Subordinate and Marginal Groups in Early India*, Oxford University Press, Delhi.

Jadhav, Narendra (2003), *Outcaste: A Memoir*, Viking, New Delhi.

Jha, Vivekanand (1975), 'Stages in the History of Untouchables', *The Indian Historical Review*, 2, 1.

—— (2004), 'Candala and the Origin of Untouchability', in Aloka Parasher-Sen, ed., *Subordinate and Marginal Groups in Early India*, Oxford University Press, Delhi.

Juergensmeyer, Mark (1982), *Religion as Social Vision: The Movement against Untouchability in 20th-Century Punjab*, University of California Press, California.

Lynch, Owen (1969), *The Politics of Untouchability: Social Mobility and Social Change in a City of India*, Colombia University Press, New York.

Mane, Laxman (1980), *Upara (The Outsider)* (in Marathi); *Paraya* (in Hindi), translated by Damodar Khadse, Sahitya Akademi, New Delhi, 1993.

Moore-Gilbert, Bart (2009), *Postcolonial Life-Writing*, Routledge, London/New York.

More, Dadasaheb (1983), *Gabal (The Household)* (in Marathi); *Deradangar* (in Hindi), translated by Arjun Chavan, Radhakrishna, New Delhi, 2001.

Naimishray, Mohandas (1996), *Apne Apne Pinjare (One's Own Prison)*, Vaani Prakashan, New Delhi.

Omvedt, Gail (1994), *Dalits and the Democratic Revolution: Dr. Ambedkar and the Dalit Movement in Colonial India*, Sage, New Delhi.

Pawar, Daya (1978), *Baluta* (in Marathi); *Achhoot* (in Hindi), Radhakrishna, New Delhi, 1980.

Prashad, Vijay (2000), *Untouchable Freedom: A Social History of a Dalit Community*, Oxford University Press, New Delhi.

Shah, Ghanshyam, Harsh Mander, Sukhadeo Thorat, Satish Deshpande and Amita Baviskar (2006), *Untouchability in Rural India*, Sage, New Delhi.

Valmiki, Omprakash (1997), *Joothan* (in Hindi); *Joothan: A Dalit's Life* (in English), translated by Arun Prabha Mukherjee, Samya, Kolkata, 2003.

Viramma (1997), *Viramma: Life of an Untouchable* (in English), translated from French by Josiane Racine and Jean-Luc Racine, Verso, London.

The Role of Judgement in Assessing Clients

A Historical Case Study of Reactivation in Sweden

Steven Gascoigne

The relationship between work and welfare has undergone a significant shift in the last two decades, as policy initiatives have increasingly sought to transform measures from passive benefits towards active programmes. Within the labour market, policy has attempted to move away from financially supporting the individual in times of unemployment and towards activating the individual so that labour market reintegration can take place as soon as possible. This move, from passive to active measures, has generated an interest in the harmonization of work and welfare in which labour market participation is the prime focus. At the European level, this harmonization has been codified within the European Employment Strategy: 'To become the most competitive and dynamic knowledge-based economy in the world, capable of sustainable economic growth with more and better jobs and greater social cohesion.'[1]

Furthermore, policy initiatives have also been recalibrated towards the individual, with localised management and design (Bonvin and Farvaque 2005). Clients are given individualized measures designed within the local context, with labour market reintegration as the goal. Benefits within this model are increasingly conditional upon appropriate behaviour by the individual, and imposing a reciprocal relationship between client and agency whereby both must play their part in the route back into work. Often described as 'workfare' or 'welfare to work', these disparate and varied schemes share a number of common attributes which Peck (2001) has used to formulate a generic definition with the following three dimensions.

First, they tend to be of a mandatory nature with no opt-out element, that is, in order to receive benefits, the client must take part in a given scheme. Second, they shift the focus away from welfare entitlements and on to labour market integration. As Peck (ibid.: 12) notes, 'the logic is to "churn" the welfare/ workfare population, to hold them close to or push them into the job market, and to systematically remove alternative means of support in order to enforce (low) wage dependency'. Third, the promotion of active measures to champion work and deter dependence on welfare – here personal responsibility for finding work

---

[1] http://www.etuc.org/a/652, accessed on 3/6/10.

is promoted and encouraged through schemes which seek to activate the client. Although it has been suggested that Peck may have exaggerated the differences between workfare schemes and previous welfare policies (Carpenter and Speeden 2007), his analysis does point to a trend in which these schemes have manifested as localized initiatives, giving rise to policy experimentation and development that depart from previous centralized structures.

This departure from a standardized or 'one-size-fits-all' policy approach to an individualized measure grounded in the locality requires an evaluation of the individual client. That is, an assessment of what characteristics are considered important and what characteristics are ignored when a client is judged in order to create an individualized solution in which work is the goal. This process is grounded in what Amartya Sen calls the 'informational basis of evaluative judgements'. 'In each evaluative structure, some types of factual matters are taken to be important in themselves, others not so. . . . In this sense, each evaluative system imposes – typically implicitly, certain 'informational constraints', which rule out classes of information from having a direct and first-hand role in evaluative judgements (Sen 1991: 16).'

This assessment process is crucial when we consider that the shift toward reciprocal workfare schemes entails an evaluative judgement to be made by officials that can dictate not only what direction a client will take within a given policy, but also what options are open and closed within a range of auxiliary services and schemes including recruitment back into the labour market. Gore (1997) identifies three aspects of this evaluative exercise that inform the process of judgement. First, the selection of valuable aspects must occur prior to any measure of their actual value (for Sen, this in itself is a 'deeply evaluative exercise'; Sen 1991: 236). Second, many disagreements within the evaluative exercise are grounded in the choice of visible objects of value (for example, physical appearance). And lastly, that differing ethical principles can be employed to exclude certain types of information in the judgement process. Within the workfare model, measures of success are in part informed by these evaluative judgements. Notions of responsibility, reciprocity and self-sufficiency are individualized, and success in these areas is based upon how the client has been assessed. To focus upon one aspect while ignoring another can have a significant effect upon how a client is treated within a welfare scheme.

Thus, in attempting to construct an individualized work-first scheme, to what extent does this evaluative judgement inform the process of re-entering the labour market? How does this process differ with regard to those considered to be the best clients and those judged to be less able? Furthermore, how are evaluative judgements affected by economic considerations: are the same judgements made in times of expansion as well as contraction?

In order to tackle these questions and draw out some implications of an active, work-focused scheme for policy delivery, this essay will present a historical case study from Sweden. This case study looks at reactivation in action before the fact – that is, an attempt to reactivate redundant workers before they became unemployed. The Swedish welfare state has been seen as having a particularly successful active labour market policy in the past where full employment and social integration are not only given equal priority but are seen as being mutually reinforcing (Kettunen 2006). Indeed, interest in the Swedish system can be traced at least as far back as 1936 to Marquis Childs' influential work *Sweden: the Middle Way*. As Arter (1999: 146) notes:

> Following Childs's analysis, Sweden became not just another state but a model for other states, its solidarity 'people's home' respected as a shining example of consensus politics and the product of an historic compromise between capital and labour. Sweden became the epitome of an egalitarian culture and pragmatic style of politics that many yearned to emulate.

This account demands a critical appraisal, not least because of its recent influence within European debates, but also due to the influence of Esping-Andersen's (1990) notion of 'de-commodification' where citizens are able to freely 'opt out of work' without the potential loss of income or welfare – this notion was found to be best represented within his Social Democratic model. Yet the notion of 'de-commodification' is problematic as the freedom to 'opt out of work' is rarely given. Rather, the system is tuned toward re-commodification whereby the most productive use of labour is encouraged and facilitated through the powerful labour market board, Arbetsmarknadsstyrelsen (AMS). Indeed, as Kettunen (2006) has noted, waged work is viewed as a social duty in which income-related welfare schemes form part of the same 'work performance model' that sees both work and welfare as aspects of social citizenship. Given this, a Swedish case study provides not only a highly topical example on account of the growing interest in work-focused schemes, but also allows for a critical assessment of an active labour market policy in action.

The case study here focuses on a company called Projekt 80 AB that ran from 1979 to the end of 1980. Its remit was to take approximately 20 per cent of the shipbuilding industry's work force in Gothenburg on the west coast of Sweden, and help them to find new work or, maybe more accurately, to avoid unemployment. As such, Projekt 80 was both an example of Swedish active labour market policy in action and an example of local policy innovation within national labour market policy. Furthermore, the project offered a range of activities and access to a range of agencies in order to produce tailormade measures for individual clients.

Background

In the mid-1970s, 14,500 people worked at the shipyards and a further 3,500 worked in local supply industries in Gothenburg (Hamilton 1980). The city was home to some of the most productive yards in the world with a reputation for quality products (Hedin 1995). The shipyards had expanded at a fast rate throughout the post-war period, but by 1975 orders had stopped arriving – they had no customers. The industry's collapse was rapid, and the first declaration of bankruptcy by a shipyard also took place in 1975. The struggling yards were nationalized in 1976, and by 1978 all the large Swedish yards were under state control. The shipping industry in general faced heavy cuts in capacity and employment. In Gothenburg, for instance, employment at shipyards dropped from the mid-1970s peak to just 3,000 in 1986, with all those employed being involved in repair and offshore work (Stråth 1987: 85). The market for Swedish ships had completely collapsed.

As far back as 1978 the Social Democratic opposition in the Riksdag had opposed a new Shipbuilding Bill presented by the Liberal minority government, by introducing a motion that not only successfully reduced the proposed cut in personnel from 30 to 20 per cent, but also introduced a two-year employment guarantee (Riksdagen 1978–79: 49, 1978–79: 141). The Social Democrats championed capacity reduction through 'socially acceptable means' that prioritized development over liquidation. In Gothenburg, however, this 20 per cent reduction in personnel could not be achieved through natural wastage over the two-year guarantee period and so it was decided to create a special project to pool the redundant workers.

The Shipbuilding Bill had demanded that action be collaborative between shipyards, the unions and public institutions. At the local level in Gothenburg, officials from the nationalized shipbuilding concern, Svenska Varv, worked with the municipality to put flesh on to the bones of the Shipbuilding Bill while keeping within the spending restraints. Visits were made to depressed areas in the Ruhr in West Germany to see how stimulation packages were working, and also to inspect a project to reduce capacity at a Swedish state-owned steel works in Borlänge. There an employment guarantee had been used to soften the blow of redundancy by allowing workers to find new work while retaining their jobs.

The officials adapted the Borlänge project for the specific needs at Gothenburg by removing individuals involved from the workplace, and engaging them instead in development activities. The logic was that decisions about future employment opportunities could be better made once the stress of immediate unemployment was removed. The development activities were to take place in a new company set up within the state-owned shipbuilding concern, which would pool the redundant workers who would then spend the remainder of their two-year employment guarantee engaged in retraining and job search exercises, leaving the company as soon as they found a new job.

Projekt 80: A State-led Solution

This is where Projekt 80 AB came in – the company was designed and set up in 1979 and functioned until the end of 1980 – to facilitate the retraining and job search process: it assisted workers in finding jobs and coordinated the collaborative efforts of the institutions involved.

Projekt 80 was designed to work to a codified system of procedures that laid out four different routes through the project and into employment. Each worker was categorized according to factors such as skill, age, health and employment history (attendance records, etc.), and then ranked in terms of how easy or difficult it would be to get him/her a job. Importantly, these categorizations were made without consulting the workers; they were 'objectively' assessed by officials and ranked on the basis of potential productive capacities. Those considered to have the best chances for employment were marked for 'Alternative 1' in the procedures and the least likely for 'Alternative 4' – or even for what was known as 'the other solution', which would involve a more intensive effort to get people into work and was reserved for the most challenging cases.

The collaborative action demanded by the Shipbuilding Bill brought together state agencies, trade unions, the nationalized shipyard concern (Svenska Varv), and other public bodies concerned with the regeneration of Gothenburg and its labour market. The labour market board (AMS) played a major role in Projekt 80 through its local job centre, vocational training school and regional employment board. AMS set up offices at the shipyards and conducted interviews with all the redundant workers to design for them a personalized route out of the shipyards and into employment, using one of the codified procedures. It collaborated closely with the white collar welfare board (Trygghetsrådet) and liaised with the adult education authority (Komvux) in placing workers. Overseeing Projekt 80 were representatives from Gothenburg municipality, blue and white collar unions, and members of the agencies working within the project.

A number of specialist work groups were also set up within Projekt 80, including the Resursgrupp which was concerned with adverse effects emerging from the transfer to Projekt 80, and the Skyddskommitté whose remit was the welfare of all workers within the project and whose scope went beyond the Resursgrupp to include work-based accidents. Worker welfare was given serious consideration; special attention was given to problems, both work-based and domestic, that could arise out of the redundancy notice; and absenteeism was followed up (Projekt 80 AB 1980).

Alcoholism, domestic violence and suicidal tendencies were concerns that had emerged during studies of the contraction process at the shipyards earlier in the decade (Herloff 1979), and, in an attempt to preempt the issues, routine contact meetings were held with all workers (Posner 1982). This formed part of a guideline on how best to secure the welfare of the workers within Projekt 80 and included the following points (see Project 80 AB 1980).

- Persons who become unemployed generally lose faith in themselves rather quickly. It becomes more and more difficult for them to do something about the situation and loss in working capacity can occur to such a degree that it may never be restored. This is bad for both personal development and the national economy. Help must be given to them to find new and permanent occupation as soon as possible. Temporary work or purposeful training pending a new job is better than being unemployed. Individual solutions for all persons concerned are a must and continuous follow-up is required until results are achieved.

- All persons have their strong and weak points – it may be that the strong points have had no chance to show up in the previous job. Try to build a new future based on on the strong points.
- A person's lack of success in his previous employment may be due to factors other than the person himself. It may be a result of unsuitable work in relation to personal qualifications, relations with fellow workers or foremen, or of conditions outside the workplace.
- Some people will not be able to handle their problems in connection with change of employment. Some of them will be so depressed that they will try to commit suicide. Prevent this with active followiup of absenteeism, together with personal welfare assistance.
- Assume that many people find security in work, that is, they want to keep their old jobs, the well-accustomed routine in the old work place and be in the company of their old fellow-workers and supervisors. Try to make them understand that security can also be found in a positive change.
- Some people may continue to be in a state of 'wishful thinking' – 'in spite of everything I think it will be okay and I will keep my old job.' Get them to understand that this will not come true and that it is absolutely necessary for them to actively search for a new job.
- For many people the greatest problems will arise in their own homes – when trying to give family and friends an acceptable explanation as to the reasons why he or she has been terminated from his or her old job.

Projekt 80: Clients

From its inception in 1979 until its closure at the end of 1980, Projekt 80 worked towards getting as many redundant workers into new jobs as quickly as possible. This reflected the long-held Swedish belief in the benefit of work, not only for financial advantage to the individual and the state, but also for the general well-being of the people and society. Furthermore, its aim was to enable securing jobs on the open market rather than devising state-sponsored relief work. Idleness was seen as corrosive by the project's designers and, as a consequence, workers were kept busy throughout the time they served in the project. A concerted effort was made to ensure that the workers had a routine in their working day. The designers argued that to leave them to sit at home waiting for a new job was to risk the emergence of various negative aspects of unemployment including suicide, domestic violence and alcoholism (Projekt 80 AB 1980). Those workers who could not be immediately placed in new jobs were offered training courses, work experience and various temporary production jobs in the shipyards.

The three main criteria for being transferred to Projekt 80 were old age, short employment service and high absenteeism (Posner 1982). Therefore, the workers in the Projeckt tended to be either relatively young or relatively old. There was also a large group categorized as 'dependent workers', those who

TABLE 1   *Outcomes for those transferred to Projekt 80*

Outcome	White collar	Blue collar	Total
New external employment	22%	43%	37%
New internal employment	23%	13%	16%
Pensioned	42%	15%	22%
Sickness pension	8%	14%	13%
Leave of absence and long-term sickness	5%	15%	12%
Total number transferred	*483*	*1331*	*1814*

Source: Projekt 80 AB (1982).

needed constant supervision at the workplace; they were typically physically or mentally disabled or alcoholics.

Transferral to Projekt 80 was voluntary; workers served with a transfer notice had the choice to transfer to the project or remain in their workplace for the remainder of the employment guarantee period. In all, only twenty-six people turned down the invitation to transfer to the project: sixteen blue collar workers and ten white collar workers. The total number of workers transferred was 1,814 (1,331 blue collar and 483 white collar workers).

The goal of getting these people into work was partially met. When the project closed, 53 per cent of its clients were employed, 34 per cent were receiving some form of pension and 12 per cent were categorized as being sick long-term. Of the 53 per cent that found work, 37 per cent found new work and 16 per cent returned to earlier held positions in the shipyards.

Criteria for Selection of Clients

During the period of expansion that occurred in the 1960s and early 1970s, the shipyards – a labour-intensive industry – suffered severe labour short-ages and needed to enlarge their work force rapidly to keep up with the growing demand for ships. Recruitment drives began targeting neighbouring Nordic na-tions and later included Yugoslavian guest workers as well (Sjölin 2003). Within Sweden, workers in poor health as well as those with disabilities and alcohol abuse problems were once again welcomed, though they required various de-grees of support to perform their jobs. Among non-Swedish workers, some needed help with language barriers, others needed special workshops or supervision, while still others got by with the help of their immediate colleagues.

Regardless of the individual's qualifications, the need for labour out-weighed any productivity concerns regarding such workers. Their personal attri-butes (age, ill-health, alcoholism, etc.) went unnoticed or, at worst, were toler-ated. These very workers, however, were 'recognized' as 'problematic' when the industry went into contraction from 1975 onwards. Capacity reduction methods deviated from the 'last-in first-out' employment laws and were entirely selective; this was because if the 'last-in first-out' laws were adhered to, the process would have removed so many welders and platers that the yards would not have been able to build any ships.[2] Therefore, the selection process for removal from jobs was based on the criterion of productivity, on removing the least productive workers from the shipyards.

Workers with special needs – the elderly and the young – again, were redefined through a stratification process as 'redundant'. The age for retirement was lowered to remove the upper-age group. The young, many of whom had just finished their apprenticeships, were now deemed as lacking in experience. Other 'problematic' workers (those in poor health, those with disabilities, alcohol abuse problems, etc.) were reidentified as 'unproductive'.

As the industry shed labour, the norms defining productive workers became even more stringent. Those at the margins of this definition were selected for transfer to Projekt 80. For some, this process occurred twice: first, when they were chosen for transfer, then again during the functioning of the project when those who were sick and elderly were rendered residual. The contraction process identified the 'least productive' in terms of those who should remain in the labour market, as well as those who were identified as the 'most problematic' in terms of re-entering the labour market.

The process of contraction was thus informed by a criterion that was relative and subjective. Stratifying the work force along the lines of productive capacity gave the selection process its terms of reference, but individual selection was based on a variety of factors of which productivity was only one. For instance, age served as a basis for stratification. Yet, if a worker was considered sufficiently skilled, such that his transfer would damage the department concerned, he was retained irrespective of his age. As mentioned above, this occurred in the case of welders and platers. For this reason, the project contained many relatively old and young workers, but not all old and young workers from the shipyards.

The selection of workers with special needs was slightly different, but still based upon relative circumstances highlighted by the stratification process. Illness, disability and alcoholism were categories based on medical judgment. But this again was relative to the environment in which the individual worked: a missing finger may be a disability but may not affect output. Thus special needs did not always impact negatively upon productivity, but productivity itself came to be understood in a narrower sense and this marginalized many with special needs. Again, it was the process of contraction that highlighted residual workers.

The selection criteria for Projekt 80 reveal how defining a person as 'problematic' was in part informed by the wider context. The categorization of workers was arbitrary, subjective and relative. During periods of expansion and growth workers were defined by their occupation: welder, labourer, shipwright, etc. During contraction these definitions changed and the 'problematic' attributes of the same workers were highlighted: old, inexperienced, disabled, etc. An eld-

---

[2] Discussion with former union official and Social Democrat politician, 10/12/08.

erly welder was seen as a welder during times of expansion and seen as old during times of contraction! Yet the worker subjected to these categorizations often had not changed at all in the time between the two definitions. Thus, perceptions of youth, old age and disability were influenced by external factors such as the economic health of the industry or the state of the economy at large.

When cuts to the work force were deemed necessary and when the principle of 'last-in first-out' was abandoned, individuals were evaluated using an entirely different information base. During growth periods the information base focused upon skill and competencies judged from an industrial viewpoint. During periods of contraction the basis shifted to age and illness judged from a medical perspective.

The initial classification system that placed all workers in one of four groups or 'alternatives', alternative 4 being 'difficult to place', was focused upon a single outcome: labour market participation. As such, this was a narrow definition that produced classifications which lacked sensitivity to difference. For instance, many older workers found themselves categorized under alternative 4, as 'difficult to place'. This categorization missed a vital element: their overall desirability to the potential employer because of their skills and experience. Thus older workers found evaluation based on solely age by prospective employers an obvious disadvantage when competing for jobs.

In order to remedy this, the unions lobbied the project to include an 'elderly guarantee'. Both blue and white collar unions argued that the elderly were at a disadvantage in the labour market, and that the project should acknowledge this by introducing a 'safety net' for clients aged fifty-five and above. The idea became official policy and came to be known as the 'elderly guarantee'. Here, then, the information base shifted from capacity to work, to a recognition that labour market participation is a two-way process needing both employer and employee. After taking union opinion into account, the over-fifty-fives were now recategorized as 'elderly'.

Within Projekt 80, another group of clients who were categorized as 'difficult to place' were those who had physical or mental disabilities, and/or suffered from alcoholism. The desired outcome here was the same as for the other three alternatives: labour market participation. Recategorization within alternative 4 came about almost by accident, late into the project's life-span. After the most desirable clients (i.e. those initially placed under alternatives 1 to 3) found jobs and left, the remaining workers were given closer attention and it was belatedly discovered that a sizeable number of them were those classified as 'difficult to place'. This 'problematic' group of clients included the disabled, for whom the union had not argued for a special clause as it had for the over-fifty-fives, as well as alcoholics.

This was a consequence of the fact that the group of the disabled was very much 'hidden': its members did not socialize with others in their department and had little contact with union representatives. This in turn was because, while employed at the shipyards, disabled workers were often located away from their departments since they had certain needs that were met by placing all of them together in one area. As a result, disabled workers found they had no network of contacts to represent them.[3]

Alcoholic workers, on the other hand, relied heavily on certain colleagues who assisted them in their jobs. Once these 'assistants' were transferred out, the alcoholics had no one around to help them. Their case too was not represented by the unions for the same reasons as for the disabled workers, and they remained 'difficult to place'.

For both the disabled and the alcoholics, recategorization was entirely a consequence of the project's realization that members of their group were not finding new jobs. The process of recategorizing was based upon medical assessment (with information already known to the project gleaned from personnel files). Recategorization here meant recognizing medical information and formulating a new classification, 'special needs'. Whereas the original procedures for difficult-to-place workers had factored in some options to explore when all other routes proved unsuccessful, the recategorization of workers now allowed these measures to be explored early rather than as a last resort, and unlike as codified in the original procedure.

Once defined as 'special needs' clients by the project, the local authority was requested to provide them jobs in sheltered industries. The data on how many clients went into sheltered industries are incomplete. Once again, though, none of the clients were consulted. Indeed, the entire process from the initial focus upon this group of workers to their eventual placement occurred without their involvement; it was conducted and informed entirely by professional opinion.

The 'elderly guarantee', created after union lobbying, and the lack of any such corresponding clauses for disabled and alcoholic workers, seems to show that the project responded better to clients who were able to unite and forward their cause. In fact there is a claim that the project responded well to groups of workers that exhibited solidarity. As the following discussion shows, this claim is inaccurate. On the contrary, the project responded well to recognized institutions: in this case the unions.

As mentioned above, both blue and white collar unions presented the case for elderly clients, but no organization existed to speak up for the disabled and/or alcoholic workers. Furthermore, the elderly as a group typically had longer service history, and were better connected to each other and to officials. The disabled and alcoholics were a disparate group with only their residual status uniting them.

Another group that was well organized were white collar workers of various ages and professions, who created an unofficial technical advisory group within the project. This group was also extremely well connected, as many members were once colleagues of officials working for the project. The group orga-

<hr>

[3] Discussion with union official, 17/09/08.

nized itself around the professions of its members, was open to all white collar union members, created a 'shadow' organization that monitored the running of the project, and offered advice and criticism whenever possible. Although the project had been designed to keep worker-clients active in education and production work, this group also met, wrote reports and planned future activities during this time.

Nevertheless, in contrast to the elderly workers, this group had a *far less responsive relationship* with the project's management. Indeed reaction to the group ranged from hostility to bewilderment. The group was never invited to participate in management and advisory board meetings, its reports were never discussed, and on the few occasions it was consulted, no one could say what the purpose was. This hostility was based on what was seen as a breach of boundaries and membership with regard to technical competence. Essentially, the management was technically competent and the unofficial advisory group was not. This highlights the strict demarcations within the project, and suggests that its largely smooth-running nature was in part due to institutions rarely crossing boundaries and stepping into others' technical domains.

The project management responded to the unions' call for an elderly guarantee scheme as the union was recognized as a body that represented its clients. The unofficial advisory group, however, possessed no such recognition and was therefore ignored. Its work breached the boundaries of both the project management and also the official advisory board. Strict adherence to procedures within the project provided no opportunity for such a group to be incorporated into the official decision-making process. Therefore, the claim that the project responded well to groups of workers that exhibited solidarity is inaccurate; the project responded well only to recognized institutions.

Conclusion

To sum up, this essay argues that the information base of judgement is contextual. The example of Projekt 80 AB shows how these bases changed with changes in the external factors that influenced them. Furthermore, the legitimation of these bases was also contextual; how a person was judged and what was considered legitimate information for making that judgement were also products of external factors.

The dual processes of legitimating knowledge and evaluative judgements dictated who was judged as redundant, what public services were available and the route back into work. The clients' first evaluative judgement occurred when they were recruited into the shipyards; here the informational bases were concerned with productivity: who can work. The second judgement that rationalized workers out of the yards was also based upon productivity, but now the focus was upon impediments to productivity: who slows down the work. The third and last judgement was informed by the medical profile of the clients. In each case it was professional judgement that informed the processes and in each case the labour market was the primary concern.

The use of professional judgement was the key. Knowledge was legiti-
mized by the state, and knowledge of any other kind was rendered illegitimate
and therefore impotent. A comparison between how elderly clients were able to
obtain concessions within Projekt 80 by using a different source of legitimate
knowledge, the union, and how white collar clients who organized into an advisory group were ignored, highlights this aspect. Again, this was contextual: the
unions were able to win concessions for their members only within the specific
context of Projekt 80. On the other hand, the white collar advisory group whose
expertise had been considered legitimate during the employment of its members
at the shipyards, was ignored within the project.

The process of recategorization shows that the information bases of judgement were fluid, and rather than producing dualities such as who can work and
who cannot, or who is fit and who is not, they reflected the wider context. Just as
when contraction deepens more people are rationalized out of the labour market,
so too during expansion more people are absorbed into the labour market. At
each stage a reclassification highlights how different information bases are contextual, and how the knowledge that informs this process is itself dependent upon
a contextual, legitimizing process.

As mentioned at the start of this essay, a shift toward individualized and
localized measures within a broad framework of 'work-first' policies necessitates
individualized evaluative judgments. Notions of productivity, old age and illness
are as fluid and contextual today as they were in 1970s Sweden. The structural
framework that informs judgements, in terms of both the wider context and legitimizing knowledge, is crucial to our understanding of individualized policy
measures.

References
Arter, D. (1999), *Scandinavian Politics Today*, Manchester University Press, Manchester.
Bonvin, J.M. and N. Farvaque, (2005), 'What Informational Basis for Assessing Job-Seekers?
    Capabilities vs. Preferences', *Review of Social Economy*, vol. 63, no. 2, pp. 269–89.
Carpenter, M. and S. Speeden (2007), 'Origins and Effects of New Labour's Workfare State:
    Modernization or variations on old themes?', in M. Carpenter, S. Speeden and B.
    Freda, eds., *Beyond the Workfare State: Labour markets, equality and human rights*,
    Polity Press, Bristol.
Childs, M. (1936), *Sweden: The middle way*, Yale University Press, New Haven.
Esping-Andersen, G. (1990), *The Three Worlds of Welfare Capitalism*, Polity Press, Cambridge.
Gore, C. (1997), 'Irreducibly Social Goods and the Informational Basis of Amartya Sen's Capa-
    bility Approach', *Journal of International Development*, vol. 9, no. 2, pp. 235–50.
Hamilton, C. (1980), *Shipbuilding, A Study in Adjustment: The cases of Sweden and Japan*,
    Institute for Economic Studies, Stockholm.
Hedin, G. (1995), *Svenska Varv: Världsledande*, Tre Böcker Förlag AB, Göteborg.
Herloff, B. (1979), *Frånvaro Bland De Arbetare, Som Flyttats Från Eriksberg till Götaverken
    Motor, Under Åren 1976–1978*, Projekt Lindholmen, Göteborg.
Kettunen, P. (2006), 'The Power of International Comparison', in N.F. Christiansen, K. Petersen,
    N. Edling and P. Haave, eds., *The Nordic Model of Welfare: A historical reappraisal*,
    Museum Tusculanum Press, Copenhagen.
Peck, J. (2001), *Workfare States*, Guilford Press, New York.
Posner, L. (1982), *Frånvaro Bland de Arbetare som Uttagits till Projekt 80*, Psykologiska Inst.,
    Göteborgs Universitet, Göteborg.

Projekt 80 AB (1980), *Principal Mark Settings for Projekt 80 AB*, Lindholmen Utveckling AB, Projekt 80 AB, Göteborgs Regional Arkiv: F6AII, Göteborg.

——— (1982), *Slutrapport*, Lindholmen Utveckling AB, Projekt 80 AB, Göteborgs Regional Arkiv: F6AII, Göteborg.

Riksdagen (1978/1979a), *Prop. 1978/79:49*, Riksdag, Stockholm.

——— (1978/1979b), *Motion 1978/1979:141 av Olof Palme m.fl. med anledning av propositionen 1978/1979:49 om vissa varvsfrågor*, Riksdag, Stockholm.

Sen, A. (1991), 'Welfare, Preferences and Freedom', *Journal of Econometrics*, vol. 50, nos. 1–2, pp. 15–29.

Sjölin, M. (2003), *Varvsindustrins för – och nackdelar*, Lindelöws bokförlag, Göteborg.

Sträth, B. (1987), *The Politics of De-industrialization*, Croom Helm, London.

Work Transformation

What Do Market Mechanisms (Really) Mean?

A Study of Bulgarian Maritime Livelihoods after 1989

Milena Kremakova

The fall of the communist regimes in Central and Eastern Europe (CEE) after 1989 saw the state-centred approach to industry management and labour distribution being replaced by democratic governance and a market economy. Institutional and economic reforms in these countries were further complicated by post-industrial developments taking place in the rest of the European Union (EU): ageing populations, declining industries, rising importance of services and increasing global competition. This presented a double challenge to EU's newest member-states[1] which have responded differently to the daunting task of marketization; it is therefore important to bear in mind their national specifics when analysing post-communist transitions. With this in mind, this text focuses on the labour market within one sector (the maritime sector) in one country (Bulgaria), using data from an indepth ethnographic study of Bulgarian maritime labour.[2]

The study follows a 'sectoral approach', similar to Tchalakov's work on Bulgaria (2008) and Greskovitz's studies of Hungary (2006, 2007a, 2007b), using the specificity of the maritime industry as an asset rather than a liability. As an autonomous sub-sector, it lends itself to a case-study approach (see, for instance, Flyvbjerg 2006). Owing to the wide range of maritime trades, professions, qualifications and types of enterprises (private, recently privatized and still state-run), it offers insight into a variety of post-socialist phenomena, from state-run measures (such as mass privatization) to spontaneous globalization of the pool of employers and flexibilization of labour conditions and contracts. Furthermore, no sector in itself is representative of Eastern European labour; in Bulgaria in particular, employees of different industries 'experienced entirely different (post-socialist) transitions' (Tchalakov 2008). Therefore, an indepth study

---

[1] Malta, Cyprus, Estonia, Latvia, Lithuania, Poland, Czech Republic, Slovakia, Slovenia and Hungary joined the EU in 2004; and Bulgaria and Romania in 2007.

[2] The study, conducted in 2007–09 as part of the author's Ph.D. thesis (in progress), uses a mixed qualitative method approach, including 52 indepth, loosely structured biographical interviews (with Bulgarian nationals currently or formerly employed in various maritime jobs); contextual content analysis of written material (news articles, laws and agreements, individual and collective labour contracts, and historical literary sources); and participant observation.

of one sectoral labour market can provide insights otherwise missed by larger-scale approaches that aggregate and generalize disparate sectors. Despite the specificity of the maritime labour market, the study also sheds light on issues pertinent to post-socialist labour marketization in Bulgaria. However, any parallels with the other CEE countries, or with maritime labour elsewhere, would require further research and remains beyond the scope of the current essay.

Methodology of the Study

The study uses several qualitative research methods including indepth interviews, contextual analysis of written documents and observation. Such a qualitative study of the maritime sector was aimed at uncovering the mechanisms of post-communist Bulgaria becoming a part of the global market economy. This, in turn, was considered essential to understand the integration of post-socialist labour with global market forces, as well as for future longitudinal studies of employment experience. Interviews with seafarers aimed at reconstructing personal stories of their working life, and their position in formal and informal professional networks (collegial, educational, familial and friendship links), as well as discussing current maritime problems. Interviews with officials and managers focused on maritime affairs, trajectories of institutional change, and comparing pre- and post-1989 labour management practices, with the aim of outlining key historical 'breaking points' between 1989 and 2009. Most of these interviews included a biographical element, allowing a schematic reconstruction of 'higher-profile' careers. Interviews were differentiated by profession and rank, and loosely grouped into two age cohorts: 'juniors' (aged 18–40) and 'seniors' (over 40). (A middle-age group could also be distinguished, aged 30–45.) A strong gender bias towards males and a slight age bias towards seniors were reflected in the sample. Participants from all key local institutions were interviewed (from businesses, non-governmental organizations, trade unions, maritime administration, and current and retired employees from all professions and hierarchical positions). A combination of stratified and snowball sampling with the help of a number of local 'gatekeepers' allowed us to construct a mini-model of the maritime community, overcoming the difficulties of access.

Documents, media reports, and historical and literary sources contextualized the biographical narratives. Unfortunately, access to pre-1989 archival data on both the Navy and the Merchant Marine was impossible: socialist shipping was a semi-military industry overseen by the Ministry of Interior, and its documents were classified and kept in secret archives that were largely misplaced or destroyed after 1989. The lack of secondary statistical data also merits an explanation. The current paucity of both regional and national data indicates that extensive research is needed to fill in the statistical and analytical gaps.[3]

---

[3] Two main international sources of data and analysis are the International Transport Workers' Federation (ITF), and Seafarers' International Research Centre in Cardiff – cf. Ellis and Sampson (2008), Wu and Winchester (2004). On five research trips over

Consequently, fieldwork and analysis was confined to an exploratory frame.

As in all ethnographic research, classifications are tentatively imposed on the 'rich ambiguity' of data (Nietzsche 1974). A serious limitation common to all research using oral histories is also the problem of memory. The non-linearity of post-socialist careers also contributed to the arbitrariness of any neat classification of interviews, and highlighted the pervasiveness and strategic importance of personal networks and multiple socio-economic roles: careers increasingly include many jobs across different workplaces in one or more industries. Successful and influential individuals tend to be proactive, simultaneously occupying various positions, and therefore evade neat classifications. On the other hand, there are also many invisible actors who do not participate in public life, are missing from the statistics and are extremely difficult to find, even in the course of a long-term ethnographic study. This is because in the maritime sector, an increasing number of young men and, since recently, women, are almost impossible to interview: they sail under foreign flags, spend little time on shore and are not a part of the geographically defined community.

Post-Socialist Bulgaria: Emergence of the New Labour Market

Post-socialist markets did not emerge from scratch; they were built on pre-existing resources, practices and conventions. Recent research refutes the previously common understanding that a market for labour did not exist in CEE before 1989. For instance, Clarke (1996, 2007), in an extensive study of the post-1989 Russian economy, argues that labour was the most marketized sphere of the socialist economy and played a crucial part in balancing its other parts.

The situation is fairly uniform across the Eastern bloc with regard to the key differences with today's labour market. A prominent feature of employment under state socialism was very narrow salary differentiation, which was compensated for by an intricate web of non-monetary means of payment (i.e. enterprise-managed provision of an extensive range of welfare services) and centralized distribution of workplaces (i.e. compulsory nationwide placements for trainees or education graduates). Another important feature of socialist societies was the resilience of what Bulgarian labour sociologist Chavdarova (2007) calls 'the market of personal connections'. This informal web, based on friendships, family connections and college networks, survived the change of regime and continued to retain crucial importance in the post-1989 evolution of the Bulgarian labour market.

The post-1989 industrial and employment developments in CEE were not qualitatively different from those that took place in the west in the second half of the twentieth century; in CEE, however, marketization was more dramatic and felt more acutely, because it occurred in a condensed time-period in less affluent societies which had little experience of the free market and less stable

---

two years, I did not find any locally available statistics, reliable or otherwise, even on such a basic numerical fact as the exact current number of seafarers.

institutional environments. Alongside new opportunities, the ensuing economic and political crisis also carried a high social price;[4] as Avramov (2001: 38) summarizes, '1989 simultaneously brought collapse and the sense of a "new beginning"'. In the early 1990s, the majority of the population (including all pensioners) found themselves sinking deeper under the official poverty line, in an environment of increasing economic and social insecurity, and unable to plan their lives in the long term. By 2009, the population had shrunk by 15 per cent due to external migration and falling birth-rates.[5] Further, due to the slow development of civil society (Kabakchieva 2001), the newly democratic state remained primarily responsible for the legal, institutional and policy reforms necessary to establish the new system of democratic governance and free market. Thus, paradoxically, market liberalization happened largely from above, even though the powers of the formerly totalitarian state had shrunk on the whole. The publicly avowed aims of the reforms were EU-like standards of governmental openness, transparency and accountability. Yet, in practice, many observers suspected that administrative reorganization and reshuffling tended to obscure the lack of indepth reform, that some reforms were driven by private interests, and that even if the wording of the law was of the highest standard, its implementation left a lot to be desired. Bulgarian analysts have noted that speedy, inconsistent, top–down and non-transparent institutional and welfare reforms in Bulgaria have frequently been carried out at the expense of long-term sustainability, social security and institutional legitimacy, have induced a more or less temporary regulatory vacuum, and have facilitated the proliferation of shady economic practices (Kabakchieva 2001; Dimitrov and Kabakchieva 2003; Dimitrov 2004; Tchalakov 2008).

Most state-run industries underwent mass privatization resulting in downsizing, closure of branches and rising unemployment through labour-shedding measures such as mass lay-offs and early retirement programmes. Parts of the new private sector emerged from what had formerly been the 'socialist black economy'. Politics and business became entangled. In the early 1990s, a small circle of private security firms became the racketeering rulers of the newly liberated but loosely regulated market rife with public and private corruption scandals, urging sociologists and journalists to speak of 'normalization' or 'chronification' of the 'post-socialist crisis'. Many more new businesses were established than could possibly survive, and many of those that survived and are still in business have operated in part in this 'second' or 'shadow' economy at some point in time.

As the private sector grew, it created some, but not enough, jobs to compensate for the demise of state-run industries; in addition, most private sector jobs were and continue to be volatile, lacking employment or welfare security although often providing a decent wage. In contrast, at least until their

---

[4] Dobrinski (2000) terms it the 'triple drain' crisis, as it simultaneously affected public finances, the banking system and the exchange rate.

[5] From 8,877,000 in 1989 to 7,585,131 in 2009 (World Bank data).

privatization, the struggling ex-socialist large state enterprises and the state administration provided a lower wage (around or under the survival minimum), but also long-term contracts and welfare security.

The post-socialist labour market emerged as fragmented, informalized and increasingly precarious, and was characterized by increased flexibility and decreased social security. Informal market mechanisms and non-standard forms of employment proliferated as means for offsetting the economic crisis. Broken career paths, multiple jobs, partially or fully undeclared (envelope) wages (Williams 2008), unemployment among highly qualified job-seekers (especially university graduates) and work after retirement became the norm. Shortening time-horizons, worsening career prospects, and the loss of job security and status brought disillusionment. Young people became less attracted to traditional professions and instead became 'permanent temporary' workers in tourism and other service jobs in the private sector, while older employees in general (though not always) tended to hold on to secure jobs.

Joining the Global Maritime Market:
Changing Opportunities for CEE Seafarers

The transformation of the Bulgarian maritime sector (and that of other CEE countries) has been dramatic, but not entirely novel: it repeated in a condensed period, the developments of non-socialist economies over the second half of the twentieth century, which has been particularly visible in the globalization of cargo shipping. Globally, the steady expansion of the 'shipping bubble' during the last few decades created an almost ideal liberal market situation (which was cut short by the financial crisis of 2009). The industrial boom in China and the Far East in the 1970s–1980s led to a rising supply of goods which needed transporting; portaging prices skyrocketed, luring new ship owners into the market; the rising demand for ships and workers to man them was accompanied by a shipbuilding boom and rise in wages. This, then, led to an increased supply of seafarers, notably from countries such as the Philippines and China. However, while the supply and demand of ratings[6] were balanced, in 2009 there was still an acute global shortage of officers.[7]

Maritime denationalization and marketization in Bulgaria began in 1989 against the backdrop of these global developments. While most other previously centralized state-owned sectors, such as telecommunications, air transport, energy, water supply, crude oil processing, etc., were urgently subjected to mass privatization, the fate of the maritime sector was different. The State Fleet[8] did

---

[6] Less qualified or unqualified seafarers (e.g. boatswains, able seamen, motormen, cooks).

[7] Highly qualified seafarers (navigators and engineers, including captain and chief engineer) requiring specialized post-secondary education (in Bulgaria, the only way to become an officer was, and still is, through the Varna Naval Academy or two engineering universities).

[8] The official Latinized brand name Navibulgar®, adopted in 1943, originates from the abbreviated French Navigation Maritime Bulgare. The Bulgarian abbreviation BMF

become leaner, and was scaled down due to deterioration of old vessels and scarce investment in new technologies; it also suffered losses due to problems in the production chain (i.e. dwindling coal production) and faced global competition much fiercer than that within the formerly jointly planned Council for Mutual Economic Assistance (COMECON) economies. Nevertheless, cargo shipping remained one of the most profitable sectors of the post-socialist economy. Company data confirm the fact that since 1990 it only suffered declining revenue growth – but never actual net loss.

The privatization of cargo shipping in Bulgaria took an unprecedented length of time. Accomplished in 2008, it lacked transparency and caused a huge stir in the maritime community (for intance, rumours spread about certain newly made local shipowners who had allegedly acquired vessels as scrap during the company's scaling down, and refurbished them). The predominant attitude in the maritime community towards privatization even today is negative. The feeling is one of loss and destruction, as seen in the hoard of catastrophic descriptives: the fleet is ruined (съсипват), destroyed/exterminated (унищожиха), demolished (сринаха), gradually drained (източиха), subjected to agony (агония), wiped out (затриха), annihilated (изтребиха), crushed (стъпкаха), sold off (продадоха), ransacked (ограбиха), betrayed (предадоха), swindled (шашма), defrauded (измама). The industry is seen as profitable enough to have deterred ten successive governments from pushing forward a mass privatization plan.[9] Yet, according to many disgruntled interviewees (both managers and seafarers), the state had used maritime revenues ('milking the cow of the State Fleet' and 'not in a rush to let go of their share of the pie' in a thriving trade) without supporting the industry (for instance, even the basic step of adopting a maritime strategy has not materialized). It must be stressed that the conservatism prevalent among seafarers (conservatism in the Bulgarian context is expressed as a tendency to defend the former, communist regime) is not rooted in blind devotion to 'socialist values'. Rather, the pessimism is firmly rooted in insider knowledge which has allowed seafarers to develop an elaborate, often articulate, understanding of how privatization works in practice. Their defence of state ownership is a defence of the only other system that they know in practice, as opposed to the current system which has not worked for them: 'Personally, I think, in two to three years from now, the Steamship Company will . . . it will be no more. At least not the way it was until now. Because in Bulgaria we haven't had a single case of normal privatization – only company 'liquidations' fraught with corruption.'

In contrast to cargo shipping, shipbuilding and especially deep ocean fishing suffered immediate decline: shipbuilding yards were scaled down and

---

(БМФ) stands for the shipping company 'Bulgarian Maritime Fleet' (Параходство Български Морски Флот); it is commonly used by employees with a definite article, 'the' ('БМФ-то'), to convey informality and familiarity, as this used to be in effect the only shipping company for several decades.

[9] In the period between the first democratic elections on 4 February 1990 and EU accession on 1 January 2009.

gradually privatized, while the national ocean fishing fleet went bankrupt in 1998 (in 2010, dozens of lawsuits by former fleet employees were still pending). Informal evidence suggests that whereas many former ocean fishing workers (those still of working age) are employed in various maritime or other jobs, no official record exists of some 30,000 dismissed workers. As an angry port agent who was laid off just one year before he was to retire, said: 'You ask where they all went? They were left out in the street! Everyone had to take care of himself and find a job somewhere.'

At the same time, the maritime market was opening up rapidly and new workplaces were absorbing excess labour no longer needed in the two shrinking state fleets. By 1992, foreign ship owners had 'discovered' Bulgarian seafarers, and by 1994 several were already established local employers. Meanwhile, dozens of small and large crew manning agencies (CMAs)[10] emerged as mediators on the maritime job market, and numerous small private maritime businesses appeared. The rapid opening of the market in 1990 liberated national fleets both from full state control and from the state's protection, as they were absorbed by the then flourishing global maritime industry. A season of unpredictable changes set in, especially for seafarers, but to a lesser extent for shore workers as well. The security of socialist seafaring careers was no longer tenable outside the encapsulated environment of a totalitarian state; maritime employment had become doubly precarious.

These factors redefined the meaning and role of seafaring professions. At first, the sudden flood of globalization propelled Bulgarian seafarers away from stable and prestigious employment in national fleets, into the global pool of cheap-waged maritime labour where they had to work for supranational ship owners in international crews dominated by other nationals – predominantly Filipino and Chinese professionals. A decade later, the new trade and labour regulations that EU candidate-member states accepted promptly reclassified CEE mariners once again: this time, as part of the expensive 'western' labour force. The EU's social model is now inadvertently causing undesired effects, as the maritime labour force in European countries is being priced out by less well-protected overseas labour.

Further, this study found that as new employment opportunities opened and old ones disappeared after 1989, inequalities and informal hierarchies among seafarers were redrawn according to their place of work. Interviews with workers show that marketization quickly resulted in a new stratification of maritime workplaces according to different types of contracts and working conditions, and, consequently, of their desirability from the workers' standpoint (while inter-

---

[10] Crew manning agents (CMAs) are private labour market intermediaries who specialize in recruiting seafarers, and mediate between job-seekers and employers; they may work with one or more ship owners, and essentially perform the function of an outsourced personnel department. In Bulgaria and other non-English-speaking countries, CMAs are typically managed (and often owned) by former seafarers who know the language and are known in the community.

view evidence is not representative, it does reveal a strong trend). Today, three distinct types of workplaces can be identified: state-owned firms, small 'local' ship owners (Bulgarian or Greek), and large international corporations.

Of these, the State Fleet and the maritime administration retain the (not uniquely) socialist practice of long-term contracts, relatively low salaries and full social security packages even after EU accession. For instance, up until its 60 per cent privatization in 2008 when over a thousand administrative jobs were shed, Navibulgar remained a symbol of security, long-term employment and the biggest sole employer of Bulgarian seafarers, employing 10 per cent of all Bulgarian nationals who own seafaring passports (it is less easy to characterize it now, a short time after the privatization).

Private employers, on the other hand, use contractually limited employment, driven by the need for a flexible work force in a global maritime market. The difference between small local and large global ship owners lies in scale, wealth and reputation. Local employers are smaller and less affluent, operate older vessels, pay less, offer only short-term contracts frequently devoid of any welfare clauses (for instance, no health care contributions beyond emergency repatriation in case of life-threatening accident or disease), subtly discourage union participation (as two interviewees indicated), and sometimes operate on the verge of the grey economy ('small firms don't pay; here in our city all ship owners are small, they have one or two boats').

Meanwhile, global firms offer the most lucrative sea jobs, but fierce competition allows them to pick only the youngest, best qualified and healthiest among Bulgarian seamen and officers.

'No Longer "The First after God"':
Globalization, New Managerialism and Deskilling of Maritime Labour

The day-to-day nature of seafaring jobs has changed little since 1989. A ship's crew still operates within a strict, quasi-military hierarchy in which every crew member knows his/her direct commander, and discipline, obedience and strict adherence to a rigid working schedule is required. Seafarers still go to sea for months on end, followed by weeks or months of shore leave. They still have notoriously troubled family lives, low life expectancy and bad health. They still receive better salaries than their friends on shore, yet their pensions continue to be extremely low. They are still mainly men, although women have been allowed to study at the Naval Academy since 2001, and there are now a small but rising number of young women employed in the Bulgarian Navy and on board foreign merchant ships.[11]

---

[11] This was primarily a response to the falling applicant rate, according to an interview with the Naval Academy's Provost: in the 1980s there were eight to ten applicants per place in the Academy; in the early 1990s, just after the economic crisis, five to six applicants; three to four applicants in the end of the 1990s; and only 1.2 applicants on an average per seat/vacancy in 2008.

All seafarers, however, have experienced the effects of the sudden globalization, new types of fleet ownership and changing managerial principles. Owing to mechanization, crews have become smaller and the workload bigger, although some jobs have become easier and more workplaces are now available. Officers – captains in particular – have also lost a significant degree of their former independence on the job, paradoxically correlated to increased responsibilities and increased accountability in an atmosphere of tightened security rules. As a 59-year-old captain noted: 'We captains don't mean much any more. I used to be "the first man after God" like in that famous novel. Now we are simple executives waiting for commands from ashore.' Captains now function as operational managers, still in charge of the unit (ship) but under much more direct command of the ship owner. Virtually all of the interviewed captains stressed their increasing loss of workplace autonomy in the last ten to fifteen years and the changing principles of management, as evident from the words of another 56-year-old captain: 'We captains feel like serfs.' According to a third seasoned veteran, a 58-year-old captain, 'All you do is sit buried in paperwork and report to shore by telex every five minutes.'

Due to reduced autonomy and the global pressure of shortage of officers, it has also become easier to reach the post of captain or chief engineer, the minimum requirement being only seven to eight years of serving as a junior officer (as compared to at least fifeen years in the 1970s and 1980s). Yet, as a result of all the above changes and the post-2000 tendency of maritime wages to grow more slowly than wages in other jobs, all maritime workers (but officers to a larger extent) have experienced a notable decrease in social standing. Less qualified and less well-paid seamen, deprived of social benefits and health care in private companies, face the necessity of using up their savings to pay for expensive seafaring qualifications and certificates. They often choose to stay on shore in worse paid but less risky jobs. The brightest of young men no longer want to be maritime officers. A 40-year-old former captain, now a manning agent, notes:

> . . . when I graduated from the English language high school in 1989, the two most prestigious places to go were the Naval Academy in Varna and International Relations (IR) in the Sofia University – not even law or economics – the only way to travel abroad was to be a diplomat or seafarer, so if your uncle was a diplomat, you went to IR, and if not! I'm joking, but you know how it was.

Though competition for places in the Naval Academy has dramatically decreased,[12] the most ambitious among those who have become officers voice disappointment, including this 26-year-old third officer working on a Greek ship:

> I've sailed on ships where it is getting worse and worse, the ship owner tries to reduce the crew, the International Maritime Organization tries to increase the

---

[12] See footnote 11 above.

workload so that everything is objective, each activity on board must be carried
out according to international standards, documents must be filled in, a thous-
and check-lists, for each teeny-weeny job you use up more paper and it takes
you more time than the job itself . . . which is not nice at all. And suddenly you
get this impression that the folks on shore consider you almost a moron and
think you need others to tell you, like, what you are to do. There is some logic
in this, generally seafarers are, how do I put it . . . well, unskilled labour. But the
stupid thing is that in Bulgaria the stupid communist system brought up the old
captains and myself in such a way that it has wasted five years of my life to study
for a degree which the west – not only in the west, but also the basic crew . . . Fili-
pinos, Indians,[13] Pakistanis, they don't waste five years in university, they directly board a ship without any education. And here I am, with my Master's
degree in navigation, stuck in a monkey job.

Some seek better career prospects on shore. A respondent who relin-
quished his career as captain at 40 to become a manning agent, with his retired
father, also a captain, as assistant, said: 'Being captain isn't as exciting as it was
in my dad's time, managers on shore know every step you take; being a manning
agent – this is real business, challenging and rewarding, even if stressful.'

All interviews with managers pointed to the falling quality of maritime
training and education as a key reason for the decreased responsibilities that can
be entrusted to the crew (the younger of whom are presumably not qualified
enough to be entrusted with the difficult responsibilities of decision-making at
sea, where expensive cargoes, tight schedules and stringent security requirements
are concerned). Most interviewees, including young graduates, professors and
seafaring professionals, agreed that the quality of maritime education in Bulgaria had worsened due to inadequate training equipment, relaxing of naval
discipline and weakened competition among aspiring seafarers (as better job
opportunities were available on shore). According to a staff member at the formerly state-owned, largest qualification centre:

Equipment costs thousands of dollars, yet people get the same document regardless of whether they take a cheaper course even though the equipment at

---

[13] The interviewee's opinion of Indian maritime specialists must, however, be corrected.
Any officer-level crew in India has to clear a merchant marine college degree course
first. Entry-level selection into the course is on the basis of a nationwide open written
examination, followed by an interview for students who pass the written exam. Selected candidates proceed to the Training Ship Chanakya, a shore-based academy
managed and maintained by the Government of India, Ministry of Surface Transport,
through the Directorate General of Shipping. The three-year degree course here culmi-
nates in the award of a B.Sc. (Nautical Sciences) degree from the University of Bombay. It is common knowledge that trained Indian merchant navy officers are in great
demand the world over for their proficiency, expertise and dedication to their profession.
It is noteworthy to mention that the nautical training imparted in this institution is of
a very high quality, and in accordance with the standards and norms laid down by
international bodies like the International Maritime Organization.

these centres does not comply with either the Convention[14] or the Act.[15] For instance, an advanced fire fighting course is taught in a lecture hall! Yet, when the European Maritime Safety Agency sends a quality-check . . . they are sent here, not to those places which totally lack equipment . . . but enough about disloyal competition! . . . This is clearly corruption at the state level and public corruption at that . . . . Whatever projects we may have, as long as the state lacks the political will to bring some order, we can't do anything. . . . There are rules – but they are only valid for us, they are not valid for somebody else.

Port specialists, such as a 60-year-old port captain with thirty-five years work experience at this job, also agree that the quality and professionalism of port workers is declining:

The job of a docker used to be a serious profession [but] with the change of cargoes, everything comes in containers now, the skill and profession got lost. . . . Dockers used to come with secondary [school qualification] and we would send the good ones to study English and port management at the Vocational College of Economics and promote them to stevedores. . . . Now stevedores come with engineering degrees in port management but they land here as if after a parachute jump, they have no clue about how a port really works . . . and discipline is generally appalling.

The quality of training and professionalism seems to be the result, not the root of the problem. The determining global force behind the rapid deskilling of seafaring labour is the changing nature of the maritime trade. The globalization and unification of cargo shipping urged a profound global change in managerial practices in shipping, making the management of maritime businesses more centralized and hyper-efficiency-oriented. Due to the overly populated shipping market, shipping companies operate on increasingly thinner profit margins, require longer-term planning, and have become so complex that they are not subject to any kind of national or supranational control. In this sense, cargo shipping is the extreme version of a liberal market left to itself.

As far as crew manning agents are concerned, they not only recruit but also manage and 'engineer' crews using neo-management techniques of keeping the staff motivated by keeping them 'on edge'. As one manning agent notes, 'If we kept them on the same ship, they'd get used to it and become complacent that they know every nook and cranny, which isn't good when an emergency invariably occurs.'

The above changes were triggered by containerization (Levinson 2006) and other positive technological developments in cargo shipping, such as cheaper and more reliable communication via telex and the Internet replacing traditional

---

14 IMO Standards of Training, Certification & Watchkeeping Convention (drafted in 1978, amended in 1995).
15 Bulgarian Maritime Specialists Training Act (2003).

radio connection based on the Morse code and performed by highly skilled radio officers both on board and on shore; constant and reliable tracking and increased safety and security became possible due to the development of the satellite global positioning system (GPS) and Global Maritime Distress Safety System (GMDSS).

What seems to be neglected by both managers and policy makers globally is that the stability provided by new technology and long-term economic planning is illusionary. Uncertainty at sea caused by weather, technological failures, human mistakes and, recently, maritime pirates has by no means been eliminated, nor is it likely to disappear any time soon. Interviews with seafarers found these problems being raised unanimously and repeatedly. Saving time and money becomes a priority and increasingly jeopardizes the 'Safety First' principle which used to be the main principle on board. In extreme cases, this takes on ridiculous dimensions. According to respondents, ships are 'ordered via telex by armchair managers' to cut through the Gulf of Aden, risking a pirate attack, instead of taking an extra few days to sail around the dangerous area; or, the new company owner chases managers around the headquarters switching off lights to save on electricity bills, etc.

Fragmented Careers and the Decline of Professional Identity

One of the most striking changes of the post-1989 period concerns the length and stability of maritime careers, which have become increasingly fragmented. Even allowing for lapses of memory and omissions of intermittent job placements in the stories of seniors, the differences are significant. In the first instance, junior participants between the ages of 20 and 35 on average report a similar number of jobs as compared to their seniors despite having much lesser work experience, while a third of all interviewed seniors cite only one workplace throughout their adult working life (excluding summer jobs at school).

Job-changing was not unknown before 1989 – about half the senior interviewees had changed industries, firms, and/or acquired qualifications later in life. Still, only two out of thirteen senior respondents had highly fragmented careers (five to ten workplaces).[16] Careers of seamen of the older generation were, in comparison to officers, more fragmented, but nowhere close to today's generation.

A second major difference is the far greater anxiety of seniors towards both actual and potential job changes. The typical senior felt like a 'fish out of water (captain, 59 years) when Navibulgar was privatized in 2008. Such seniors faced the necessity of having to forego their lifelong loyalty to their employer in order to find a job after (or in anticipation of) redundancy, or after taking voluntary early retirement. The interviews were replete with stories of distress, with many interviewees and their colleagues aged over 45 fearing redundancy for years without finding a job in the private sector. A 56-year-old chief officer in

---

[16] Both these men had low qualifications and had worked mostly as seamen; one of them added qualifications later in life.

Navibulgar, speaking to the author in 2008, a few months before privatization was announced, said: 'Your dad and I, we grew up in this company, so to speak, and I see the way things are going now: they are not going well.'

In comparison, young people, like the 26-year-old third officer on a Greek ship (quoted in the previous section and whose career began after 1989), whose short but unsatisfying career has prepared them for radical professional change, are far less anxious:

> I've changed three ships, three companies in less than two years. That's not exactly what I call stable, but what can you do. I am quitting this one too, the conditions are not good. In fact I'm disappointed with seafaring altogether, I want to work on a small coastal boat, I've already got the Certificate and everything; or I'll get a job on the coast or start my own business.

There is more than one explanation for this gap in generational attitudes. The first is the objective difficulty of finding a job: as in Russia (see Clarke, 1996, 2007), the window of employability, especially for jobs in industries, is quite narrow, between 30 and 45 years of age; 45-plus job seekers are less well placed on the labour market. So are young people under 30, yet the attitude of young seafarers towards change and risk on the labour market, as seen above, is far more relaxed.

Second, the sheer lack of choice of workplaces before 1989 resulted in a uniform, predictable work experience, and had a profound effect on the way in which today's seniors view their workplace. They speak about their profession emotionally, either with pride like this 50-plus captain: 'People are different today . . . they do not cherish the sea, the maritime, any more'; or with disillusionment, like this 57-year-old captain: '[Navibulgar] is one of the largest shipowners in Eastern Europe. It will shrink with privatization but will still remain a pretty impressive company. It reached 2.5 mln tonnes dwt, and had 5,000 employees, of whom 3,000 were seafarers. You know, for a small country like ours . . .!' Even interviewees who had been laid off or felt otherwise mistreated by the employer were not indifferent, and all of them equated seafaring with national pride – at least with regard to the past.

Before 1989 the inspirational image of seafaring as an honourable job and as service to the nation, akin to the armed forces, was somewhat transferred to the only possible employer: Navibulgar. For instance, Dimitrov (2003) says (author's translation):

> Thirty years at sea have sailed by, for twenty-two of which I have sailed as captain . . . It might be naive, but I was never attracted by a foreign flag. It never even occurred to me to leave Navibulgar. Whatever we may call it, loyalty, duty, gratitude, or pride – the Steamboat Company is among the most prestigious companies in the world. Or at least it was, at its peak.

All seniors started their careers in Navibulgar, including those who 'broke off' and sailed under foreign flags, and all continue to use the same set of familiar names for their former employer: the BMF,[17] 'the steamship company' (Параходството), 'the firm/company'; 'the Fleet' (Флотът); even 'the company-mother' (компанията-майка).

In contrast to the seniors, none of the young interviewees expressed any attachment to the workplace or firm. The typical young seafarer is instrumental-ist and disinterested, has had several job placements with different companies, has worked in international crews, and declares readiness to change his work-place (or has already done so) if the conditions do not suit him. As one of them said: 'This is a profession just to give you a start in life, it allows you to fix yourself a small flat, buy some stuff . . . and then . . . like I have started this part-time M.A., you can finance some further education and quit before you're com-pletely bonkers.'

Most interviewees among the younger generation did not refer to any kind of stable community either, with the exception of those related to senior seafarers, who recognize that seafaring is still an 'honest trade' (27-year-old second engineer) despite all the shortcomings, and mentioned that a maritime community used to exist but no longer does (their views were clearly influenced by their seafaring fathers or relatives). They speak today of seafaring as a means to an end, declare plans to only sail 'for a few years' and then find a job or establish a business, and are generally cynical about future prospects otherwise: 'there is no life in the sea' (multiple interviews). The 27-year-old second engineer quoted above asked, 'Do you reckon we go to sea because we like it? Okay, you tell me – what else can a bloke do in this city? I mean, as an honest job?'

The differences here are not purely generational. They also, to some extent, reflect the fact that the free market demands and rewards a more de-tached kind of adaptability, a more individualized career strategy and a more efficiency-oriented set of work skills, such as the ability to communicate in basic English (which implies being able to sustain a working community without the deeper shared understanding of a mother tongue) and to cope with the novel pressures of highly automated, sparsely manned vessels.

Marketized Maritime Labour: A Success Story?

On the surface, maritime employment appears to be a happy exception amidst the overall industrial decline in post-1989 Bulgaria. Maritime jobs, espe-cially seafaring ones, are among the country's few highly professional, competi-tive and fast-developing spheres that remained afloat and prospered. Other such spheres include the new information technology (IT) and telecommunication ser-vices, building and construction, tourism, and some other service industries.

The quick influx of foreign employers (directly after 1990, much earlier than most industries) and the emergence of local maritime businesses in Bulgaria counterbalanced the sudden neglect by the state, and created jobs at least until 2009 for unemployed seamen and officers. This rapid internationalization kept

---

[17] See footnote 8.

the maritime industry afloat despite the fast demise of some of its sub-sectors such as ocean fishing and shipbuilding, and the slow shrinking of the profitable cargo transport sub-sector. Swift internationalization allowed the industry to pick up momentum and develop even during the first decade of transition, when most other sectors were in decline. As a result, the maritime industry, which is now 80 to 90 per cent foreign-owned, remains a staple regional employer in coastal areas and is crucial for the coastal economy. It provides employment to large numbers[18] as well as relatively high standards of living to many families, along with starting capital for a number of small businesses.

There are a number of reasons why cargo shipping and its auxiliary trades 'remained afloat' during the economic chaos of the early 1990s. The first was the international nature of shipping: the economic implosion of the state was not enough to bury an already 'well-oiled' cargo transport industry. While, for example, deep ocean fishing became non-viable after Bulgaria lost access to the vast Soviet food market, carrying goods by sea had been a competitive business operated on an international scale even under the socialist state. It was a well-equipped and well-manned industry: as early as 1960, degrees from the Naval Academy had received worldwide accreditation (Ivanov 1996), which now enabled its officers, unlike most other East European professionals, to seek jobs abroad.

The second reason was time: due to the long planning lag peculiar to the very large-scale business of maritime transport, the state fleet still had up to two years ahead before its old contracts were completed and consequently had the breathing space to seek new business partners. As the opening up of the Bulgarian economy occurred in a favourable maritime environment of growing demand for shipping, the transition from predominantly Soviet cargoes to a more international selection was relatively cushioned, and happened without the abrupt shock common to industries more reliant on either the national or the joint COMECON markets.

However, shipping is not simply the success story it may seem to be. Since 1989, the choice of employers has broadened, but at the expense of fierce competition. It has also diminished, or outright removed, legal and welfare protection for workers, especially those working under foreign flags. By 2009, very few firms, if any, offered long-term contracts and the few that did, reserved them for senior high-ranking officers (captains and chief engineers who constitute less than 10 per cent of all maritime professionals). Today, risk-aversion is never rewarded and seafarers have to be ready to take responsibility for their own careers: research the market, change employers, and pay for their own qualifications and certificates. This emphasis on risk in the labour market creates an important paradox: despite all the recent technological advancements and the importance of economic planning and profit, caution and avoidance of risk

---

[18] The geographically compact maritime work force includes 22,000 registered seafarers and a further 1,32,000 onshore workers in related industries (ECOTEC 2006).

remain important components of good seamanship, and are essential for survival, security and safety at sea. Interviews show that risk-averse behaviour at sea and in the labour market are correlated. Risk-averse and cautious seafarers (more typically, though not always, seniors) are bad at 'selling' themselves on the labour market, while the less risk-averse (typically younger, but again not always) are better placed to find jobs, though they are not always better professionals.

Further, there are now fewer maritime jobs on shore due to the 'optimization' demanded by a competitive global market. Seafarers' placements are entirely outsourced to crew manning agencies, and for those seafarers no longer able or willing to sail, neither state-run nor private job offices offer any kind of placement or reintegration programme. Whole sub-sectors (such as ocean fishing) have also imploded, leaving tens of thousands of specialists unemployed. The seafaring community in general is dissolving due to the internationalization of the profession and the individualized, job-hopping career strategy of young maritime workers, most of whom are employed abroad; yet it also survives in the form of personal networks (largely involving people over the age of 40) which serve to provide an informal channel for information and communication regarding jobs and other maritime developments in an otherwise profoundly non-transparent informational environment.

Globalization pressing in from the outside coupled with the consequent denationalization made maritime employment doubly precarious – or, rather, it revealed the absurd security of socialist seafaring careers, unattainable outside the artificial environment of a totalitarian state. At first, globalization propelled East European seafarers from their national fleets into the global pool of cheap maritime labour, working for supranational ship owners in a mixed crew, mainly coming from 'developing' countries such as the Philippines or China. A few years later, the new trade and labour regulations that some Eastern European countries accepted upon accession to the EU pushed them into the expensive 'western' maritime labour force. Thus, even though the opening up of the Bulgarian maritime industry to the international market of goods and labour happened in just a few years, when examined closely, the post-communist liberal market is hardly rational, self-regulating or efficient, nor has labour (or a maritime career) necessarily become any more fulfilling or promising.

What is clear is that two decades after the fall of the Eastern European socialist regimes, the world of work needs to be reimagined, because neither old socialist ideas of work and employment nor post-socialist neoliberal ones fully explain the new reality. Contrary to the predictions of pre-1989 socialist theorists, communism was not achieved; contrary to the expectations of western neoliberal policy advisors and Eastern European policy practitioners in the 1990s, a labour market on which labour would be traded as a commodity like any other has failed to emerge. Labels such as 'post-socialist' or 'transitional' applied to labour markets are insufficient since these labour markets are more than carbon copies of West European ones. Nor are imported preconceptions, such as unemployment or inactivity rates, corruption, moonlighting, black (or grey, shady, second and so on) economy, sufficient tools of analysis. As Standing points out in his analysis of the babble of euphemisms (Rainnie, Smith and Swain 2002: 28–35), the prevalence of the prefix 'post-' in descriptions of almost any aspect of the 1990s betrays an inability to engage with the real nature of the changes by limiting the analysis to the collapse of the previous historical period. In order to understand the workings of new capitalism on the everyday level in the lives of individuals, the analysis must not only go beyond valid but incomplete judgements such as the comparative efficiency of the liberal market and similar large-scale generalizations; it must also critically decompose interactions among key and marginal actors, and determine the forces and principles that govern these interactions.

References

Avramov, Roumen (2001), *The XXth Century Bulgarian Economy* (in Bulgarian), Centre for Liberal Strategies, Sofia.

Chavdarova, T. (2007), 'The Small Entrepreneur: Culture and economic action (the case of Sofia and Skopje)', in *How to Think about the Balkans: Culture, region, identity*, Centre for Advanced Studies Working Paper Series, Sofia Academic Nexus, CAS, Sofia; http://www.cas.bg/uploads/files/Sofia-Academic-Nexus-WP/Tanya%20 Chavdarova.pdf

Clarke, S. (1996), *Labour Relations in Transition: Wages, employment, and industrial conflict in Russia*, Edward Elgar, London.

—— (2007), *The Development of Capitalism in Russia*, Routledge, Oxon.

Dimitrov, G. (2004), 'Institutional Resources for the (Non-)Accomplishment of Social Reforms', in G. Dimitrov, ed., *The State against Reforms*, Iztok-Zapad, Sofia.

Dimitrov, G. and P. Kabakchieva (2003), *A Short Story about a Reform that Never Took Place: Strategies of the policies of education and science* (in Bulgarian), Sofia University Press, Sofia.

Dobrinsky, R. (2000), 'The Transition Crisis in Bulgaria', *Cambridge Journal of Economics*, vol. 24, pp. 581–602.

ECOTEC (2006), *Report on Maritime Employment*, European Commission, Prague.

Ellis, N. and H. Sampson (2008), *The Global Labour Market for Seafarers Working aboard Merchant Cargo Ships 2003*, Technical Report, Seafarers International Research Centre (SIRC), Cardiff University, Cardiff.

Flyvbjerg, B. (2006), 'Five Misunderstandings about Case-Study Research', *Qualitative Inquiry*, vol. 12, no. 2, April, pp. 219–45.

Greskovitz, B. (with D. Bohle) (2006), 'Capitalism without Compromise: Strong business and weak labor in Eastern Europe's new transnational industries', *Studies in Comparative International Development*, vol. 41, no. 1, Spring, pp. 3–25.

—— (2007a), 'Neoliberalism, Embedded Neoliberalism, and Neo-corporatism: Towards transnational capitalism in Central–Eastern Europe', *West European Politics*, vol. 30, no. 3, May, pp. 443–66.

Greskovitz, B. (with D.L. Brown and L. Kulcsár) (2007b), 'Leading Sectors and Leading Regions: Economic restructuring and regional inequality in Hungary since 1990', *International Journal of Urban and Regional Research*, vol. 31, no. 3, September, pp. 522–42.

Ingham, M. and H. Ingham (2002), 'Gender and Labour Market Restructuring in Central and Eastern Europe', in A. Rainnie, A. Smith and A. Swain, eds., *Work, Employment and Transition: Restructuring livelihoods in post-communism*, Routledge, London.

Ivanov, T. (1996), *Maritime Merchant Shipping of the Third Bulgarian State* (in Bulgarian), IK Galaktika, Varna.

Kabakchieva, P. (2001), *Civil Society against the State* (in Bulgarian), LIK, Sofia.

Kapelyushnikov, R.I. (2001), *The Russian Labour Market: Adaptation without restructuring* (in Russian), State University, School of Economics, Moscow.

Kotzeva, T. (1999), 'Re-imaging Bulgarian Women: The Marxist legacy and women's self-identity', *Journal of Communist Studies and Transition Politics*, vol. 15, no. 1, pp. 83–98.

Levinson, M. (2006), *The Box: How the shipping container made the world smaller and the world economy bigger*, Princeton University Press, Princeton.

Manolova, Tatiana, S. Bojidar, S. Gyoshev and Ivan M. Manev (2007), 'The Role of Interpersonal Trust for Entrepreneurial Exchange in a Transition Economy', *International Journal of Emerging Markets*, vol. 2, no. 2, pp. 107–22.

Nietzsche, F. (1974), *The Gay Science*, Vintage: New York.

Standing, G. (2002), 'The Babble of Euphemisms', in A. Rainnie, A. Smith and A. Swain, eds., *Work, Employment and Transition: Restructuring livelihoods in post-communism*, Routledge, London.

Tchalakov, I., A. Bundjulov, I. Hristov and L. Deyanova (2008), *The Networks of Transition: What actually happened in Bulgaria after 1989* (in Bulgarian), Iztok-Zapad, Sofia.

Valkanov, V. (2003), *Maritime History of Bulgaria* (in Bulgarian), Albatros, Sofia.

van der Ende, Martin, Marius van der Flier and Ewout Bückmann (2009), *Study on the labour Market and Employment: Conditions in intra-community regular maritime transport services carried out by ships under Member States' or Third Countries' Flags*, ECORYS Report for European Commission, Directorate-General Energy and Transport, Directorate-General Maritime Transport, Rotterdam.

Williams, Colin C. (2008), 'Envelope wages in Central and Eastern Europe and the EU', *Post-Communist Economies*, 20:3, pp. 363–76.

World Bank, http://data.worldbank.org/indicator/SP.POP.TOTL?page=4, accessed on 11 January 2011.

Wu, B. and N. Winchester (2004), 'Crew Studies for Seafarers: A methodological approach to global labour market for seafarers', *Marine Policy*, vol. 29, pp. 323–30.

Becoming a *Grihasta*
Hierarchies of Work among Handloom Weavers in Early Twentieth Century United Provinces, India

Santosh Kumar Rai

Studies about weavers and artisans in modern Indian history usually dwell on the dichotomy of deindustrialization (through globalization) versus modernization and commercialization (Chandra 1966; R.C. Dutt 1906: xxv; R.P. Dutt 1949: 165; Roy 1993, 1999, 2002: 507–32). Since the experience of those most affected, i.e. the artisans, is not central to such explanatory frameworks about craft industries, they miss out on ways in which traditional artisans concretely and hieratically appropriate the external constraints posed by industrialization through reconfiguring the internal spaces of 'community', 'work' and 'forms of labour'.

This essay argues that the work process in the handloom sector was produced by, and productive of, changes in life cycle and social differentiation within local weavers' communities in the course of the nineteenth and twentieth centuries. The entire community chain, active in the process of handloom production in a micro-region, was appropriated in a new relation of commodity production. Therefore, this essay discusses the emergence of capitalist conditions that enabled connections, affiliations and exclusions in networked relationships in social communities. The community was converted into capital to be utilized for marginalization of wage–work relations. The transformation revealed itself in rapid internal differentiation among the weavers, with the emergence of the merchant artisan capitalist on the one hand, and the loomless weaver on the other.

Colonial interaction with weavers in India began in south India in the seventeenth century, when the East India Company (EIC) began trading there. The category of master weaver rose to prominence in south India between the eighteenth and nineteenth century, as a part of the commercial network of the EIC. S. Arasaratnam suggests (1986: 257–82) that in late eighteenth-century south India, the 'head weaver' or elected caste leader (*nattar*) in a weaving village, mistakenly thought to be a master craftsman employing many journeymen, was only a social mediator with no control over production.

The EIC wanted to repeat the successful experiment it had carried out in south India in parts of the then United Provinces – areas that today fall in the eastern part of the modern Indian state of Uttar Pradesh. The Company faced a totally different scenario up north, however, since the trading nexus of weavers in the south as well as their working circumstances were altogether different from the situation in the United Provinces. Moreover, the Company's commercial penetration into the United Provinces began at the end of the eighteenth century – nearly two centuries after their entry into south India. Unlike the south which had weaving communities of different castes, there existed only a single caste of weavers in the United Provinces called *julahas*, who belonged to the Muslim community. Further, the exposure of these *julahas* to the outside world was quite limited, unlike that of the weaving communities in the coastal areas of south India.

Muslim *julaha* weavers (still extant) were lower-caste, semi-urban artisans who had converted to Islam during the fourteenth to seventeenth centuries. Though nineteenth-century deindustrialization was also a story of dislocation of the handloom textile industry in this region, local handloom weaving nevertheless survives to date. *Julaha* weaver communities were, and still are, located in the weaving centres of Azamgarh, Gorakhpur and Faizabad divisions, especially in places such as Maunath Bhanjan, Mubarakpur, Kopaganj and Tanda in eastern Uttar Pradesh (Naqvi 1968: 121–22).

The word 'community' in the colonial context had multilayered economic connotations for its meaning and uses. Local terms were often captured and used to signify something they had originally not meant. The word *grihasta*, for instance, stemmed from the ancient terminology to mean a Hindu householder. By the late nineteenth century, however, in the Muslim-dominated weaving hubs of eastern Uttar Pradesh, *grihasta* had come to refer to senior members of the Muslim weaver or *julaha* caste-community.

While the continuing relationship with the occupation of weaving kept Muslim *julaha* weavers attached to their traditional skills, limited local job opportunities and possession of a traditionally valued skill tied them to their hereditary occupation during the period under study. They were unable to shift into other, possibly more lucrative occupations, even though this would have been at the expence of at least short-term economic instability and displacement. Nevertheless, a sense of dispossession and lost opportunity prevails among such communities in this region, which has been explained away in terms of Hindu–Muslim antagonism. The author's research, however, indicates that this scenario was a result of complex praocesses such as underutilization of traditional skills, inflow of new techniques, changing patterns of cloth consumption, and capital requirements for reproduction of labour and raw material, all of which ensured the emergence of new capitalist relations within the ambit of social hierarchies.

The Rise of the *Grihasta*

It is a matter of speculation whether the appropriation of the word *grihasta* by senior master weavers of the *julaha* community, as mentioned above, reflected an earnest desire to become an 'independent' prosperous householder (as indicated by the original meaning of *grihasta*), or whether it was intended to subvert the status of the exploitative Hindu merchant *grihasta* (householder). Either way, by the late nineteenth century Muslim master weavers or *karkhanadars* (*karkhana* loosely means a factory, so *karkhanadar* refers to 'one who ran/owned a factory' but at the cottage industry level) had started employing the term *grihasta* to refer to a senior master weaver who had extra resources, and who was a mediator between the community, and traders and merchants. In this context *grihasta* came to be used for organizers or trainers of handloom production, who were like the guild 'masters' and 'merchant manufacturers' of the 'putting-out' system in Europe.

Even as one draws a parallel with the European guild system, however, one has to be cautious in explaining the vocabulary and circumstances of the indigenous system of production. The terms master weaver and *grihasta* are generally taken as synonymous. But it is important to note that the organization of handloom cloth production in India was quite different from that of the medieval European guild. European guilds were characterized by centralization of production and trade under a single 'master'. The English master weaver was the guild head or trainer of the local occupational group; he was not bound by hereditary and community considerations with regard to apprentices. He specialized in the teaching of a particular craft to a fixed number of apprentices and journeymen specifically in an urban context.

In the Indian context, particularly in the erstwhile United Provinces, the *grihasta* was a senior weaver whose role was transformed under the EIC to a supervisory one. The Indian *grihasta* was far more than an economic category of 'master trainer'. He was the hierarchical head of the production process. He connected the producer and the marketing network by participating in both production and marketing. He enjoyed a higher status not just because of his economic and technical superiority, but also because he was part of the occupational and kinship bonds of the 'community' and often its leader.

Transformation of the work culture of the *grihasta* and the corresponding exploitation of the loomless weaver indicates that *grihastas* used community as social capital to form new relations of production and maintain control over labour. This community-based capitalist relationship became possible due to the generational conditioning of those associated with this traditional skill and the sense of prestige associated with the trade. Nevertheless, the rise of the *grihasta* from among the *julaha* weavers proved subversive for both the *julaha* weaver community as well as for the new 'capitalist' relations.

The story of the rise of the *grihasta* in the United Provinces was linked to the expansion of European trade in this region. In a commercial inquiry constituted by the British East India Company in 1787, Secretary to the Bengal government, G.H. Barlow, observed (1778) that *khasas* (or *baftas*), *garhas*, *imertees* and *lakhauris* were the four main varieties of cotton piece goods being manufactured in the region of Banaras (which falls in present-day Uttar Pradesh), to be exported to Bengal. In the late eighteenth century, weavers interacted with merchants (either private merchants or EIC employees) only through *dalals, gumashtas*

and other intermediaries (discussed further below). We learn of a private merchant, J.A. Grant, purchasing cotton cloth in Ghazipur and discussing with a Mr
Duncan (see Grant 1790) the prominence of the *dasturias* and *dalals* in the process of cloth marketing in Mau town in Azamgarh (which today falls in eastern
Uttar Pradesh).

In the first half of the eighteenth century, the EIC had no legal monopoly
over the cloth trade in Banaras. However, regulations implemented by it in the
Bengal Presidency (which included Banaras) from the second half of the eighteenth century led to indirect control over the weavers through a system of paying
'advance' (*baki*) to fulfil its trading engagements. These regulations were also
implemented in the ceded districts of the United Provinces (ibid.; Sinha 1961:
164–66), and in the Diwani areas given to the Company, which included the
Banaras region (Naqvi 1968: 111). Thus the work of weaving was institutionalized under the command of the EIC.

Till the last decades of the eighteenth century, the Company had to pro-
cure cloth either through private merchants or contractors in the eastern provinces of the then state of Awadh (in modern-day Uttar Pradesh). John Scott, a
private merchant who had established a cotton piece goods *aurung* or factory at
Tanda, had worked in both capacities for the Company (Millet 1880: 41). In
1801, it was reported that 'weavers and artisans, as they are all freemen; they
work by the piece, by contract or by the day, as they can agree one with another
(Henchman 1801: 55). Just within two years of ceding the eastern districts, the
EIC's Commercial Residents were posted to a number of trading centres replacing contractors and agents of the Company, and were ordered to begin cloth
purchases. *Aurungs* were opened at the manufacturing centres of Azamgarh,
Mau, Maharajganj, Kopaganj and Gorakhpur on the lines of existing centres in
Bengal. Now the production system was institutionalized with the establishment
of a hierarchy over the weavers.

The office of the *gumashta* acted as an interface between the native
producers and the procurement network of the EIC. C.R. Crommelin, Commercial Resident of Mau, Azamgarh Residency, had demanded that the office of
zilladar be instituted at all *aurungs* to ensure that the advance was applied to the
purpose for which it was made and to monitor the quality and timely delivery of
the handloom cloth. *Zilladars* were also the official source of information for
what went on in the *aurungs*. The Board of Trade that had accepted the appointment of *zilladars* observed (*Board of Trade [Commercial] Proceedings*, vol. 166,
part 2, no. 66, paras 8 and 33):

> . . . it would be highly impolitic to delegate to such people any control over the
> advances received by the manufacturers. Their inspections will probably not
> help, rather the sorting out and rejection of poor quality cloth, when submitted
> will keep up the quality. . . . Otherwise authorities like *zilladar* would abuse their
> power oppressing the weavers and for 'occasionally interested purposes excit-
> ing weavers to acts of contumacy' injurious to Company's interests.

The weavers resisted such attempts of the authorities to dominate the production process. In 1803, J. Ahmuty, Judge and Magistrate of Gorakhpur, wrote to the Commercial Resident at Mau and Azamgarh (Ahmuty 1807) expressing concern over the behaviour of the refractory weavers of Mau (Dewar 1919: 434). So, while the penetration of the Company's agents in the United Provinces led to control over the production process by the establishment of the Commercial Residency, this process, upon its culmination, reduced the producers to a 'stage of absolute bondage' (*Board of Trade [Commercial] Proceedings*, 18 August 1807). Usually, with the establishment of each *aurung*, the hierarchy of native officers was as follows: *gumashta, tavildar, zilladar, mohurer*, peons and *chaukidars*. However, at Mau one head weaver, and at Kopa one head weaver and one assistant head weaver, were also appointed (*Board of Trade [Commercial] Proceedings*, vol. 172, no. 33, para 7).

By the second decade of the nineteenth century, the Company began winding up its textile business in India. The role of 'indigenous' master weavers and *zilladars*, until now working under the auspices of the EIC, was recast. Over this period the *grihasta* emerged as a separate category, distinct from the independent weaver owning more than one loom. Outwardly, the *grihasta* or master weaver seemed a continuation of an older category. But internally that role had changed remarkably, due to changes in the nature of work and the support mechanism.

Instead of focusing on weaving, *grihastas* had begun to emphasize controlling production more as a business concern. They acquired the space vacated by the Company *gumashtas*, and became the interface between the production system and marketing. Even though they did not have the exigencies of state power, the nature of production, credit and the marketing chain ensured their dominance over the mechanism of production. By the late nineteenth century the United Provinces had seen the emergence of independent master weavers or *grihastas* in a big way. There emerged a hierarchy among labourers and weavers in the process of weaving:

1. Unpaid household labour: women and children.
2. Paid weavers without their own means of production, including low-caste Hindu weavers.
3. Weavers who had looms but were dependent on the master weaver or *grihasta* for raw material.
4. Self-employed weavers who had a loom and other means of production.
5. The master weaver or *grihasta*: the interface between the production and marketing.

Overall, the shift from household production to *karkhana* production meant transformation of familial apprenticeship to forms of wage and child labour. The master weavers began hiring paid and *bani* (explained below) workers to operate the looms owned by them, a role that had earlier been in the hands of Hindu mediators – *gumashtas* or brokers. By the early twentieth century the organization of the production-marketing mechanism had been taken over by Muslim *grihasta* mediators, who used their religious identity to claim that they were countering the exploitation of Hindu brokers.

Sari designing and manufacturing was a monopolistic trade in the hands of a small number of *nakshabandhs* or pattern makers. Common weavers could not meet the expenses of these designs on their own; they were unable to afford the raw material. Once again the *grihasta* stepped in: weavers who owned looms worked a system locally called *bani,* where they received the raw materials to manufacture cloth, the design and other wherewithal to produce the design from the *grihasta*. Often, the yarn had to be arranged by paying a higher price on credit. This was also provided by the *grihastas* who lent both yarn and money (*Report of the United Provinces Provincial Banking Enquiry Committee, 1929–30*, vol. III: 386). Weavers were bound to give the cloth they produced to the master weaver and they received fixed wages in return. *Baki* or advance was also given on a systematic basis by these employers in order to retain a skilled labour force. This system, also called *bakidari* or deferred payment, was based on partial payment of wages to the workers as a guarantee of them staying on to repay the loan.

It was now *grihastas* who supplied workers with raw materials and paid for the finished product on a piece-rate basis. Loomless weavers were also employed as daily wagers by the *grihastas* who supplied them with raw materials, and at times even a loom, to work either at the *grihasta*'s house or in their own homes.

The *grihasta* was the essential design and marketing link in the system. It was he who selected the design (based on market preferences), determined the production structure, provided all costs related to design-making, suggested the colour, purchased the silk and gold yarn, set up the loom and ensured the quality of the final product. A weaver could function well only if the *grihasta* understood the constraints of the loom, and appreciated and provided quality yarn. The *grihasta*'s ability to supply raw material and provide the weaver with regular work even in low seasons sustained a patrimonial bond between the two. Paid as well as independent weavers were given advances or interest-free loans, which were then deducted from the piece-work payment. Even when the workers remained in debt to the master weaver, this relationship acquired the status of 'moral debt' or 'moral economy' as the master weaver was the only person to whom a weaver could turn in illness, death or other such contingencies. For Muslim weavers the relationship with the *grihasta* had a stronger sense of solidarity, as the *grihasta*, being a Muslim, generally did not practice usury, which is prohibited by Islam. Nevertheless, the condition of the weaver was pitiful.

This may also be illustrated through the plight of the *kamkhab* (thick woven brocade) weavers of Banaras in the 1880s. A weaver who produced brocade worth two hundred rupees received a pittance of two *annas* a day as wage. An 1882 *Report on the Railway Borne Traffic of the North-Western Provinces and Oudh* stated that weavers were bound by 'hopeless indebtedness to the firms who employ them and their remuneration depends as little on the demand which may exist for their goods as if their condition was one of actual slavery'. According to the same report, trade in both *kamkhabs*, and saris and *dupattas* was 'in a flourishing condition, but the workmen are miserably poor. Even those styled independent for want of a better word are in reality in the hands of *mahajans* [moneylenders], who advance them what is necessary for support of life and absorb all the profits of their labour.' The report showed that hardly any independent weavers survived in Banaras in 1881–82 in the segment specializing in production of expensive *kamkhab* cloth, while independent weavers were outnumbered two to one in the less expensive sari and *dupatta* segment.

In 1918, the Indian Industrial Commission (Appendix II: 3) took note of the fact 'they [weavers] are entirely out of touch with [the] outside cloth market and their poverty has subjected them to the moneylender'. Being cheated at the hands of trader due to illiteracy and being the last link in the demand–supply chain of production condemned weavers to a life of poverty. The system of payment for the manufactured cloth was planned in such a way that the manufacturers had to wait till the sale of the cloth was completed, and only then receive their monies after the usual reductions and cuts in payment. In one of the first official references to a *grihasta* in the 1880s it was observed that 'the *julahas* who carry on the manufacture of the fabric are miserably poor, but the master weavers are not; some of them are very well off. Three of them are landholders and own indigo factories.'

'Corporatization' of the weaving industry had established itself in Banaras by the 1880s, with firms engaging weavers on wage payment for the manufacturing of silk cloth. It is also pertinent to note that independent weavers were to be found in larger numbers in the relatively cheaper sari and *dupatta* segment. In Azamgarh district, cheaper silk, and satinette or *galta* of silk and cotton mixed were produced predominantly in rural and semi-urban settings. This innovation provided cheap and comfortable material for ladies' dresses and led to a strong demand from the European community. Most important, however, was the silk fabric called *sangi*, which was in demand by Muslims for pyjamas. 'Mubarikpur and Khairabad, two villages eight and twelve miles respectively from Azamgarh, were the manufacturing centres' (ibid.).

As indicated in Table 2, in the 1880s, independent weavers in the villages of Azamgarh manufactured cheaper varieties of cloth as compared to those

TABLE 1   *Types of silk woven in Banaras in 1881–82 and 1882–83*

Year	Types of cloth	No. of firms	Employee weavers	Independent weavers	Total weavers
1881–82	Kamkhab	138	757	15	772
	Saris and *Dupattas*	270	1358	621	1979
1882–83	Kamkhab	131	913	–	913
	Saris and *Dupattas*	286	1386	627	2013

TABLE 2 *Types of silk weavers in Azamgarh in 1881–82 and 1882–83*

Year	No. of firms	No. of workmen employed			No. of independent workmen			Total		
		Ist class	IInd class	Total	Ist class	IInd class	Total	Ist class	IInd class	Grand total
1881–82	65	53	262	315	6	2,162	2,168	59	2,424	2,483
1882–83	69	164	189	353	–	2,154	2,154	164	2,343	2,507

available in urban Banaras. Further, the number of independent weavers in Azamgarh was much higher than the number of employed weavers. Independent weavers worked largely under the advance or *baki* system. Wage labour-based employment relations were less in evidence, as were organized firms, in comparison with Banaras. In Banaras, production structure hierarchies in silk weaving came to be fairly entrenched by the first decade of the twentieth century. These hierarchies were strongly correlated to the segmentation of the industry by type of cloth, cost of raw material and degree of organization of investment and marketing. Availability of costly yarn and gold thread made skill-based work subordinate to the mediators.

In the above circumstances, community networks gradually ensured that the *grihasta* should come from the weaving communityand should be a Muslim as well. Even when the master weaver became a merchant or trader of cloth, his basic training in weaving on account of it being a family profession meant that his association or identity as a *julaha* weaver remained a part of his personality. The mechanism of advances and loans given to the weaver/labourer by the *karkhanadar/grihasta*, coupled with the resources at the disposal of the latter and his role of mediating between the production process and the market by supplying raw material, providing designs and undertaking procurement, ensured that the weavers/labourers remained under constant moral and social pressure to succumb to 'capitalist relations'.

At the beginning of the twentieth century, the government of the United Provinces tried to introduce improved weaving technology, but *julaha* weavers who professed 'a religious prejudice against the paying as well as receiving of interest' (Chatterjee 1908: 30), were not responsive to this move since they would have to rely on taking loans to buy this technology. Community spirit and religious commonality kept the Muslim weaver bound to the *grihasta*. Thus, even as the *grihasta* had occasion to help a *julaha* weaver, he had the chance to exploit him as well. If a weaver wanted to change his employer but had no money to repay his debt, the new employer repaid his debt and the weaver worked off this repayment with the new employer. Also, to resort to a market moneylender meant exorbitant interest rates (*Report of the United Provinces Provincial Banking Enquiry Committee, 1929–30*, vol. III: 386).

The textile industry of the districts that today fall within eastern Uttar Pradesh had become synonymous with the silk sari industry by the 1920s. The fusion of local designs with external ones, coupled with the local climate which was conducive to silk handloom weaving, put this region at the helm of silk-weaving activities. Weavers undertaking silk sari production in this region adapted to new patterns of demand and fashion in the early twentieth century. The artistic ingenuity of the artisans and the changing market trends resulted in a great variety of fabrics. The quality and type of fabrics indicated the weavers' occupational status and artisanship. Better quality and higher priced fabrics required greater artisanship, labour and financial investment. Each fabric was unique in terms of quality, colour combination, design and pattern. As a result, there could be no uniformity in rates, which in turn became a cause for rampant exploitation. The production system was now based on two methods: *bani* and *adhiya* or *lagaar*.[1]

So the *grihastas* got saris woven by the weavers on contract or *bani*, and also bought the finished saris woven by self-employed weavers and daily-wage weavers. *Grihastas* could be distinguished from general weavers on the basis of capital, resources and raw material capacity. They owned anywhere between two to hundreds of looms. By providing *katan* (raw material) to the weavers working on *bani*, they became the owner of the product. When the ready cloth produced by the weaver was given back to the *grihasta*, he would deduct some money from the weaver's wages in the name of *cashar* or *batta*. The margin incurred due to deduction of *batta* or *cashar* from the price of cloth was the perquisite of the purchasers. Therefore, they tended to evaluate cloth piece goods as inferior (Interview with Qazi Zafar Masood in Mubarakpur, 31 January 1998; Bismillah 1987: 16–17). This mode of functioning was noted in the *Report of the Fact Finding Committee (Handloom and Mills)* (1942: 73) in the following words:

> In the *katiauti* system prevalent in the United Provinces, the price of the yarn is debited to the weaver's account in the *mahajan's* books and when the cloth is delivered its price is credited. Interest is not usually charged, but the *mahajan* is able to realize not only interest but a good profit by calculating the price of yarn at a slightly higher rate than the market price, and by making certain customary deductions from the purchase price of cloth.

This deduction was made for 'apparent' deficiencies in the cloth such as stains (*daag*), *rafoo* (near-invisible stitching of a rip or tear), or uneven colour (Bismillah 1987: 11; Interview with Qazi Zafar Masood in Mubarakpur, May 2007; Barlow 1778: 3241).

---

[1] The term *bani* is an occupational expression for handloom weaving and for weft. *Bani* consists of a putting-out system by which a master weaver provides his labourers with handlooms, raw materials and sari designs. Weavers give finished *saris* to the master weaver and receive fixed wages in return. As for *lagaar*, in the post-independence period, due to the increased demand, the relation between the *grihasta* and his *karigar* or worker also changed. Instead of *bani*, in Mubarakpur, the system of *lagaar* prevailed. In this system too the *karigar* shared the profit in the sale of cloth, especially *saris*. However, if any defect was detected, then the profit of the *karigar* was reduced.

Interestingly, certain practices among the weaver community that began at that time continue even today. For instance, in Banaras, Hindu traders at Kunj Gali (the oldest silk market) had started the practice of deducting fifteen *paise* for every hundred rupees of purchased product for a *puja* (called *phenuk*) for Hindu gods. This religious deduction became an obligatory offering for Muslim weavers too, who reconciled the enforced tithe with *zakat* (a portion of the earnings which go to serve the poor and needy as per the Qur'an). In Mubarakpur, low-caste Hindu weavers also had to pay this deduction. The tradition (and the existence of Muslim *grihastas*) continues to this day, though interviews by the author in Banaras and Mubarakpur reveal that in the recent past, rightist forces who are oblivious of the origin of the tradition, have been provoking Hindu weavers into not paying this religious deduction to Muslim *grihastas*.

A narrative of the early twentieth century establishes the process of appropriation of community hierarchy as a form of capital for handloom production. Sheikh Abdul Majid (1864–1934), a weaver of a locality called Muhalla Pura Sofi in Mubarakpur, maintained a dairy which gives us fascinating insights into the forces at play. His narrative focuses on the *julaha* weavers' community of Mubarakpur and the diary records events from 1902 to 1934. It establishes Sheikh Majid's credentials as a prosperous member of the weavers' community, in all probability a *grihasta*. Most of his entries list the prices of different kinds of cloth, and of various types of thread and other commodities, but he never refers to a loom. This well-to-do weaver reveals himself as a government sympathizer and police informer. His major concerns are about his business (not the work), the cloth trade, community issues and the *panchayat* (locally elected self-government), notorious personalities, scandalous affairs of the *qasba*, local politics, and the Non-Cooperation movement launched by Gandhi during the freedom struggle. His references to weaving are more about the politics of product marketing and raw materials, than the work and labour involved in handloom production. His diary reveals that all such issues were resolved through the agency of the community, which was converted into capital to be utilized by *grihastas*.

Sheikh Majid's social and political concerns appear to have been mainly focused on the business of weaving and the community involved in this work. He makes it clear that he was not in favour of the Non-Cooperation and Khilafat movements, or the idea of '*swaraj*' (self-rule). In a diary entry November 1921, he nevertheless evinces sympathy for participants in the Khilafat movement from Mubarakpur, when six were convicted and sentenced to six months rigorous imprisonment for picketing the cloth shop of one Babu Bal Kishan Aggarwal. His sympathy with the Khilafat volunteers is not because they are nationalists but because they are fellow-Muslims. Majid appears displeased about the fact that evidence against these six was given by five witnesses belonging 'to the community'. He condemns the prosecution witnesses: 'these people got Musalmaans imprisoned in spite of themselves being Musalmaan'.

In 1922, disagreements within the Muslim community over the Non-Cooperation and Khilafat movements were explicit, and Sheikh Majid, a *grihasta* and therefore a powerful opinion-maker in the *qasba*, states in his dairy that he opposes all such 'anti-government' activities. His business interests and affiliations shaped his opinions on the picketing of a Hindu merchant's shop.

Meanwhile, by 1920 intensified commercialization had redefined the role of community institutions as well as the leadership of *grihastas*. The resurgence of the community was not limited to the negation of technological innovation and restrictions over its members; commercial alliances were also being reviewed and reformulated in favour of the *grihastas* via community panchayats. In an entry dated 12 December 1919, Sheikh Majid notes that weavers of *atthaisi* (twenty-eight) *mauzas* of Mubarakpur met at Haji Abdur Rehman's house in Gajhadha village°and decided that henceforth they would not transact with three Hindu traders: Babu Mahabir Chaudhary, Kothi Babulal and Babu Kamta Prasad Aggarwal, who dealt in yarn and silk. The diary also take of notes a resolution that Muslims would trade exclusively among themselves.

An entry dated 8 January 1920 notes that a panchayat meeting of the *atthaisi* was held at a house in Pura Dulhan locality in Mubarakpur because Mahabir Chaudhary, Kothi Babulal and Babu Kamta Prasad Aggarwal had opened their shops. Fines were also imposed for cloth sales from certain houses of weavers. Sheikh Majid notes that he too was fined a hundred-and-one rupees, the heaviest fine of the lot, but we are not told why – was he not supposed to sell cloth from home? His diary does not make this clear.

An entry dated 8 February 1920 states that the panchayat assembled at Gola Bazar where the shop of Chaudhary (probably Mahabir Chaudhary, mentioned earlier) was found open and he was fined two hundred rupees by the panchayat, which also took another twenty-five rupees from him to pay for expenses incurred on assembling the panchayat. The entry states that the panchayat collected another two hundred rupees as a fine from Karim Baksh Dalal of Sarian village and punished him by making him stand for two hours˙doing *gosh maali* (pulling his ears); only then was he forgiven, although what the offence was, we do not know. We learn from the same diary entry that Sabir, son of Ismail of Sarayin, was expelled from the *biradari* (loosely brotherhood; normally used to refer to 'community') for the same mysterious offence.

To strengthen production relations in their business, *grihastas* always tried to mobilize the community and gain leadership through their newly acquired status and wealth. Sectarian polarization and community leadership were thus dependent on these resourceful *grihastas*. This also transformed the nature of the work of weaving as an activity to be safeguarded within the community. however, *grihastas* becoming the flag-bearers of the community and their dominance over production as well as marketing, did not result in improvements in the fortunes of the common weavers as well.

Instances of *grihastas* acquiring community leadership are recorded in Sheikh Majid's diary entries. He informs us in a 1932 entry that Mohammad Amin, a powerful *grihasta* of Mubarakpur, had been a renowned *zamindar* famous for his womanizing, drinking and lavish lifestyle in the 1920s. One of the

most important men in the *qasba* market, Amin remained chairman of the local
municipal board for a long period. He was also the leader of the Barelvi sect of
Muslims and always moved around with a large entourage. It appears, however,
that he came to a sad end, losing his fortune and dying in a miserable condition,
'begging a few pennies from all and sundry but still drinking'.

Continuing, the entry states that his rival was another *grihasta*, Maulvi
Shukrullah, who was a leader of the Deobandi sect in Mubarakpur and secretary
of the Mubarakpur Khilafat Committee. Sheikh Majid notes that Maulvi
Shukrullah 'was said to be the grandson of a Hindu woman taken from Kopaganj
and therefore a familial rascal'. The inherent bias of the writer and his antipathy
to the neutral stance taken by the Khilafat movement comes out in the following
description:

> During the period of Khilafat movement this Maulvi Shukrullah was a very big
> leader, he began speaking rough and foul to the people and started closing their
> shops. In ultimate result a case was charged against Shukrullah and he went to
> jail for six months. After coming back from jail, he maintained a low profile for
> four or five years. Later, he began his old deceptiveness and began targeting the
> big *alims* and earned the support of big people of town particularly the wealthier
> [ones]. Later he became a big religious preacher.

He adds that in the 1930s 'there were frequent *lathi* fights between the Deobandi
group of Shukrullah and the Barelvi group of Mohammad Amin *grihasta*. In this
contest Shukrullah was subdued and began calling Amin *grihasta* a good man
'which shows he was a familial rascal'. These entries serve to show that *grihastas*
influenced local politics and social alliances as well.

In the 1930s, moving beyond the usual role of the *grihasta*, a few Muslim entrepreneurs began to make inroads into traditionally Hindu-dominated
businesses. The monopoly of Muslim weavers played a major role in this transformation. The Hindus, on their part, tried to resist the religious polarization of
the occupation of weaving. In 1939, after Hindu–Muslim riots in Banaras, a
Hindu cloth firm led by Lala Mohan Lal sacked Muslim weavers and tried to
hire Hindu weavers in order to create an alternative Hindu occupational group.
But this conscious attempt to segregate the occupation of weaving on Hindu–
Muslim lines failed to succeed, as Hindu weavers' expertise in handloom weaving was limited.

The new inroads made by a few Muslim entrepreneurs into traditionally
Hindu-dominated businesses led to the emergence of a class of Muslim merchants, over and above the already dominating Muslim *grihastas*. The organization of the Muslim Tanzim movement became more prominent in the early 1930s,
a period that coincided with a slump in demand and price of artisanal products,
exposing artisans to economic hardship and increasing their dependence on
karkhanadars, financiers and merchants.

In the early twentieth century, nationalist politics tried to establish a
relationship between the handloom industry and *khadi*. But Muslim weaving

communities could not be successfully roped into this mobilization. This led to further polarization between Hindu merchants and Muslim weavers. By the late 1920s, Muslim sub-contractors in Mau also were edging out Hindu middlemen who controlled the handloom business. In Banaras, one out of every five *kothidars/ gaddidars* in the wholesale silk trade was reported to be an Ansari (Muslim) weaver (Offredi 1996: 303–36). *Julaha* weaver-traders were now found to be competing with the established traders and merchants in the handloom business. Being skilled craftsmen, they had an edge. They did not need to employ additional experts (as did the Hindu merchants) to deal with their contract weavers or to perform quality checks on the goods under negotiation. Moreover, contract weavers preferred to work for their co-religionists as they found it easier to complain and arbitrate with them on matters such as unjust deductions and under-priced goods. In this context, Baba Khalil Das (*Secret Police Abstract of Intelligence, United Provinces,* no. 41) of Banaras advised weavers to practise thrift to avoid indebtedness as well as to gain literacy so that they could unite against the merchants. He also advocated a bank for Muslim artisans to decrease their dependence on Hindu financers (ibid., No. 28). Through large processions, he hoped to demonstrate the strength of the local weavers to the local Hindus (ibid., no. 27). But such attempts only further strengthened the hold of the Muslim *grihastas* over Muslim weavers in the form of kinship patronage, ensuring weavers' dependence on them.

This overlapping of complex identities led to the initiative for Muslim entrepreneurship and, later, community action had to be taken to strengthen and safeguard the economic position of these Muslim merchants and traders. In 1945, a Weavers Committee was formed at Mau to look after the interests of Muslim yarn and cloth dealers, under a local leader named Rizwanullah. Weavers in Azamgarh registered their grievances at a meeting held on 23 January 1945 (Central Intelligence Department, United Provinces, *Weekly Appreciation Ending January 1945*). One thousand weavers from Mau held a meeting at which it was decided to elect a representative and subscribe at the rate of twenty-one rupees per handloom for the purchase of yarn (ibid., *Weekly Appreciation Ending February 1945*). At a meeting of their provincial working committee, the Muslim religious organization Jamait-ul-Ulema formalized a demand for a proportionate share of the cloth trade to Muslim dealers (ibid., *Weekly Appreciation Ending March 1945*). At the district Momin (another term for Muslims) conference held in Gorakhpur, attended by three hundred people and presided over by Abdul Qayum Ansari of Bihar, an appeal was made to the government for more yarn and adequate representation of Muslims in the state legislature (ibid., *Weekly Appreciation Ending April 1945*). The Provincial Muslim '*soot* and *kapra* committee' conference was held at Mau on 5 and 6 June, attended by around eight hundred people. Rizwanullah and Fakhrul Islam condemned the existing supply and control systems of the government, and a demand was made for the allotment of at least twenty yards of cloth per head to Muslim weavers (ibid., *Weekly Appreciation Ending June 1945*). Yet the mediating role played by *grihastas* as community leaders ensured that any such arrangement would benefit them alone. They fixed arrangements with *arahatias*, *mahajans* and firms for execution of orders. They had enough surplus capital to invest in raw material and to provide advances to the ordinary weavers. As A.C. Chatterjee (1908: 19) observed in the first decade of the twentieth century: 'In the town of Tanda there is a large proportion of master weavers who employ a number of journeymen weavers earning from three to five rupees a month and one meal.'

Their professional expertise and experience, as well as command over the organizational set-up, led to a diversification of the *grihasta*'s role, both in the market and in terms of their predominance in the community. By the 1940s, the *Report of the Fact Finding Committee* (1942: 72) found that the *grihastas* had become entrenched in the yarn and wholesale cloth markets.

> In some parts of the United Provinces (e.g. Mau), the bigger broker-weaver is called a *grihast* [*grihasta*]. The leading *grihasts* are also yarn merchants as well as wholesale cloth merchants. Some of them engage *dalals* for distributing yarn and collecting cloth; others directly deal with the weavers. The *grihast* is regarded by the workers with some affection as they are all of the same caste and are bound by something more than mere cash nexus. He and the weaver-workers have to cooperate in their caste festivals and other functions. They are bound to each other by various ties. The workmen are in need of advances and the employer is able to give them with confidence as the weavers are easily within his reach. The system, therefore, works well for both parties.

By the 1940s, observations on the technical backwardness of weavers came to be reflected in the official records. This was an outcome not of 'the community's' backwardness, but due to lack of knowledge and capital. Now even independent workers were at the receiving end and the system of 'ready purchase' was held responsible for the plight of the weavers (*Report of the Cottage Industries Committee*: 3). This traditional nexus, despite being exploitative of the *julaha* weaver, smacked strongly of paternalistic bondage. It was observed that the community network tied up with patrimonial exploitation by the community leadership was guiding the pace of changes. According to the *Report of the Weaving Schools Committee* (1920: 43) 'they [the weavers] are habitually led by the nose [by] leaders of the community who generally profit by their industry and therefore assist the independent organizations. . . . They are easily led to oppose joining societies on religious grounds that these work on interest.' Commissioner of Fyzabad Division, E. Rogers (1908), observed that in the case of Tanda, 'all the *julahas* are bound hand and foot to a *mahajan* or some rich employer of their own caste. Neither of these classes are at all anxious that the *julahas* should secure their independence.'

Conclusion

In the early nineteenth century, in the eastern part of the erstwhile United Provinces in India, the role of the *grihasta* (master weaver), as a senior weaver performing the work of a trainer of apprentice weavers, was transformed under the East India Company. He began to function more as a supervisor of the Company's impressed export production. The subsequent extinction of exports and breakdown of the formal procurement system of the EIC led to reconstitution of the *grihastas* as well as a change in the life-cycle of weavers. By the early twentieth century, a relative informality was introduced into the procurement process through the use of primordial bonds. New hierarchies caused by the removal of Hindu merchants and changing patterns of fashion and demand redefined capital investment, the hold over resources, professional expertise and the hereditary position of the *grihastas*.

Now, instead of the official agency and investment of the EIC, the community of weavers itself was appropriated as capital by the *grihastas*. This subversive change effected to the capitalist character of the professional exploitation of weavers was institutionalized through community networks. Thus, to sum up, this essay argues that societies produce material goods through reproduction and reorientation of social relations according to changes in the contextual scenario.

References

Ahmuty, John (1807), 'John Ahmuty to the Secretary to the Government', 22 June, in *Board of Trade (Commercial) Proceedings*, 18 August, microfilm form, West Bengal State Archives, Kolkata.

Arasaratnam, S. (1986), 'Weavers, Merchants and Company: The handloom industry in southeastern India, 1750–1790', *Indian Economic and Social History Review*, vol. 17, no. 3, pp. 257–82.

Barlow, G.H. (1778), *Report on the Trade of Awadh*, 6 June, in Foreign Department, Secret Consultations, OC No. 5, Appendix No. 1, National Archives of India (NAI), Delhi.

Bismillah, Abdul (1987), *Jhini Jhini Bini Chadariya*, Delhi.

Central Intelligence Department, United Provinces (1945), *Weekly Appreciation Ending 26th January 1945.*

———, *Weekly Appreciation Ending 28th January 1945.*

———, *Weekly Appreciation Ending 23rd March 1945.*

———, *Weekly Appreciation Ending 20th April 1945.*

———, *Weekly Appreciation Ending 8th June 1945.*

Chandra, Bipan (1966), *The Rise and Growth of Economic Nationalism in India: Economic Policies of Indian National Leadership, 1880–1905*, New Delhi.

Chatterjee, A.C. (1908), *Notes on the Industries of the United Provinces*, Allahabad.

Dewar, Douglas (1919), *A Hand Book to the English Pre-Mutiny Records in the Government Record Rooms of the United Provinces of Agra and Oudh*, Allahabad.

Dutt, R.P. (1949), *India Today*, Bombay.

Dutt, R.C. (1906), *The Economic History of India*, vol. I: *Under Early British Rule, 1757–1837*, second edition, London.

Grant (1790), 'Grant to Duncan, 16 October 1790, BCSC, 15 December 1790, Range 155, 83, No. 15, paras 11–13'; cited in K.P. Mishra, *Banaras in Transition (1738–1795): A Socio-Economic Study*, Delhi, 1975, pp. 106–07.

Henchman, Thomas (1801), *Observations on the Report of the Directors of the East India Company, respecting the trade between India and Europe*, London.

Indian Industrial Commission, Minutes of Evidence, 1916–17 (1918), Appendix II, Calcutta.

Interview with Qazi Zafar Masood (1998), Mubarakpur, 31 January.

Interview with Qazi Zafar Masood (2007), Mubarakpur, May.

Millett, A.F. (1880), *Report on the Settlement of the Land Revenue of the Fyzabad District*, Allahabad.

Mishra, K.P. (1975), *Banaras in Transition (1738–1795): A Socio-Economic Study*, Delhi.

Naqvi, H.K. (1968), *Urban Centres and Industries, 1556–1803*, Bombay, 1968.

Offredi, Mariola (1996), 'The Muslim Weavers of Benaras and Mau in the Seventies', *Eurasiaica*, vol. 40, pp. 303–36.

Parthasarathi, Prasannan (2001), *The Transition to a Colonial Economy: Weavers, Merchants and Kings in South India, 1720–1800*, Cambridge.

'Reply of Board of Trade to the Commercial Resident Mau, Azamgarh' (1803), 29 August, in *Board of Trade (Commercial) Proceedings*, vol. 166, part 2, no. 66, paras 33 and 8, microfilm form, West Bengal State Archives, Kolkata.

Report of the Cottage Industries Committee.

Report of the Fact Finding Committee (Handloom and Mills) (1942), Delhi.

Report of the United Provinces Provincial Banking Enquiry Committee 1929–30 (1930), vol. III, Evidence: 'Witness, Sheo Narayan Juneja, Principal, Government Central Weaving Institute Benaras', Allahabad.

Report of the Weaving Schools Committee (1920), Industries Department File No. 407.

Report on the Commerce and Customs of the Ceded Provinces (1804), 27 April, in *Board of Trade (Commercial) Proceedings*, vol. 172, no. 33, para 7, microfilm form, West Bengal State Archives, Kolkata.

Report on the Railway Borne Traffic of the North- Western Provinces and Oudh during the Year ending 31st March, 1882 (1882), Allahabad.

Report on the Railway Borne Traffic of the North- Western Provinces and Oudh during the Year ending 31st March, 1883 (1883), Allahabad.

Rogers, E. (1908), 'E. Rogers, Commissioner, Fyzabad Division to J.W. Hose, Secretary to Government, United Provinces', Industries Department File No. 64, Box No. 87, UPSA.

Roy, Tirthankar (1993), *Artisans and Industrialization: Indian Weaving in the Twentieth Century*, Delhi.

—— (1999), *Traditional Industry in the Economy of Colonial India*, Cambridge.

—— (2002), 'Acceptance of Innovations in Early Twentieth Century Indian Weaving', *Economic History Review*, Vol. 55, No. 3, pp. 507–32.

Secret Police Abstract of Intelligence, United Provinces (1930), No. 27, 12 July, Police Intelligence Department, Lucknow.

—— (1931), No. 28, 18 July, Police Intelligence Department, Lucknow.

—— (1931), No. 41, 17 October, Police Intelligence Department, Lucknow.

Sinha, N.K. (1961), *The Economic History of Bengal*, vol. 1, Calcutta.

Precarious Hopes
Labour Remittances, Family Investments and the Effects of the Global Economic Crisis in Senegal

Dennis Galvan

This essay is an exploration of labour, migration, family, community and crisis in Senegal. It is a story that is macroeconomic, set in the broad sweep of historical change and rooted in large-scale movements of culture and society; at the same time it is centrally about people's lives, hopes and experiences. So, as a way to frame the issues and the analysis, the essay begins with the account of a migrant whose story is representative of typical migrant experiences, and whom the author knows reasonably well.

An Illustrative Migration

Had Waly Faye returned home to Senegal in 2010, he would have become part of the financial crisis that threatened to swamp the small boat that is Senegal. Waly has been in the US (northern California), working semi-legally and sometimes studying, for about twenty years. He sends home a reasonable sum of money, helps his family, extended kin and their children whenever he can. His family's compound is in a village in the Serer area (in the Sine or Fatick region). It was built decades ago by Waly's father (himself an international migrant, a colonial gendarme, who used his pension to build the main house in the 1970s), but now has new walls, fresh paint and some remodelling, thanks to Waly's earnings in California.

When Waly left in the early 1990s, things were different for migrants. He made a choice as a relatively young man to leave, to get school degrees and the tools he felt he needed to get ahead in life. His extended family helped him with the ticket and carried some hope that Waly might some day help them. But in contrast to contemporary migration planning, he was not their only, not even their primary investment.

When Waly left almost two decades ago, he planned to stay for six months and do a training programme in sustainable agriculture. Soon he was in a community college and then pursuing a four-year degree at University of California, Berkeley. While he was away, circumstances changed in Senegal and in the world, and being abroad became a lot more lucrative than it had once been. So, degree earned, visa expired and status illegal, it simply made sense for Waly to stay on in the US and keep working. He rode the wave of boom times in dreamy California. Even though he worked near the bottom of the ladder, tending the gardens and lawns of the rich, he sent money home, he saved, he paid for a wife he had never met to come from Senegal, they had kids, and, in the *piece de resistance* of living the 'American dream', he bought his own no down-payment, low-interest home in the new suburbs outside San Francisco. Odds are that before he wrote his first monthly payment, his mortgage had been sliced, diced, bundled and re-bundled into a tradeable commodity. On the unclear value of these mortgages, derivatives – i.e. bets on whether traders would drive up or down the value of the now tradeable or securitized packaged bits of many mortgages – could be bought and sold in a now infamously booming market (once worth the fantastical sum of $40 trillion).

Without knowing it, this lone Senegalese labour migrant was right inside the belly of the beast, i.e. speculation on fanciful new financial products fuelled by a remarkable boom in cheap housing. In Waly's case, that beast was surreally situated inside the belly of an even bigger monster: a global economic system swift and nimble at moving capital and production to low-cost locales, desperately in need of equally flexible movements of low-wage workers, but unwilling, for cultural and political reasons, to make the movement of people open and official. The predictable result: constant unofficial flows of labourers, a bizarre system of surmountable formal obstacles to migration, winks and nods in enforcement and employment, and considerable legal and personal insecurity for those who came to exist and work in the semi-legal shadows in destination countries. Perhaps only (or mainly) in California with its fast capitalist combination of boom, anything-goes investment, cultural flux and hopeful, superficial cosmopolitan self-imagination, could an African migrant in such a state of insecurity end up living the dream and feeding his earnings straight into the machine that would produce the worst global economic disaster since the Great Depression.

Waly's story does not end there. For most of his time outside of Senegal, even as he married, had children, bought a home and settled, he was convinced that as soon as he saved enough, as soon as his nest egg was big enough to go home and really make a difference in his village, he would return to Senegal and 'start something', making a permanent positive impact for the country, community and family he so clearly missed. It would take a long time, but eventually he always hoped to go home.

Forces beyond Waly's control intervened in 2007–08 as the housing bubble burst and the crisis unfolded. By 2007, Waly was losing work. By early 2008, most of his best landscaping clients could no longer afford to have their lawns manicured and their gardens tended to quite so often. By early 2009, many of those same clients had lost their homes. In that same year, Waly's own house value fell; he was now 'under water' with the value of his mortgage debt well above the market value of his house. What little equity there might have been evaporated as the bubble popped. It was now uncertain if Waly could make his monthly payments, though the bank had little incentive to reclaim the low-value house.

How much longer would it make sense for Waly to remain in these conditions? The nest egg was not getting any bigger and house values might not recover for a decade. Work did not look promising, and Waly was putting on years and scars from his long absence from home. Maybe, in 2010, it was time to just walk away from the mortgage and the dream, cash in the nest egg and return to Senegal.

As we will see later, the available data, although sketchy, shows that remittances from Senagalese migrants in 2009, the first really bad year of the crisis, were down by 4 per cent. According to many informed observers, because so many Senegalese migrants repatriated their nest eggs in 2009, they produced a one-time artificial boost that temporarily hid the magnitude of the decline. The World Bank, the International Monetary Fund (IMF) and the Ministère de l'Economie et des Finances (MEF) predicted that this would not be the case in 2010 (World Bank 2010; IMF 2010; MEF 2010).

To get a sense of what this means, and to move beyond an individual story and see the interplay among labour migration, family and social investment strategies, global financial crisis and changing economic prospects of countries like Senegal, this essay proceeds in three steps.

- It places Waly Faye's story in the social and historical context of the evolution of labour migration and socio-economic relations in Senegal.
- It considers recent shifts in labour migration that place increased importance on family and social investment strategies.
- It explores the global financial crisis and its effects on Senegal as transmitted through the channel of labour remittances. The story there is disquieting and grim. Seen, however, in the context of the historical modes of labour migration, there are some grounds to expect a resilience that might otherwise go unnoticed.

Contextualizing Labour Migration in Senegal

Senegalese labour migration, as seen at the end of the twentieth and beginning of the twenty-first centuries, is nothing new. Destinations of choice, logistics, duration and the work itself have taken on new forms especially in the last two to three decades. Yet, movement to take up new residence for the sake of economic opportunity is a well-established feature of the history of the region. It was woven into the political economy established under colonialism, and has since been reworked in the post-colonial period. Across these time-scales, it is especially striking how social, familial and cultural patterns have changed in ways that continually facilitate the dispersion of people across a range of landscapes, ethno-scapes and production-scapes (to borrow and torture Appadurai 1996).

As Jean François Bayart notes (1993), in the Braudelian *longue durée*, migration represents a well-established social, cultural and political trope. Given generally low population densities and high land availability, a range of social and political tensions (contestation over inheritance; leadership succession; internal family conflicts particularly between siblings and children of different co-wives; tensions over control of various resources, skills and positions of status, etc.) have resulted in a general tendency to cleave, migrate and found new settlements. Numerous communities and histories in the Senegal–Gambia region reflect this *longue durée* trope.

Take, for example, the Serer of Sine in today's Fatick region in the west-central Peanut Basin in Senegal. Oral histories and archival records suggest that the progenitors of the Serer of Sine left the Senegal River Valley around the eleventh century when Islam first arrived. While the Pulaar-speaking peoples of that zone began to convert, the Serer moved away rather than convert. Some claim this move gave the group its name, derived from the Pulaar verb *sererabe*: to divorce or formally separate. Village-founding tales among the Serer of Sine include migration by a heroic first founder often from the north, fitting nicely into the basic cleavage–migration–resettlement trope (Becker 1984; Dupire *et al.* 1974; Lericollais 1972).

We find a similar model in the subsequent conquest of the Serer people by a Mandé matrilinial splinter group, the Guelwaar, who appear to have left the core Mali empire region in the thirteenth or fourteenth century as a result of tensions associated with the gradual decline of that state (de Kersaint-Gilly 1920). Eventually the Guelwaar migrated to the area that had been settled by the Serer, conquered them and imposed a Mandé-style centralized state system. Over time, the Guelwaar intermarried and assimilated Serer language, culture and religion, becoming a noble caste rather than a distinct cultural group.

These stories of conflict–cleavage–migration–resettlement are generic, as one can glean from the cultural and social structures that provide ideational, behavioural and organizational scaffolding to support the general pattern of migration. Two examples illustrate this point. First, conflict–cleavage–migration–resettlement appears as a cultural pattern in the foundational text of West Africa's oral history and mythology, the Sunjata epic (Niane 1965). Sunjata cannot come into his true inheritance and destiny until he resolves a conflict with his half-brother Dankaran Touman and Dankaran's mother Sassouma Bérété. The conflict festers throughout Sunjata's youth, exploding when he comes of age and is exiled along with his mother and allies. During the exile he gains long experience of wandering migration, which proves essential in helping Sunjata forge alliances and discover skills that he will bring to bear when he returns to found the empire of Mali. The trope of migration also lies at the foundation of Sunjata's very existence. The wandering hunter from Do foresaw Sunjata's birth, instigating a search outside Mandé for the mythic Buffalo Woman whose daughter Sogolon must leave home, migrate to Mandé, marry the king and give birth to the new heir Sunjata.

Likewise, social and familial organization, values and practices afford similar scaffolding to the conflict–cleavage–migration trope. This is especially clear with regard to perceived pairings of patrilinear clans linked by fictive bonds of joking kinship that are said to cover the West African region.[1] Rafäel Ndiaye (1992) has argued that joking kinships linking major families in the old empire of Mali can be matched to the migration patterns and adoption of new names as founding families left Mali and moved westward to present-day Senegal, and southward to what is now Côte d'Ivoire. Thus the Traorés, once allied in joking kinship in historic Mali with the Coulibalys, became the Diops when they made it to Senegal and took up joking kinship with the Falls, themselves associated with the Coulibalys of Mali. In the present day, such correspondences between paired patrilinear clans linked by joking kinship facilitate intra-regional migration. If as a Diop I move to Mali, I can 'become' a Traoré, effectively reworking my identity within a migration-generated identity rubric. I can then insert myself in relations of reciprocity and conviviality with my new joking kin, the Coulibalys. The same happens with migration to other places in the origin matching up with other patrilinear clan names. Practices associated with historical memory and the fluidity of cultural identity thus have long helped support and manage processes of migration.

As in so many domains of life, the colonial order built directly on pre-existing patterns of economic and social action, reinforcing patterns and relations it found useful. With peace under colonial rule, there was a significant reduction in full-scale cleavage and the establishment of new communities (in Senegal, the Mouride expansion into the east for peanut production constitutes an important exception, to which we will return). The old trope shifted to something more complex and more artificially ordered, with four modes of reorganization of labour: assimilation, *corvée* or forced labour, market, and brotherhood. Over time, as we will see, the first two merged into and informed the third. So, by the end of the twentieth century, we are left with a market logic of labour migration which contains concatenated elements of the older assimilation and *corvée* logic, and the dominant alternative: a religio-commercial logic of labour migration expressed through the Islamic Sufi brotherhoods, especially the Mourides.

The assimilationist project of the French colonial administration with its on-again, off-again partial self-governance for culturally transformed Africans in the four coastal towns created a new dynamic of migration to these emerging cities (Crowder 1967). It was of course artificial, in that it was at first coercive (the Ecole des Otages took children of chiefs to the French school for cultural reprogramming; it did not ask for volunteers) and later highly restrictive. In spite of the artificiality, the myth of *citoyenneté* (citizenship) mattered (Gellar 2005), and only those who had gained the right and difficult-to-obtain education or the right access to urban employment stood a chance of moving into this new status.

---

[1] Joking kinship generally consists of widely-held notions of perceived relatedness that may link large extended families or ethnic groups. It typically centres on patterns of mutual teasing, ribbing and insulting, with primary themes of historic subordination/ slavery and food insecurity.

It established an ideal of movement to the urban coast as a form of almost fantastic economic possibility associated with crossing a significant cultural divide. It founded and cemented a kind of schizophrenia still characteristic of Senegal today: to cross that divide into a place of material hope and cultural transformation is a prized goal and a mark of achievement, but the passage is always two-way. In a non- or semi-acknowledged way, one always goes back to the non-*assimilé* world, usually the rural world. One always receives visitors from that other world and takes care of people from the place of origin. It is a facile truism in Senegal to simply declare, *à la* Leopold Sedar Senghor, that one is truly of both worlds: a truism that masks the tensions and contradictions that proliferate with this particularly artificial form of cultural–material partial migration.

Further, the colonial order, in its other more general guise as an authoritarian regime that positioned bodies and other resources for useful purposes, reorganized labour using *corvée* gangs. Forced labour conscription and mobilization was a tool in the hands of colonial officials who needed manpower to build roads, dig wells, clear and cultivate fields, and engage in dozens of other tasks (Fall 2010). *Corvée* represented another way of forcing labourers leave their homes and take up work in new locales. The obvious resentments it instilled precipitated a fairly novel, reactionary, traditionalist defence of place and custom. Workers wanted to get free of the labour gang and go home, and now home was held up, even reified, as a more ideal, extant and well-bounded locale than it had once been.

At the same time, *corvée* brought people to new areas, created new contacts and sometimes opened up new opportunities. In rare instances, these created new possibilities for migration and work beyond and after the *corvée* experience (Interview with Diouf 1992). Perhaps, more importantly, *corvée* began to establish an ontological distinction between home as a fixed place of affective attachment and choice, versus work elsewhere as mandatory, unwelcome economic obligation. This new affective migration map would correspond reasonably well to labour relations and migration experiences instilled not by violence, but by parallel and more subtle market incentives.

Market forces, new technologies (especially the railroads, from the 1920s onwards) and new opportunities for work drew massive numbers of migrant workers from distant places in Senegal, and from neighbouring French Soudan and Haute Volta, to booming peanut fields in the country. As time went on, the same forces drew steadily increasing numbers to the coastal cities, at first Rufisque and Saint Louis, later Dakar, and still later the various provincial capitals within Senegal (David 1980).

At a superficial level, this reflected a free choice to take up new residence to earn resources, and possibly to send some back home. But the exigencies of new commodification (and taxation) make it awkward to talk of free rational choice and utilitarian calculation behind migration without acknowledging the forces that pushed people, against their will, into the cash economy (Galvan 2004, Chapter 2). In recognizing the complex interplay of human agency and structural coercion behind marketization, it is helpful also to keep in mind the changing social and cultural valence of marketized labour migration as it emerged throughout the twentieth century and later as it became increasingly internationalized.

Marketized labour migration was something akin to assimilation – partially luck and partially deliberate effort, which produced an ambivalent cultural passage into a new life with new economic opportunities and status markers. At the same time, marketized labour migration was a kind of wage slavery (Roediger 1991; Rogin 1991) more akin to *corvée*, a necessary evil that also reified the imaginary cultural place of family, tradition, home and fixed place. Market-driven labour migration thus entails an ambivalent mix of voluntaristic hope, disordering cultural passage, shame over cultural loss, resentment over loss of pre-capitalist freedom, and reification of traditions and places left behind. In that sense, it is unsurprisingly an excellent window into the nature of postcolonial modernity itself.

If the twentieth century, then, saw the fusion of assimilationist and *corvée* logic of labour migration with the emerging market logic, it also witnessed the emergence of a fourth wholly different mode and logic of moving workers to new locales, which we might refer to as the Mouride model, although it applies to Islamic Sufi brotherhoods besides the paradigmatic Mouride group founded by Cheikh Amadou Bamba. As *navetanes* or temporary migrant workers were moving via market forces to fill labour needs in the western or core part of the Peanut Basin, a new political economy and political culture were emerging in the Mouride heartland around Touba, Mbacké and Diourbel, and in the newly settled lands to the south and to the east. Here, religious followers of the Mouride founder Amadou Bamaba and his lieutenant Ibrahima Fall[2] turned remote religious schools into peanut farms. Using slash-and-burn agricultural techniques, these farms thrived, expanded and then, having exhausted the already poor soil, relocated to fresh lands to the east and the south along the new railroad line.

Using the hard labour of religious devotees whose work earned them favour from the Sufi leader, and by extension entry to heaven, these were dynamic economic enterprises. They fostered a new mode of migration which built on patterns of family investment akin to an older practice known as pawning, whereby a child would be conferred into the care of a family with more resources or opportunities for education, or would simply be used as a means to cement an

---

[2] Fall was a former member of the *ceddo* warrior caste in a defunct Wolof kingdom that had been shattered by French conquest in the 1870s. He negotiated with Bamba special terms by which he and many of his fellow ex-warriors would convert to Islam and become not just followers, but the backbone of the emerging Mouride Sufi brotherhood. Fall and his followers were granted exemption from the requirement that they pray five times a day, undertake the pilgrimage, give alms, and read and master the Qu'ran. Instead, their special mark of devotion would be extreme loyalty to the Sufi leader or *marabout* (Bamba), and zealous, hard labour on his behalf. As it turned out, this lent itself well to the eventual spread of the peanut economy (Cruise O'Brien 1971).

alliance with another lineage. The Mouride mode of migration built in part on this model, in that many children were conferred to the Sufi leaders for religious training, thus cementing alliances between families and the new brotherhood. Spiritual services could then flow from Sufi leaders to the relatives of the conferred child (Behrman 1970; Villalón 1995).

As Mouride peanut farming became increasingly important in the rural economy of Senegal, this religious mode and rationale for moving people took on greater emphasis and emerged as a distinct alternative to market logics of migration, and their attendant assimilationist and *corvée* frameworks. The 1980s and beyond saw the international expansion of the Mouride pattern and rationale for migration. The brotherhood was no longer only in the business of growing peanuts, but had diversified into international commerce. They set up religious communities (*daaras*) no longer in the semi-desert but in urban outposts at the far end of long-distance trading networks in Paris, Rome, Madrid, New York and, later, many other cities. These religious communities attracted devotees, set up housing, and made connections to jobs and social services for new migrants. They also provided a ready labour pool for selling goods (in the usual micro-retail ambulant manner of Senegal) and for conducting larger-scale transactions including trust-based loans of considerable magnitude (Bava 2003).

Both nationally and internationally, then, we work our way into the late twentieth century with two distinct types of labour migration. The first, market-based migration drawing on both assimilationist and *corvée* roots, entails an aspirational cultural passage, regret over loss, and a nostalgia for obligation towards a reified home, culture and place. The second, the Sufi Islamic (especially Mouride) mode, entails a smoother, more syncretic integration of new aspirational religious culture with prior links to family and origin, from which one was literally or metaphorically conferred in an alliance.

The market mode promotes dualistic investments (material and affective) in both the aspirational target socio-cultural order and the reified anterior one. The Mouride mode is arguably more integrative and intensive, creating less bifurcation between the material and the affective, with labour more fully concentrated in the service of a capital-accumulating organization, and greater possibility of providing social and economic services for those who experience loss in difficult times. As we will see, these two modes become important not as a dichotomous pair but in tandem, when we consider the effects of the global financial crisis on Senegal in the last section of this paper.

Migration, Remittances and Family Investments

Remittances sent home by overseas migrants became a very significant part of the Senegalese economy in the 1980s and 90s. In much earlier periods, the international migration profile consisted of those seeking educational opportunity, an associated brain drain of the most employable, and a growing low-skilled migration flow, seeded by but not limited to religious commercial networks. By the time of the 1994 devaluation of the regional common currency

(CFA franc), the number of Senegalese living and working abroad was already quite significant. As Figure 1 shows, remittances sent home by migrants became a significant part of the Senegalese economy in the last decade, now exceeding the combined total of development assistance and foreign direct investment.

The 1994 currency devaluation was an important watershed for Senegal's political economy as well as for international migration. The CFA franc had been established as a regional common currency for French West Africa in 1945. Its value had been fixed in relation to the French franc, and, after 1999, to the euro. While a regionwide common currency shared by fourteen small countries was a partial boon to regional integration and commerce, the exchange rate peg always entailed a loss of autonomy in macroeconomic management and ran the risk of overvaluation (*Africa Recovery* 1999). By the mid-1990s – the time of the Washington Consensus around neoliberal macroeconomic policies – most developing countries focused their economic strategies on cheap exports and attracting foreign investment with low costs, low taxes and cheap labour. But a CFA pegged to the reasonably strong French franc, and later to the quite robust euro, wiped out these natural comparative advantages for Senegal and its partners in the common currency. By the early 1990s, a consensus had emerged among international donors and local policy makers on the pitfalls of an overvalued CFA. After much wrangling, the CFA franc was devalued by 50 per cent overnight, effective 1 January 1994.

Social unrest was ensured as incomes halved and import prices doubled. Social spending by the government to cushion these shocks proved quite limited. The hope in a country like Senegal was that these adverse economic effects would be offset by a boost in exports and even a shift away from expensive imported foodstuff and toward local production. There was a modest rise in

FIGURE 1   *Value of resource flows (millions of US$)*

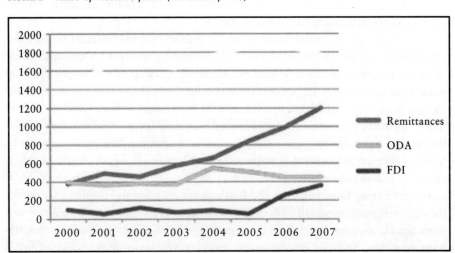

Sources: Zupi *et al.* 2009; Direction de la Prévision et des Etudes Economiques (DPEE) 2010.

exports and economic growth was restored (though it remained uneven). The hoped-for big leap in foreign direct investment (FDI), however, never materialized, in part because the devaluation still left the currency pegged at a fixed rate, ensuring a gradual return to overvaluation (Daffé 2009).

Devaluation also operated at a psychological and cultural level: in popular perception, the exchange rate adjustment amounted to an injurious and insulting negative assessment of Senegal as a country and even Senegalese as individuals ('*je suis devalué*' – I am devalued – was the frequent refrain, which spilled over into social and interpersonal relations). Senegal after 1994 seemed like a place where 'things had suddenly gone from bad to worse' (Interview with Ngom 2002).

At the same time, devaluation instantly doubled the value of remittances. In the real and perceived crisis that followed January 1994, this was the lifeline. Families lucky enough to have a relative abroad had hopes of making it through the difficult times. Those without such links worked creatively with flexible notions of kinship to make friends and associates who were overseas into quasi- or fictive kin (Interview with Touré 2000).

Remittances and outmigration climbed after 1994. Even as devaluation and other changes eventually led to economic growth in Senegal, good times seemed to have little impact on migration. Numerous interviews conducted in Dakar and in the rural Sine region since the mid-1990s reflect a few common themes: Senegal remains a 'difficult place to live'; 'there is nothing to do here'; 'the educational system continues to churn out well-trained graduates, too many of whom sit idly or drive taxis'; 'I know so and so who is doing well overseas (many Waly Fayes), so it's worth the risks and costs to get myself over there', 'can you as *toubab* (white person) get me a visa?' The core logic of migration remained fairly immune to the salutary effects and hopeful signs associated with growth in the Senegalese economy from roughly 1999 to 2006. Some argue that was because the benefits of growth were rather unevenly distributed (Zupi *et al.* 2009). Others venture that it is the reverse – growth actually stemmed in large part from the increasing flow of remittances.

A decade and a half later, on the cusp of the global financial crisis, there can be no doubt about the importance of remittances not just for growth but for the basic functioning of the Senegalese economy. Official estimates put the total value of remittances at 12 per cent of the entire Senegalese economy in 2008–09 (World Bank 2010; IMF 2010; MEF 2010). This figure is fairly conservative in that it includes only official, easily traced transfers (proverbial Western Union flows); but a rather significant portion of all remittances flow more informally, in ways that are not included in the official 12 per cent figure. Some of this is certainly individuals entering the country with cash and other valuables. Most observers agree, however, that the lion's share of informal remittances comes through religious, especially Mouride, networks. These are trust-based transactions among members of a shared community of belief, who can count on long-term relations, and can thus manage complex and sizeable transfers of funds based on word-of-mouth arrangements. In a transcontinental update of the historic Dyula trading networks (Cohen 1971), money that needs to go from, say, New York to Dakar, is exchanged between brotherhood members (in the proverbial exchange on 116th Street in Harlem, Little Dakar). Or it may be that no money changes hands at all, just the promise of payment. The recipient in New York calls or texts a trusted confidant in Dakar (a friend, a brother, someone in the same Sufi brotherhood), who then draws from his funds to make the necessary payment to a final recipient in Senegal, who meets the intermediary to get the money at Dakar's downtown Marché Sandaga (in the proverbial transaction). Intermediaries simply remember the amounts in question. The sum might get credited against another transaction at some future point. Flows are wide and steady enough in these relationships for many individual transactions to simply wash out over time.

Reliable, though conservative estimates put these informal flows at about half the total for formal transaction (Direction de la Prévision et des Etudes Economiques [DPEE] 2009). The real figure is probably larger than half. So a safe estimate of remittances as a fraction of the overall economy in Senegal is 18 per cent (12 per cent official, 6 per cent informal). In the context of limited resources and very narrow in-country economic opportunity, Senegalese have cobbled together a makeshift way of making ends meet that draws on their unique international positioning and their long history of labour migration. They have, in local parlance, *goorgoorlu'd* their interaction with the global economic system (*goorgoorlu* in Wolof literally means to 'man-man-it'; figuratively, to make do, improvise, jerry-rig).

This new remittance economy is more than an accident of a well-networked Senegalese global diaspora. It builds on the logics of migration described above, both market-centred and religio-commercial, involving individuals, families now functioning more like investment-making firms, and, of course, large-scale religious organizations.

In the days of Waly Faye, before the boom in remittances, migrants got help from relatives to get abroad, but this was not necessarily a deliberate or very crucial strategic investment by families. As one middle, aged female relative of an international migrant put it (Interview with Gning 1993):

> Sure, when Aminata was thinking of going to France [in the early 1990s] she talked to me and I did what I could to help her. She's my niece, kind of like my niece, or I think that's what you would call her in French, and I wanted her to succeed and have a good life. Who doesn't want that for their child?

Once, as in the case of Aminata's 'aunt', the logic of assistance had been more personal, affective, and focused on the success and well-being of the migrant as an individual. Of course there was certainly some degree of expectation of financial return from the migrant. But in thirty-seven interviews conducted on this topic in the rural village of Toucar (Sine/Fatick region) in 1992–93, only eight respondents (22 per cent) made any explicit reference to the financial benefits to relatives who stayed behind. Contrast this to twenty-three interviews conducted on this topic in 2008–09 in the same village, in which twenty respondents (87 per cent) made explicit and detailed references to the uses and benefits of remittances sent by relations and friends abroad.

Although there is relatively little in the way of comprehensive data on uses of remittance monies by recipients in Senegal, what little research has been done supports the anecdotal observation that household budgets are quite remittance dependent. As shown in Figure 2, based on a survey of some fifty Dakar households, family aid and school fees take up 41 per cent of remittance funds, with vaguely defined categories such as goods and services constituting another 41 per cent.

Figure 2 contradicts the widely shared anecdotal perception in Senegal that the primary household-level use of remittances is real estate investment and construction of new homes, often associated with storefronts and small shops as family micro enterprises. Wherever the money for such building is coming from (remittances; capital flight from crisis regions of West Africa; licit proceeds of internal economic growth; illicit money from shadowy European or American activities laundered into officially unprofitable Senegalese real estate investment; illicit redirection of aid and development funds), this kind of small and medium-scale construction has indeed dramatically altered the landscape of Dakar. Moreover, categories in Figure 2 such as 'family aid', 'goods' and 'services' may in fact contain resources destined for housing and real estate investment.

A 2006 study in the village of Touba Toul in the Thies region of Senegal likewise confirms the degree to which the number of households receiving remittances has mushroomed in recent years, and also reveals the increasing dependence of these households on funds sent by relatives from abroad for both basic needs and new investments (Petersen 2007).

FIGURE 2   *Remittance uses (2004–05)*

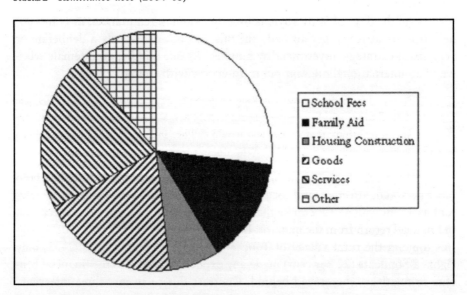

My own research in and around the village of Toucar in the Sine/Fatick region confirms this same impression. Although the proportion of families benefiting from remittances ranged from a low estimate of 5 per cent to a high of 21 per cent (relatively low figures that correspond with the overall economic and educational marginality of Toucar and the environs), hopes of international migration and tapping into the remittance flow remain quite widespread. In 63 interviews conducted from 2008–10 on the development situation and how to improve conditions in Toucar, 58 respondents (92 per cent) mentioned finding a way to get someone from their family out of the village, and of these more than half (32 respondents) expressed hope that the migrant would go abroad. Even discounting the likelihood that these comments were directed at me as a foreigner, these data point to two remarkable features of contemporary hope surrounding migration and remittances.

First, international migration has now become more of a family investment than an individual choice or personal means to improve one's situation. Respondent Awa Sarr (Interview 2010), a mother of five, offers these thoughts about her younger brother who is trying to get to Italy.

> Every family is thinking about this now. We all see our neighbours with a kid or a relative outside. They get a new roof; they can send another child to school in Fatick or Dakar; they can buy rice even in the hungry season (months before the harvest, June–September). We all want this and we know nothing is happening here in this village to help us get this. We put our hope in this person because it can work, we see it happening all the time.

Or, in the words of this middle-aged male respondent in Dakar's Usine neighbourhood (Interview with Diouf 2009):

> . . . there's not a lot of hope here right now . . . things are bad . . . we have hope in one person, and we send him with our blessings and our prayers and our money to go to America or Europe and we hope, God willing, that he'll do well and he'll remember us.

As migration has become more of a family investment strategy, it evokes, and in some sense appears propelled by, prior historical logic. The exigencies of limited means force a kind of exile, like Waly Faye's six months becoming two decades. Families are making a calculated, hopeful investment to get someone across a major geographical and cultural divide to, in effect, confer them to another society or to the global market system. There is not necessarily any expectation that the individual in question will come back. In some sense, return undermines the logic of the investment. As Waly Faye's cousin told me recently, '. . . he's gone, we know we will never see him again in this life. He is doing what he has to do and we're doing what we have to do. If he can lend us a hand, that's the best thing for everyone' (Interview with Faye 2010).

This market logic of migration, fusing older assimilationist cultural passage and *corvée* exigency, has now become a family investment strategy. Of course this is not the only style of social investment in international migration. Mouride and other religious networks partake of a different logic centred on communities of shared values, internal trust and solidarity, and alliances with families cemented as children are conferred as *talibés*[3] to religious leaders.

So, naturally, families invest in migrants who do not go on their own but link up, through brotherhoods, to well-established and resilient networks of migration, social support and capital flow. Likewise, the brotherhoods are not so pervasive in Senegalese daily life as to fully recruit members and migrants on their own. They rely on both family investments and the fact that new migrants who go abroad on their own need camaraderie, familiar language and food, as well as a job and place to live. The best organized source of these necessities are Mouride religious communities (*daaras*). So, even those who left West Africa without a strong Sufi religious affiliation often become much more closely affiliated, more religious and more organizationally integrated in the course of their migration experience.

It would be a mistake to think of contemporary international labour migration strategies, logics and processes in terms of a false dichotomy between family investment informed by a market logic and Mouride/brotherhood investment informed by a religio-commercial logic. At best these are ideal types which tell us something about the range of real-world variation. But all real-world instances are some mix of the ideal-type categories.

As we shall see below, especially in the case of international migration as a family investment strategy, hopes have been made quite precarious by the global financial crisis. But it is precisely the intertwining of family/market and religio-commercial migration investment logics that may help Senegal sidestep the worst effects of the crisis.

Remittances and How the Global Crisis Hit Senegal

Ironically, the typical reaction in Senegal to the global economic crisis has been: 'What crisis? You mean a new one in addition to all the crises we've already been dealing with?' (Interview with Ndiaye 2009). Ongoing, everyday crises of underdevelopment are of course familiar in this society: lack of employment, crumbling infrastructure, sparse natural resources, desertification, soil depletion, climate change, and insufficiencies in education, provision of primary health care and housing, to name a few.

---

[3] Children serving as *talibés*, or religious disciples of a Sufi leader or *marabout*, is a phenomenon that has gained considerable notoriety of late in the western media, thanks to the attention drawn to cases of abuse in which *marabouts* forced Qur'anic school students to take up street-begging, and to suffer beatings, drug addiction and other humiliations in the service of the religious leader (Adigbli 2008). It is probably as widespread and systemic a phenomenon as child abuse by Catholic priests. That is, it is a real, serious and tragic social issue that nevertheless does not describe the complete reality of the entire religious social order. Despite western media accounts to the contrary with regard to abuse of *talibés*, the part should not be mistaken for the whole.

On top of these, new shocks rattled Senegal's economy and society in the years leading up to the global financial meltdown. A World Bank economist stationed in Senegal for many years describes the five 'F crises': food, fuel, floods and fiscal disorder, followed by the global financial crisis. Senegal imports about 80 per cent of its main staple crop, rice, primarily from Thailand. The global crisis in food prices and supply began in the rice market in 2005–06, shortly after which the Thai government limited exports. Prices soared worldwide, and Senegal was no exception. Even though the government took a significant budgetary hit as it continued to subsidize staple prices with an eye toward keeping urban consumers happy, nevertheless the increases that were passed along hurt. Rioting took place in Dakar in response to the price shock, with the worst episodes in March–April 2008.

Further, Senegal has no petroleum resources, and is fully dependent on imported oil for transportation and for 90 per cent of its electricity production. Steadily increasing oil prices in the years prior to the global financial crisis naturally hit Senegal quite hard. Again, the state absorbed some of these increases. In the electricity production sector, this meant that budget resources that might have been used to upgrade and maintain production and transmission equipment were used to maintain subsidized consumer prices. By 2007, electricity output in the high-demand summer months proved unreliable thanks to equipment failures. The Dakar housing boom of the previous decade had considerably increased demand for power, with little or no matching upgrade in output or crumbling infrastructure. Rolling brownouts became increasingly common. By summer 2009, they were more widespread than ever before, resulting in social protest by ordinary people. Muslim religious leaders even took to the streets. The country's most popular pop icon, singer Youssou Ndour, released a song mocking the government's handling of the crises, which became wildly popular and captured a simmering mood of discontent (Kandji 2009).

To add to their troubles, unusually heavy rains in August–September of 2005 and 2009 caused massive flooding in Dakar. As the city has expanded in the last two decades, areas once considered uninhabitable, low-lying lands have filled up, unsurprisingly with makeshift housing for the poorest (see Figure 3).

These regions were most affected by flooding. In 2009, 450,000 people (out of a total Dakar population of some 3 million) saw their homes flooded, and as late as December, some 30,000 people were and continued to be inundated. In both years, the government promised rapid and direct relief, but delays and lack of resources left most flood victims feeling abandoned and deeply frustrated with how the crises were handled.

By late 2008, just as the gravity of the global financial disaster was becoming apparent in the North, Senegal experienced a fourth crisis in public finance. Expenditures associated with response to the food, fuel and flooding crises, as well as the costs of seven years of massive public spending in new infrastructure, came together at this time in the form of a short-term crisis of arrears. The government typically ran a budget deficit, with aid and inter-

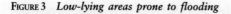

FIGURE 3 *Low-lying areas prone to flooding*

national loans from the IMF and other sources to cover the gap. The arrears crisis, however, was unrelated to this public debt. Rather, the state had 'lost track' of a series of obligations to pay out contracts, most of them associated with large-scale construction projects and public works. By December 2008, the IMF and World Bank estimated that the total cost of the unpaid obligations was almost 6 per cent of Senegal's entire gross domestic product (GDP) (World Bank 2010; IMF 2010; DPEE 2009). State fiscal coffers were running bare just at the time when the global financial crisis was expected to deal a significant blow to public revenues and to add to social service expenditures.

The World Bank, IMF and other donors folded their response to the arrears crisis into their overall plan to prepare the West African region to respond to the global economic storm. For Senegal, this meant direct support to cover the arrears in exchange for an unusual degree of opening of books, allowing external donors to intervene fairly directly in public accounting and allocation of public resources. By the beginning of 2010, the arrears were more or less fully paid up. Nevertheless, when the global financial crisis began to hit in 2009 the government was 'on its knees', in the words of a highly placed government economist (MEF 2010). It had no capacity to engage in stimulus-spending to keep the economy from slipping into a deep recession.

Prospects looked quite grim going into 2009, especially given growing disenchantment with the government of President Abdoulaye Wade and his Parti Democratique du Senegal (PDS). Wade had come to power in 2000 as a heroic figure, winning an election which marked the first ever defeat for the party that had ruled since independence in 1960 and unseating an incumbent President from that same party. Since then, Wade's regime has been marked by steadily authoritarian and personalistic tendencies: harassing and jailing critical journalists, a practice almost unknown in pluralist Senegal; antagonizing the Catholic minority and seeming to favour his own Islamic Sufi brotherhood (Mourides) at the expense of several others (especially the large Tijane brotherhood), again unheard of to date in tolerant and secular Senegal; a steady drumbeat of accusations of corruption among key allies and in the office of the President; fairly overt efforts to position the President's unpopular son Karim as a successor; a series of increasingly arbitrary changes to the Constitution, including reworking presidential terms in a way that made it possible for Wade to hold office for at least nineteen years, as opposed to two five-year terms as of the time of his first election (Foucher 2010).

At the time of the President's re-election in a contest deemed by observers from the Economic Community of West African States (ECOWAS) reasonably free and fair in February 2007, the public seemed to discount the accumulating signs of personalism and authoritarianism in light of Wade's aura as the leader of a major movement of democratic change, and his real success in garnering donor and private investment funds for a massive public works construction programme to rebuild and expand roads, seaports, airports, schools and clinics. Not long after the February 2007 re-election, however, the public mood against the President shifted. In the March 2009 elections for municipal and local offices, the PDS was trounced, with the President's son defeated in his bid to become mayor of Dakar, and the President's party losing mayorships and other local offices in many rural districts and all but one provincial capital (AFP 2009). Thus, as the 'five F' crises compounded in 2009, the government had few tools to manage the economic situation, and faced a restive, suspicious and increasingly angry populace.

As it turned out, there was a temporary upside for Senegal in the global financial crisis: food and fuel prices dropped for the first time in half a decade. Moreover, the main channels by which the crisis spread from the US to other Northern economies, and then to some emerging markets, left Senegal mostly out of the loop. In this case, being on the margins of the global economy proved an asset: Senegal's eighteen banks did not participate in the high-flying complex investments from which the crisis originated. They thus avoided the major credit crunch that slowed growth elsewhere in the world. Exports, especially fish products and phosphates, as well as tourism, did suffer, but they were already in decline and are expected to bounce back fairly quickly in 2010, as Figure 4 reveals.

FDI and official development assistance (ODA) to Senegal also suffered as a result of the crisis, but, as Figure 5 reveals, declines in these areas were not as severe as expected.

The critical point about FDI and ODA, in fact, is how little they actually

FIGURE 4   *Value of major exports (USD million)*

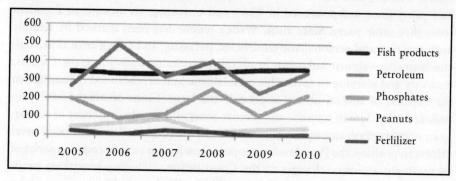

FIGURE 5   *Value of resource flows (USD million)*

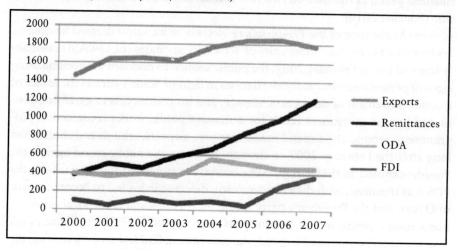

FIGURE 6   *Remittance growth rate*

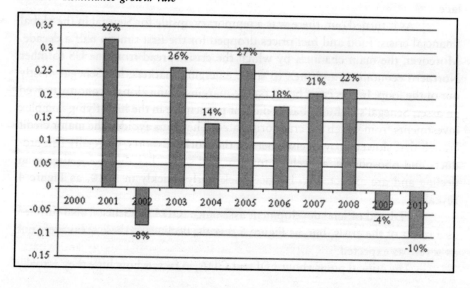

contribute, relative to remittances, to the Senegalese economy. By 2007, remittances were of greater value than FDI and ODA *combined*, a major shift in the structure of the Senegalese economy over the last decade. Given this shift, remittances represent the major channel of transmission by which the global financial crisis could impact Senegal.

Remittances have grown at a fast clip for most of the last decade but dropped by 4 per cent in 2009, and are expected to plunge by 10 per cent in 2010 (Figure 6).

As noted above, as Northern economies took a rapid nosedive into severe recession in 2008–09, Senegalese migrants like Waly Faye were among the first of millions to lose jobs or experience a significant slowdown in their semi-formal and illegal work patterns. As a result, most observers expected a decline in remittances much larger than 4 per cent.

The relatively mild reduction appears to have resulted from a nest-egg effect, in which newly unemployed or underemployed Senegalese abroad returned home and brought their accumulated savings with them, just as Waly Faye is thinking of doing. Similar phenomena have been observed in other settings, such as Central Asia, when, earlier in the decade, cultural and political conflict led to a rapid repatriation from Russia of many migrants, whose return brought a one-time boost to struggling economies in that region (IMF 2010).

In 2010, World Bank, IMF and Senegalese government economists envisioned a worst-case scenario in which the temporary cushioning effect of nest-egg repatriation faded, and Senegalese households experienced the full brunt of a 10 per cent drop in a sector that now accounts for as much as one-fifth of the entire economy. Combined with the government's shaky finances, the likelihood that the summer of 2010 would witness power shortages and brownouts on a scale similar to or greater than 2009, a government losing legitimacy fast, and an increasingly frustrated and angry populace – and one had the recipe for a dangerous social and political situation.

In thinking about the potentially volatile social and political brew in Senegal in 2010, it is worth delving briefly into local politics. Although it might seem to be something of an idiosyncratic, local issue, the scandal surrounding the state's construction of the Monument of the African Renaissance may be illustrative of the ferment and potential crisis in Senegal.

The large statue perched on a hilltop near the westernmost point of Africa (Illustration 1), visible from many points in the capital, was conceived by the President himself (who, on this basis, has claimed 35 per cent of the proceeds from entrance ticket sales to the statue and museum/exhibit space in and under the monument), built with public funds and North Korean engineering and labour. Controversy broke out as soon as the statue itself took shape and became visible (an athletic and vigorous man holding aloft a young baby and embracing, behind him, a woman with bare breasts and barely covered hips and buttocks). Muslim leaders took to the airwaves to denounce the partial nudity and what some called the idolatry of this sculptural celebration of the human form. Cathol-

ILLUSTRATION 1 *Monument of the African Renaissance*

ic leaders made similar complaints, to which the President replied in December 2009 by denouncing the 'hypocrisy' of Catholic leaders who themselves, he said, worshipped a human figure on a cross. Outrage from the Catholic community and rioting in Ziguinchor, a majority Catholic provincial town, added to that community's simmering sense of injury at the hands of the President. Commentators who avoided aesthetic and moral questions nevertheless challenged the use of public funds and the President's assertion of intellectual property rights to 35 per cent of revenues associated with the state.

In February, Wade backpedalled and declared that he would donate all of his proceeds to a newly established foundation to assist preschools across the country. The highly visible monument and the mixture of personal power, corruption, sexuality and religion created a compelling iconography that kept Senegal in the international media in a way that almost no other issue has since independence (more *New York Times* stories on Senegal in 2009–10 thanks to the statue, than on any other single issue in any equivalent prior period).

The details of the statue controversy are less important than its staying power. Unlike other scandals and controversies surrounding President Wade and his government, this one has stayed in the news and remained a favourite subject of conversation, the number one national topic of gossip and complaint, for the better part of a year. It is clearly not the most important issue in the country, nor do critics of Wade see it as his worst offence. But because it is large and visible from much of Dakar, it is as if the monument serves as a daily reminder of many accumulated frustrations with this government's management of the economy, its corruption, authoritarianism and personalistic tendencies. It is as if the state built a lightning rod, a tool, to focus and direct wide-ranging social frustration which had been diffuse and difficult to concentrate before the statue went up. Now, one need only look to the west or turn on the TV to see its image and gain a fresh reminder of the government's arrogance and incompetence.

The statue controversy is important as a window into the scale of public frustration with the Senegalese government and its declining legitimacy. A regime that seems to have exhausted its population will have limited room to manoeuvre should Senegal experience the global financial crisis more acutely than it has to date. There is a general sense of anxiety among informed observers as well as on the street in Senegal, that the country could be headed for a serious crisis. Given its increasing dependence on resources sent home from Senegalese migrants abroad, the anticipated large drop in remittance earnings, if combined with anticipated crises this summer in electricity production, could prove volatile. Further ham-handed moves by this government (more constitutional shenanigans; rearranging the timing of the next election; pushing too hard to promote the President's son as successor; a new round of major corruption scandals) could provide a spark that ignites a situation rendered combustible by economic decline and social frustration.

However, the structure and logic of labour migration itself offers a countervailing source of some potential resilience that could mitigate the looming crisis. Of the two modes/logics of labour migration – market logic of family investment; religio-commercial logic of brotherhood, especially Mouride investment – the former is probably more vulnerable to the global financial crisis. To the extent that individual and family investments in labour migration are driven by some combination of *corvée*-style economic exigency or *assimilé*-style hope for socio-cultural transformation, individual migrants take calculated risks, or, as seen more recently, families make reasonable investments to get a relative into the circuits of international migration.

Within this logic (at once both cultural and utilitarian), it makes sense to come home when life becomes unviable in the target society, when there is an economic depression and little prospect for future growth, and when, unsurprisingly, xenonophic hostility fuelled by economic uncertainty is on the rise in the North. Assimilationist dreams and practical money-making become especially uncertain. One then should expect many migrants to return to Senegal, and a corresponding major decline in remittance flows.

The other logic of migration is more organizational, and perhaps, in that sense, more resilient. The religio-commercial logic of the Islamic brotherhoods as enterprises is far less individualistic. Because of its capacity to spread risk across a wider social pool, as well as its capacity to direct resources to alleviate temporary crises, it is reasonable to assume that Mouride and related migration networks will be somewhat less vulnerable to the global financial crisis than migration networks organized on a market-based individual or family investment strategy.

Given that the best available estimates place informal religious network remittance flows at 6 per cent of the Senegalese economy and more formal flows at 12 per cent, it might seem reasonable to assume that only about one-third of remittances are structured by this more resilient religio-commercial logic.

This assessment, however, underestimates the importance of this mode of labour migration for two reasons. First, migrants embedded in religious networks make both formal (Western Union-style, traceable) and informal (trust-based Dyula style, untraceable) transfers. Moreover, the two logics of migration are hardly separate but fully intertwined, as explained previously. Family investments are central to migration strategies, to be sure, and they partake of and follow the market-based logic described above. But these family investments are in no way sealed off from religio-commercial logics and modes of migration. The two naturally intertwine. Family investments lead to migration within Mouride and other religious channels. Perhaps more importantly, migrants who get to destination countries on their own find their way quickly into support networks that link them to religious communities of commerce, labour and migration. Sometimes they change identities, even names (as in the case of Waly Faye, now Cheikh Ibrahima Faye), when they make this move. To the extent that these networks and logics are indeed intertwined, more international migrants may draw on the risk-pooling and social service resources of the brotherhoods to ride out the effects of the global financial crisis, stay in destination countries, and help maintain the flow of remittances that has become such a mainstay in the Senegalese economy to date.

Data on logic and modes of migration are thin at best, and much research remains to be done to tease out how this logic affects migrant choices at a time of crisis such as the present. As we nevertheless do the best we can to make sense of the interaction between a fast-moving global economic meltdown and a struggling economy strikingly dependent on labour remittances, it is important to try to capture the full depth of the historical and cultural context that animates the contemporary flow of labour out of and perhaps back to Senegal. Doing so opens an additional deeper layer of analysis that can help account for an unexpected degree of resilience in the Senegalese economy and society in years to come.

References

Adigbli, Koffigan E. (2008), 'Senegal: Street Children at Risk of Exploitation', *IPS News Service*, 22 September; available at http://allafrica.com/stories/200809230014.html, accessed on 26 April 2010.

Appadurai, Arjun (1996), *Modernity at Large: The cultural dimensions of globalization*, University of Minnesota Press, Minneapolis.

Associated France Presse (AFP) (2009), 'Opposition Claims Victory in Sénégal Elections', 23 March; available at http://www.google.com/hostednews/afp/article/ALeqM5gVBQru 535fJPRwvHbkZ1mT9g, accessed on 26 April 2010.

Bava, Sophie (2003), 'De la "baraka aux affaires": Ethos économico–religieux et transnationalité chez les migrants sénégalais mourides', *Revue européenne de migration internationale*, vol. 19, no. 2.

Bayart, Jean François (1993), *The State in Africa: Politics of the belly*, Longman, New York.

Becker, Charles (1984), *Traditions Villageois du Siin*, CNRS-LA, Dakar.

Becker, Charles, Mamadou Diouf and Mohamed Mbodj (1987), 'L'Evolution Demographique Regionale du Sénégal et du Bassin Arachidier (Sine–Saloum) au Vingtième Siècle, 1904–1976', in Dennis D. Cordell and Joel W. Gregory, eds., *African Population and Capitalism: Historical perspectives*, Westview Press, Colorado.

Behrman, Lucy (1970), *Muslim Brotherhoods and Politics in Senegal*, Harvard University Press, Cambridge.

Cohen, Abner (1971), *Custom and Politics in Urban Africa: A study of Hausa migrants in Yoruba towns*, University of California Press, Berkeley.

Crowder, Michael (1967), *Senegal: A study of French assimilation policy*, Methuen, London.

Cruise O'Brien, Donal (1971), *The Mourides of Senegal*, Clarendon Press, Oxford.

—— (1975), *Saints and Politicians: Essays in the organization of a Senegalese peasant society*, Cambridge University Press, Cambridge.

Daffé, Gaye (2009), 'Signes inquiétants dans la marche de l'économie Sénégalaise', unpublished manuscript.

David, Philip (1980), *Les Navetanes: Histoire des Migrants Saisonniers de l'arachide en Senegambie des origines à nos jours*, Les Nouvelles Editions Africaines, Dakar.

de Kersaint-Gilly, F. (1920), 'Les geulowars: Leur origine d'aprés une légende trés en faveur dans le Saloum oriental', *Bulletin du Comité des Etudes Historiques et Scientifiques de l'AOF*, vol. 3, no. 1, pp. 99–101.

Direction de la Prévision et des Etudes Economiques (DPEE) (2010), 'Situation Economique et Financière en 2009 et Perspectives en 2010', DPEE, Ministère de l'Economie et des Finances, République du Sénégal, January.

Dupire, Maguerite, André Lericollais, Bernard Delpech and Jean-Marc Gastellu (1974), 'Résidence, tenure foncière, alliance dans une société bilinèaire (Serer du Sine et du Baol, Sénégal)', *Cahiers d'Études Africaines*, vol. 14, no. 3, pp. 417–52.

Fall, Babacar (2010), *Sénégal: Le Travail au XXè siècle*, Karthala, Paris.

Foucher, Vincent (ed.) (2010), *Sénégal de Wade*, Karthala Press, Senegal.

Galvan, Dennis (2004), *The State Must Be Our Master of Fire: How peasants craft culturally sustainable development in Senegal*, University of California Press, Berkeley.

Gellar, Sheldon (2005), *Democracy in Senegal: Tocquevillian analytics in Africa*, Palgrave, New York.

International Monetary Fund (IMF) (2010), Interview with high-ranking IMF official, IMF Country Office, January.

Interview with Diouf (1992).

—— (2009).

Interview with T. Faye (2010).

Interview with Gning (1993).

Interview with Ndiaye (2009).

Interview with Ngom (2002).

Interview with Sarr (2010).

Interview with Touré (2000).

Irving, Jacqueline (1999), 'For Better or for Worse: The euro and the CFA franc', *Africa Recovery*, vol. 12, no. 4 (Department of Public Information, United Nations), April.

Kandji, Souleymane (2009), 'Album sur les Coupures de Courant et le Monument de la Renaissance: You Ndour s'Engage aux Cotes du People', 2 Xibar.net, 2 septembre 2009; http://www.xibar.net/album-sur-les-coupures-de-courant-et-le-monument-de-la-renaissance-you-ndour-s-engage-aux-cotes-du-peuple_a18217.html, accessed on 30 September 2011.

Lericollais, André (1972), *Sob: Étude geographique d'un terroir sérèr (Senegal)*, ORSTOM Atlas des Structures Agraires au Sud du Sahara, vol. 7, Mouton, Paris.

Ministère de l'Economie et des Finances (MEF) (2010), Interview with high-ranking economist, MEF, République du Sénégal, January.

Ndiaye, Raphäel (1992), 'Correspondances ethno-patronymiques et parenté plaisantante: une problématique d'intégration à large échelle', *Environnement africain*, vol. III, nos. 3–4, pp. 97–128.

Niane, D.T. (1965), *Sundiata: An epic of old Mali*, Longman, London.

Petersen, Dann (2007), 'The Impact of International Migration on Wives of Migrants in Touba

Toul, Senegal', unpublished M.A. thesis, International Studies Program, University of Oregon, June.

Roediger, David (1991), *The Wages of Whiteness: Race and the making of the American working class*, Verso, New York.

Rogin, Michael ([1975] 1991), *Fathers and Children: Andrew Jackson and the subjugation of the American Indian*, Transaction, New Brunswick/New Jersey.

United Nations Development Programme (UNDP) (2007), *Human Development Report*.

Villalón, Leonardo (1995), *Islamic Society and State Power in Senegal: Disciples and citizens in Fatick*, Cambridge University Press, Cambridge.

World Bank (2010), Interview with high-ranking World Bank economist, Senegal Country Office, January.

Zupi, Marco, Alberto Mazzali, Gafe Daffé and Anna Ozorio de Almeida (2009), *Trade, Investments, Debt, Aid and Remittances*, International Finance for Development in Africa.

Haalpulaar Labour Migration to America
Paths of Socio-Cultural and Economic Insertion in New York, Cincinnati and Memphis

Abdoulaye Kane

Migration by the Pulaar-speaking people of Senegal (called the Haalpulaar or Haalpulaar'en) has spanned more than a half century.[1] There has been internal migration (both rural–rural and rural–urban), intra-African migration (to Cote d'Ivoire, Gabon, Cameroon and the two Congos), and transcontinental migration to France, Belgium, and, more recently, Italy and Spain. Of late, Haalpulaar labour migrants have also arrived in the United States. The relatively long history of labour migration in the Senegal River Valley has resulted, over time, in the creation of a culture of migration in which young men are increasingly expected to travel to more or less faraway places in order to realize their dreams of becoming socially successful. The long experience of migration has also resulted in the creation of enduring social networks based on kinship, social class, religion, ethnicity and village of origin, which are instrumental in the socio-cultural and economic adaptation of newcomers.

In this essay, I examine how Haalpulaar labour migrants have negotiated their socio-economic insertion in three different American cities. To what extent were their previous experiences of internal migration or intra-African migration instrumental in their ability to successfully adapt in the United States? I also examine the process by which the Haalpulaar migrants left New York City in the mid-1990s to settle in Cincinnati and Memphis where they are currently employed in food processing plants on the border between Ohio and Kentucky or in casinos on the border between Tennessee and Mississippi. I wish to analyse the processes by which Haalpulaar migrants explore, capture and occupy new destinations. I shall also specifically address the relations between the pioneers of

---

[1] Pulaar is the Senegalese dialect of the Fula language. Fiona McLaughlin (1995) refers to a 'significant population of Fula speakers who together number at least ten million and who are spread out over a two thousand mile stretch of West Africa. . . . The vastness of the space inhabited by Fula speakers belies the actual sociological and political strength of the language: because state boundaries and linguistic boundaries do not coincide. Fula is a minority language in every country in which it is spoken. Such is the case within the Senegalese context where results of the 1988 census show that speakers of Pulaar, the Senegalese dialect of Fula, constitute 23.2% of the population, a far second to the Wolof who comprise 43.7% (République du Sénégal 1990).'

Haalpulaar migration to America and the successive waves of migrants that came later with the help of the former.

This essay will first examine the history of labour migration among the Haalpulaar of the Senegal River valley. The outcome of this relatively long history of mobility has been an expansion of the geography of Haalpulaar migration from Dakar to other parts of Africa, Europe and now America. The second part of the essay will review the arrival of Haalpulaar migrants in New York City and the challenges these pioneers faced. The third part will look at the spread of Haapulaar migrants to other cities and states in America, as also the reasons behind them deciding to go to Ohio, Kentucky and Tennessee in the mid-1990s.

Extending the Geography of Migration

It is important to examine the long history of Haalpulaar migration, spanning more than half a century, to trace how the Haalpulaar progressively moved from rural–rural migration to rural–urban migration in Senegal, and then to international migration, first within Africa, then to France as early as the 1960s, and more recently to the United States. One can delineate the successive and sometimes overlapping phases of this evolution in Haalpulaar migration.

The first phase started in the colonial period with the participation of Haalpulaar labour migrants in the *navetanat*, a rural–rural type of labour migration whereby farmers migrated to the colonial site of peanut production in the central region of Senegal. The *navetanat* was a seasonal type of movement that provided Haalpulaar households with cash to pay taxes, and to buy manufactured goods and imported food products (coffee, sugar, cooking oil, milk, etc.), to complement their agricultural production of cereals (corn, millet and sorghum), beans, melons and sweet potatoes in the highlands (Deri) during the rainy season and on the flooded lands near the Senegal River (Walo). This type of migration continued in the 1950s but progressively lost momentum after the Second World War, when seasonal migration become more oriented toward urban centres in Senegal and in the West African region, especially Côte d'Ivoire.

The second phase saw the participation of the Haalpulaar in a rural exodus from the 1960s to the 1980s. The goal of migration remained unchanged during the early years of this rural–urban migration. Haalpulaar labour migrants were involved in seasonal migration, combining farming activities during the rainy season with jobs and petty trade during the dry season in urban centres. Migration from the Senegal River Valley to Dakar, however, did not concern only labour migrants, menial workers and traders. Due to the limited number of secondary and high schools in rural areas, students had no option but to migrate to major cities like Matam, St-Louis and Dakar, to pursue their education. Also, the migration of patients in search of good quality health care was, and still remains, very common. The concentration of well-equipped hospitals in Dakar attracted rural patients to the city for medical attention.

Over time, some of these categories of people started dwelling in urban areas. Traders, civil servants and teachers were the first urban settlers. The arrival of their families (wives and children) and their investment in urban housing turned some of the Haalpulaar into urbanites who spent more time in Dakar and who visited their rural homes mainly on occasions such as funerals, marriages or religious celebrations (Ferguson 1999; Manchuelle 1997). From the mid-1960s, their presence in large numbers in specific neighbourhoods in Dakar, and the creation of hometown associations, and family-, corporation- and ethnic-based social networks were clear indicators of the stabilization of Haalpulaar labour migrants and traders in Dakar (Diop 1965).

Central Africa and France also became attractive destinations for Haalpulaar migrants at the end of the 1960s. The so-called *diamentaires* went to the Democratic Republic of Congo (previously Zaire), Angola and Botswana, and worked as diamond diggers and dealers, while a large majority of the Haalpulaar went to Côte d'Ivoire, Gabon, Congo-Brazzaville, Cameroon and the Central African Republic where they worked as traders, retailers and shop-keepers. In the 1960s a few Haalpulaar went to France, following in the footsteps of their Soninke neighbours who had migrated in significant numbers even before independence. They were employed as *plongeurs* (dishwashers), janitors or factory workers in and around Ile de France. Haalpulaar emigration was reinforced in the 1970s by ecological challenges stemming from successive droughts in rural Senegal, which pushed a number of able-bodied men to leave their villages and go to urban centres in Africa, Europe and North America. The 1970s and early 1980s were a period that saw the highest number of Haalpulaar arrivals in France.

The last phase corresponded with economic crises in urban centres in Africa. The prospects of finding lucrative jobs in African cities became slim in the 1980s and 1990s, forcing Haalpulaar labour migrants (like many other Africans) to find new destinations in Europe and North America. The family reunification laws enacted in France in the early 1980s gave Haalpulaar migrants an opportunity to bring their families across, and created the conditions for the emergence of Haalpulaar communities in the host country. This trend, however, was reversed in the beginning of the 1990s, when the progressive tightening of immigration policies in France made it difficult for a large number of candidates to get visas from the French embassy in Dakar. Despite this obstacle, many Haalpulaar managed to cross the European borders through Spain, Italy and Greece, paying large sums of money to human traffickers and taking enormous risks to cross the Mediterranean. It was North America that emerged as a popular destination for Haalpulaar labour migrants and traders in the 1990s. Most of them went on business visas, and then decided to overstay and look for refugee status as Mauritanians.

The arrival of large numbers of Haalpulaar migrants in Europe and North America and their relative success as compared to living and working conditions back home, prompted young Haalpulaar men in an Africa devastated by poverty, unemployment and a volatile economic situation, to migrate in search of a better future. In the perception of Haalpulaar youth and their families, migration became the only hope of, and secure path to, social success. This progressive change in the perception of migration was reinforced by remittances and the behaviour of returnees who, through their lavish consumption styles, fancy attire, generous gifts and growing social status, embodied the local standard of social success.

So, in less than a half-century of labour migration, the Haalpulaar of the Senegal River Valley moved from viewing migration as a means of support to the local economy to considering it as a central element of household revenues. It is difficult today to find a household in the villages of the Senegal River Valley that does not have at least one member living and working outside, and remitting a significant proportion of his earnings to family members back in the village. It is also clear that the more members a household has as migrants living outside the country, the better it does in term of living standards as compared to households with only one migrant.

After this brief outline of the history of Haalpulaar migration, I shall now focus on its latest phase by looking specifically at the ways in which Haalpulaar labour migrants negotiate their socio-cultural and professional insertion in America. While the Haalpulaar labour migrants in France have remained mainly workers since their arrival there, in America they veer between trade and factory or combine the two depending on local economic circumstances. The rest of the essay will therefore offer an analysis of the experiences of Haalpulaar migrants in three American cities: New York, Cincinnati and Memphis.

Arrival of Haalpulaar Migrants in the United States

Haalpulaar migrants came in large numbers to the United States from the mid-1980s to the end of the 1990s. It is possible to distinguish three important phases in their migration to the US. The first was the arrival of pioneers, most of whom were traders in other parts of Africa, especially Central Africa. They established themselves at specific places in the US, where subsequent migrants were welcomed and helped to find their way. The second phase commenced from the mid-90s and coincided with the arrival of large numbers of young migrants, mostly inexperienced, including students who had stopped their studies and become migrants. If the pioneers came to America on their own, the wave of young Haalpulaar migrants who came in the mid-90s received a lot of help from family members already established in Europe and in the United States. The great majority of this group got their American visas from Burkina Faso through a network of paper traffickers with connections to Burkinabe people working at the American embassy. The third wave was characterized by women coming to join their husbands, including French girls of Haapulaar origin married to first-generation Haalpulaar migrants in America.

The First Haalpulaar Migrant in New York City: A Profile

Siley, 47, a taxi driver in New York, regarded in the community as one of the first migrants in America from Thilogne, is respected in the community as most of the later migrants are indebted to him. Siley in fact claims that he is one of the first three Haalpulaar in New York. The other two are his close friends, one from Golaya and the other from Thilogne. Siley arrived in New York in 1985 from Libreville, where he owned two retail shops. He left the shops in the care of his cousin and nephew. When he got his business visa, he intended to return to Gabon after exploring some business opportunities in America. After meeting with some African businessmen in Broadway and getting to know New York a little better, however, he decided to stay and set up trade. He ran a stand in the African open market in Harlem, where all African traders had their stands.

I met Siley in his two-bedroom apartment in Brooklyn in 2004. Friends who knew about my research had referred him to me as one who could tell me the whole history of the Haalpulaar community in New York. Though I hailed from the same village as he, I did not know him very well. I had heard about him during my frequent visits to Thilogne. Entering his apartment, I found two young Haalpulaar boys watching a Nigerian film. Siley asked one of them to make some tea. We sat in his bedroom, I on a chair, he on the bed. He was wearing a blue Nike jogging suit. After discussing the reasons for my visit, Siley smiled and said to me, 'you better let that story rest!' Then one of the young boys entered with two tea. After drinking my tea, I asked Siley to tell me about his early days in New York. 'Where should I start?' he asked. 'Why did you come to New York? And is it true that you are the first to come here from Thilogne?' Siley then narrated in detail.

> You know, we young Haalpulaar are travellers. I left Thilogne when I was 18 years old. Since 1976, I have been travelling to different destinations: Dakar, Ouagadougou, Abidjan, Yaounde and Libreville. I was in Gabon before coming here to New York. I came here with a business visa and I was intending to go back but I realized that business was really good here and the currency was very strong. When I came here the dollar was very strong. When you sent a little bit of money it became a fortune in Senegal. It was also very easy to get money in New York selling in the streets. I used to set up my stand right in front of my building. So, as I said, what took me to Gabon was to make money and now I realized I can make more money here. I decided to stay and I sold my shops in Libreville.

'Was life in New York difficult for you as a newcomer? How did you manage to survive?' I asked.

Siley took a deep breath and continued:

> It was a little difficult to find a place because the rent was rather high for one person. However I arrived here with a lot of money and I was also making a lot of money. It was very cold and that was the hard part for me. My first winter was brutal. When you sell in the street, at some point you can hardly feel your feet. The fact that my place was just at the entrance of my apartment was very helpful. From time to time I would ask a neighbour to look after my place while

I went inside to gain from the heat. Apart from the cold, the first years were very lonely. There were very few Haalpulaar migrants. I did make some good friends among Fulani from Guinea who speak Pulaar like me and who had a large community in Brooklyn. I regularly ate in their restaurants along Fulton Street.

The pioneer Haalpulaar migrants had both the financial resources and the experience of migration to easily adapt to New York. They were crucial in creating conditions that enabled and eased the arrival of larger numbers of young Haalpulaar who could count on their support to find their way in the city. In fact, soon after Siley decided to stay, he talked to different friends in Central Africa who came to join him. He vacated his room in the small hotel in Harlem and together they moved to Brooklyn in 1988. At the end of 1988 he went back home and was able to build a house in Dakar in less than a year. His return was triumphal and raised a lot of interest about America as a new destination among the young Haalpulaar in the Senegal River Valley. He had brought back a lot of electronics. True to his *ceddo* identity, he took the opportunity to make his name known in *griot* and *nyeenyo* circles by giving generous donations to those who came to greet him.[2] He also organized at his house in Thilogne several *kirde*, during which *griots* sang glory of him and his ancestors. In Thilogne everybody was talking about Siley's success. He created, through what was perceived as a very successful return, the myth of America as the best destination for Haalpulaar migrants.

After four months in Senegal, Siley returned to New York City with a long list of young people from his extended family, whom he intended to help bring to the United States. Haalpulaar migrants in other African cities, hearing about Siley's success, also started exploring the possibilities of migrating to the United States. Starting in 1989, Siley and his friends received more than twenty people from Central Africa and Senegal. Among the young Haalpulaar who arrived in 1989, seven were from Thilogne, Siley's home town, four from Central Africa and three from Dakar with his sponsorship (these three were related to him). At that time all arriving Haalpulaar migrants had a single address in Brooklyn where they were housed and helped to start earning money in the streets of New York City.

Siley can tell who came after whom among the Haalpulaar migrants in New York between 1985 and 1990, when there were only a small number of people from his village. He welcomed them all to his two-bedroom apartment which became a sort of village house, like the Cheikh Ahmadou Bamba houses across Europe and North America that welcome Mourides newcomers (Carter 2002; Babou 2001). He said to me that at one stage the apartment looked like a

---

[2] The term *ceddo* has diverse meanings, ranging from 'warrior' or 'courtier' to 'drinker of alcohol' and 'non-Muslim'; it is, however, usually used in opposition to Islam. *Griots* traditionally refer to West African story-tellers who are considered a repository of oral tradition. *Nyeenyos* refers to Haalpulaaren men who belong to the social rank of *nyeenybe*, which includes craftsmen, musicians and praise singers.

small training camp and that they named it after a war zone in Chad. As a pioneering migrant, Siley played a pivotal role in making the lives of those who followed him easier. He acknowledges now that the living conditions then were quite difficult, but it was better than living on the street. At least the newcomers were not left to fend for themselves. They had a place to stay and often some start-up money or inventory to earn a living and contribute to the community fund to pay for rent and food.

Gradually, the network of migrants from Thilogne came to be organized at the neighbourhood level: newcomers were taken care of by pioneers coming from the same neighbourhood in the village of origin. In some cases neighbourhood intersected with kinship ties. Samba, who arrived after Siley, took all migrants from his neighbourhood of Golera and some family members from Halaybe and Molle that belong to the Torobbe group, while Sam took migrants from Molle and Jawanbe who for the most part hailed from the extended Jawanbe family. Siley continued to receive young migrants from Diabe Sala, Dioufnabe and Badel neighbourhoods which are inhabited mainly by the Sebbe families. These three pioneers were the pillars of village community solidarity in New York. They extended help to people from other neighbourhoods and from different social groups as well.

Samba is my neighbour from Thilogne. He hosted me in his two-bed-room apartment in Fulton Street for two weeks. He shares the apartment with five other migrants from the same home town. They regularly receive Thilognese guests on their way home from Ohio, Colorado, Michigan, Kentucky and Tennessee, or the other way around. The living room would be filled with mattresses for the guests coming from or returning to Senegal to sleep. The evenings were very lively. One of the occupants of the apartment would cook dinner while the rest sat in the living room, some watching TV, some making phone calls home. After dinner, they discussed news from home over tea, their travel experiences, their businesses, their preferred basketball teams, their fears, their hopes and their dreams.

On one of those evenings I asked Samba to retrace for me his journey to America. He enthusiastically talked about the 'long and tortuous route' that brought him from Thilogne to New York. Samba, forty-two years old, had started out as a *bethiek* man in Dakar at the end of 1980. He sold beauty products in the popular neighbourhoods of Pikine for five years. In 1986 he went to Ouagadougou where his uncle, who sold sun glasses and watches, managed to find him a place in the central market. He also gave Samba his first inventory as a loan. Samba saved the profits from his business and paid back the total value of the inventory to his uncle over a period of one-and-a-half years. In 1988 he decided to continue his adventure to Central Africa. He travelled by car and crossed about five countries before arriving at his final destination in Libreville, Gabon, after four months. There, he set up a shop with financial help from his brother who was in France. Like many Haalpulaar shopkeepers, he was very successful. In 1992, however, he decided to go to New York after getting good feedback from a friend who had left Libreville and started street-vending in New York. His reason for leaving Libreville was the insecurity that plagued Haalpulaar migrants in the city, where they were often targeted and injured or killed by criminals. Between 1992 and 2002 Samba settled down in Brooklyn, where he became a street vendor selling shoes, baseball caps, gloves, scarves and sun glasses just outside his apartment building on Fulton Street. He used the small bazaar as a cover for his more lucrative business of selling counterfeit products, and pirated copies of film and music CDs. After the Brooklyn open market on Fulton Street was dismantled, Samba rented a small space on Fulton Street from where he sold cell phone accessories.

Samba's story reflects, in many ways, the typical journey of many Haalpulaar pioneers in New York. They came with a great deal of travel experience, as a result of crisscrossing Africa. Their patterns of settlement and adaptation in American cities owed a lot to their previous experiences in African cities. Most of the Haalpulaar pioneers in New York were a part of this group of experienced travellers who learnt and honed the skills of trading. After finding their feet in the US, they provided money and information to family members, neighbours and friends back home who wished to join them. A majority of the newcomers received help from pioneers like Samba in one form or another. It was thus chain migration that led to the rapid rise in the numbers of Haalpulaar migrants in the mid-1990s.

For instance, forty-year-old Ka, one of the pioneers, helped more than ten people come to New York. He explains why:

> The first person I helped was my cousin who dropped out of school and could not find a job in Senegal. I was the only one who could help him. Since I was helped by my uncle in Ouagadougou on my way to Central Africa, I felt responsible for his sons. By helping my cousin I only started paying back the help I got from his parents. I arrived in Ouagadougou in 1982. I was welcomed in my uncle's house. I did not have to pay rent, I ate for free and my uncle gave me my starting-up money. He found a place for me in the central market where I sold watches and glasses. I stayed there for two years before continuing to Central Africa. I learnt a lot from my uncle who had a great deal of experience in trade. He is the one who taught me how to sell, how to manage my money and how to keep good relations with valuable customers. So helping his son was the least I could do for my uncle.

In 1994, Ka sent $2000 to his cousin, who used the money to secure a US visa. He also sent him the plane ticket and took care of him until he got a job in New York. His cousin stayed with him till 1995, when he decided to move out and rent an apartment with other Haalpulaar friends. In 1995, Ka helped a nephew, a brother and a friend to come to New York following the same procedures. All pioneers from Thilogne practised chain migration. Ndiaye, one of the first immigrants to New York from Thilogne, claims to have helped more than thirty people in one way or another to come to America. Pioneers like Ndiaye are seen by people in their home villages as models of success for the youth. They are admired by neighbours and friends, and their families are very proud of them. By helping young Haalpulaar find their way to America, the pioneers increased their social capital and therefore enhanced their social status among villagers.

In many cases, young migrants who received help from the pioneers paid them back. Only neighbours and friends are expected to repay debts, not close family members. Even after paying back the money spent to help the young villagers migrate, however, they remain indebted towards the pioneers, in a way, since the Haalpulaar think you cannot completely pay back someone who helped you to enter Europe or the United States. The pioneers use this moral debt to exercise control over the newcomers.

As is evident from the life stories presented above, all the pioneers were traders. It is only in the second wave of migration to America that one finds migrants taking up jobs as unskilled workers. Contrary to the pioneers who came with a great deal of experience in travel and trade, Haalpulaar who arrived in New York in the mid-90s were mostly students who had dropped out of school, and second-generation Haalpulaar boys from Dakar whose first sojourn from home was to go to Burkina Faso to apply for an American visa. There were also some migrants from other parts of Africa and Europe who decided to make the US their destination after hearing the success stories of Haalpulaar pioneers in America. Many of these later migrants started street-vending in Canal Street, Battery Park and Fifth Avenue before moving towards paid jobs and services.

The Second Wave of Haalpulaar Migrants to America

When I visited America for the first time in 1999, I was surprised by the large presence of people from Thilogne in New York and Cincinnati. As is customary, my cousins in Cincinnati organized a dinner for me. To my surprise, over forty people from Thilogne showed up. The following Friday, I met with other people from Thilogne who had not made it to the dinner. The next day I met yet more Thilognese people in a Senegal grocery/restaurant complex in Cincinnati. I also visited Mulberry Square where hundreds of Haalpulaar from around the Senegal River Valley villages live in a single building with a mosque and a classroom, where people pray on a daily basis and study Pulaar and English during the weekends. It is clear that chain migration has resulted, in less than two decades, in the establishment of Haalpulaar communities in American cities.

The second wave of Haalpulaar immigrants to America helps us understand the reorientation of Haapulaar migration from West and Central Africa and Europe to North America. The increased migration of students with high school and university degrees, as well as of urban youth, most of whom are early school dropouts, is a result of the implementation of World Bank-led structural adjustment programmes in Senegal. Subsequent to these programmes, it has become increasingly difficult to find a job in the Senegalese administration since

the state is required by international financial institutions to retrench civil servants to solve the problem of a bureaucrat-heavy public sector. At the same time,
the increasing number of people entering the informal sector saturated it: everybody is a street vendor of some sort, selling something, anything, and working
tirelessly, as is evident around the Sandaga, Harbor, Tilene and Colobane markets, and the Independence Square in Dakar.

The second wave of Haalpulaar migrants arrived in the US in the mid-
1990s. As mentioned earlier, many Haalpulaar youth arrived in New York through
chain migration with the help of pioneers like Siley and Samba. The existence of
very well-established networks of visa traffickers in Burkina Faso (and also the
Senegal River Valley) who exploited, for years, the loopholes in the American
visa application process, facilitated the arrival of the second wave. Migrants in
New York who wanted to bring a member of their family or a friend sent money
directly to one of the traffickers in Burkina Faso, who then helped to arrange for
the papers required by the American embassy for a business visa, including,
when required, formal papers of a business registered under the name of the
applicant, receipts of previous transactions, statements of bank accounts, etc.
Hundreds of young Haalpulaar received their US visas between 1993 and 2000.
Siley and Samba collaborated with Sada and Momo, the visa traffickers in Burkina
Faso, to bring to America as many people from their village as they could. Those
who got help from them were asked to pay them back when they made it to New
York and started to earn money, so that other people in Senegal could be helped
to come to the US. The visa traffickers charged 4,00,000 F CFA (about $1000) in
the early 1990s. By the middle of 1990s the cost had jumped to 1,200,000 F CFA
(about $3000). The traffickers accepted payment in instalments from visa appli-
cants backed by a financial guarantor established in America. Despite the high
costs, and with the help of these agreements between pioneers and visa traffickers, over a hundred people from Thilogne entered America between 1992 and
1999.

The group of young Haapulaar that came during these years was very
diverse in its composition. It is, however, possible to place them in three categories: high school and university graduates, urban Haalpulaar youth, and
Haalpulaar migrants from Africa and Europe changing their destination. The
first category, also the most significant, consisted of students and second-generation Haalpulaar migrants from Dakar and other African cities. Between 1995
and 2001, more than twelve students from the village of Thilogne alone arrived
in the United States, not to pursue their studies, but to earn a living for themselves and their families back in Senegal. Some of them had a Bachelor's or Master's degree. Although all Haalpulaar migrants in the US faced the language
barrier, this category was able to improve its language competency significantly
after a year or so of stay. Consequently, they could find jobs that were relatively
well-paid, as compared to the kind of jobs available to the pioneers. But many
also experienced a downward mobility in labour market opportunities. For in-

stance, Haalpulaar migrants with a Master's degree from their home country were no match for those with degrees from American universities. They did not get jobs in their domain of expertise and often had to take up jobs like taxi-driving or janitorial work.

Another significant category of the second wave of Haalpulaar migrants is that of the young urbanite born and brought up in African cities like Dakar and Ouagadougou. Most of these young Haalpulaar dropped out of school before they could get their high school certificates. The reason that these students chose to migrate rather than pursue their studies was because of the general feeling among the Senegalese youth that migration to Europe and North America pays better than studying in Senegal, where there is no clear path to a promising future.

These two categories of the second wave of migrants had neither any migration experience within Africa nor any trading experience. Consequently, they relied heavily on the pioneers to find their feet in the United States.

Students

Students and 'boy-Dakars' – as the second generation of Haalpulaar migrants from Dakar are called – have a very different lifestyle from that of the pioneers and the Haalpulaar migrants coming from the Senegal River Valley villages. In the mid-1990s, students and boy-Dakars relied on the pioneers to find their way to and in America. They accepted the pioneers' lifestyle and living conditions, but only till such time as they were able to strike out on their own. Now, they are very critical of what they call 'Modou's lifestyle'.

Sow, a law student, who was a doctoral student in France before moving to the United States, described the 'Modou's lifestyle' as unhealthy and very degrading.

> I do not get it. Why are the Modou so eager to accumulate money to a point that affects their health? They do not try to get decent housing and they do not spend money on healthy food. If you care about having decent housing and eating good food, people start criticizing you as someone who does not know what brought you here. I think they are wrong. My position is that I want to live a good life with the money I earn. I do send some money back home to support my parents but I will never compromise my well-being in order to save and send more money home. The Modou who are accepting terrible living conditions to accumulate will not profit from their saving because they are certainly damaging their health by so doing.

Most of the Haalpulaar students who migrated to America in the 1990s came from the University of Dakar. Although some had a Bachelor's or Master's degree, the majority had only a high school diploma (*bacalaureat*). A large number of students came from the Senegal River Valley and were first-generation migrants in Dakar. As mentioned earlier, unlike the pioneers, they had neither work experience nor travel experience outside Senegal. As a result, when they started working on the streets of New York City as street vendors, many of them found that they were not good at selling.

Ibra, 27, arrived in New York in 1996. He was a Natural Science student at the University of Cheikh Anta Diop in Dakar. After two years of failing to pass the first year examination, he dropped out and started exploring ways to pursue his studies outside Senegal. He wrote to several French universities but never got a positive response. In 1995, he decided to go to Ouagadougou to try and get an American visa. After a few months he secured a visa and came to the United States. Ibra recalls his mindset back then: 'When I got the visa, I was so happy and I thought that my suffering was over. Since I arrived here, I have changed my mind. Life is not as rosy here as I used to think back then.'

Ibra, like many of the other students, had little patience and wanted to make a lot of money quickly. However, when they discovered that the pioneers were making money by taking enormous legal risks, they started looking for alternatives. Although only a few of them came with good language skills, the students had an enormous advantage over the pioneers because they had learned English at school in Senegal. Ibra, like most of the others, started looking for paid jobs. His first job was at an Indian bazaar, and it paid very little. He helped his boss put merchandise on the shelves. A number of Haalpulaar students were also employed by Clean Services, a company based in New York, which provided services to local companies from floor, carpet and window-cleaning to janitorial work.

Omar was among those first employed by Clean Services as a window cleaner. He remembers getting a two-week training before going out with his team to clean windows in Lower Manhattan. He told me that 'the work was paying well compared to my poor street-vending. It was also physically very demanding. When I come back from work, I just want to lie down and sleep. I need to find a way to go back to my studies.'

Thus, in contrast to the pioneers who were mostly traders, the second wave of migrants opted for paid jobs. Students as well as boy-Dakars are in a better position to get these jobs because they often require a certain level of communication skills in English. In some cases, the students are able to rapidly rise to higher positions because of their language skills. For example, Baba, who studied Economics and Management in Dakar, became a senior supervisor at Schwans Food, where he then recruited many Haalpulaar workers.

I met Baba for the first time in 1993 at the University of Dakar in my cousin's room. He was a second-year student at the Faculté des Sciences Economiques et Gestion. In 1995 he graduated with a Bachelor's degree. Like many Senegalese students in the 1990s, Baba was disillusioned about the prospects of finding a job after university studies. He was contemplating the idea of continuing his studies outside the country. When he heard, in 1996, that it was easy to get a US visa in Ouagadougou, he convinced his mother to give him the money to go to Burkina Faso and get the visa. In less than six months he had secured a visa and came back to Senegal to bid goodbye to his family and friends, before going to New York City.

Baba is a second-generation Haalpulaar migrant in Dakar. He was born and raised in the Senegalese capital city and knew little about his parents' home town. He had two uncles, his mother's brothers, already in New York prior to his arrival. Both contributed towards Baba's visa fees and ticket. When he arrived he lived with one of his uncles for the first year before finding an apartment with other friends. He soon improved his English and got a job at a shoe store, where he worked for four years before moving to Cincinnati. With his English skills and work experience, he found a job at the Schwans Food factory in Florence, Kentucky. After a year, he was promoted to the position of team leader. He helped to recruit many Haalpulaar migrants into the company.

He also helped the community in a number of other ways: filling their tax returns, translating their letters, filling in their forms, accompanying them to hospital, etc. He soon became well known among the small Haalpulaar communities in Cincinnati and Florence. After six years in the United States without a legal status, Baba got married to a cousin who is a second-generation Haalpulaar migrant in France. Their marriage took place in Les Mureaux, a suburb of Paris, without the physical presence of the groom. Baba's wife visited him twice in Cincinnati for limited periods of one to two months. After the birth of their daughter, Baba decided to leave the United States for France, where he could easily get legal status.

Baba's case is not isolated. There are over fifteen Haalpulaar migrants from Thilogne alone who abandoned their university studies to come to the United States. Common to them is a certain sense of having wasted their time in studies that did not serve them at the end of the day. They recognize, however, that their schooling equipped them with English language skills that serve as an advantage in adapting to the American way of life. Most of them can read English and start to speak fluently after a couple of years in the US. Consequently, they act as intermediaries between Haalpulaar migrants and American institutions and services, thereby assuming leadership roles in the community.

Another category that one finds among the Haalpulaar migrants in the United States is second-generation migrants coming from Haalpulaar communities outside the Senegal River Valley. While the large majority comes from Dakar, some young men also come from other African countries and Europe.

Boy-Dakars

In the parlance of Haalpulaar migrants, boy-Dakar means a young man who was born or grew up in Dakar, the Senegalese capital. Most boy-Dakars among the Haalpulaar migrants left school before getting their high school diploma. What characterizes boy-Dakars is their urban style, their use of the Wolof language rather than Pulaar, and a heavy accent when they speak their mother-tongue. Like the students, they too have received help from the pioneers in settling down in the US. While they rapidly integrate into American society,

Haalpulaar migrants from rural areas carry stereotypical notions about them, including a lack of perseverance and the love of an easy-going life. They are often criticized because of their expensive lifestyles, viewed by the elders among the Haalpulaar migrants as a waste of money that can serve to improve life back home.

Sow, twenty-eight, is a good example of a boy-Dakar. He was born and brought up in Dakar. His knowledge of Pulaar is basic, but he speaks Wolof as if it were his mothertongue. He dropped out of middle school, and for years waited for his uncle in France to finance his trip to Europe or America. So when the opportunity of getting a visa opened up, he asked his mother to put pressure on his uncle so that he would agree to send the money charged by the visa traffickers. His uncle agreed eventually and Sow received his visa in 1998. Unlike many Haalpulaar migrants wo stayed for a long time in New York, Sow spent only two nights in the city before continuing to Cincinnati, Ohio. Soon after was taken in as a worker by Schwans Food in Florence, Kentucky.

In Cincinnati, Sow and Omar are viewed as typical boy-Dakars who spend their entire pay cheque on branded shoes and clothes such as Nike, Adidas, 501 Jeans, Gap, etc. They also spend a lot of money on entertainment, like going to night clubs every Saturday night, buying music and films and sophisticated electronic goods such as fancy cellular phones, DVD and CD players, and loudspeakers. Migrants from rural Senegalese homes whose goal has never been to follow the frenzied consumption styles of the host country, but to try to accumulate money for a triumphal return home, feel that the boy-Dakars do not know what brought them to America.

Like the students, boy-Dakars are also indebted towards the pioneers who financed their visa and plane tickets, and took care of them when they first arrived in America. The pioneers are often exasperated by their costly lifestyle. They sermonize to them about how they need to conduct their lives in America in order to take care of their families in Senegal. Due to their lack of experience in trading, they too, like Sow, become workers in food processing factories in Columbus and Cincinnati, Ohio and in Florence, Kentucky. We also find a large number of Haalpulaar migrants from these two categories (students and boy-Dakars) in Memphis, Tennessee, working in the casinos on the Mississippi river.

Changing Destinations

Among people who arrived in New York in 1990 as part of the second wave, there are also those who were already migrants elsewhere and decided to change their destination. There has been, for instance, a significant flow of Haalpulaar migrants from Europe to the United States; migrants were repatriated because of new restrictions in European immigration policies and those who were living a clandestine life in Europe decided to change course to America. This category of the second wave of migrants has much in common with the pioneers in terms of extensive experience in travel and migration. Many like Rouna, whose story is discussed below, have had a very complex itinerary, visiting and working as a trader and a worker in several countries in Africa and Europe before landing in America.

Rouna's Itinerary

In the summer of 2004, I met Rouna in Memphis, Tennessee. I had known him since we were children. Seeing him after more than ten years brought back a lot of memories. We belonged to the same age-group and came from Golera, one of the larger neighbourhoods in Thilogne. He is my cousin from my mother's side: his mother and mine are half-sisters. Age-group plays a major role in a boy's initiation to manhood in the Haalpulaar society. After families, age-group constituted the most important social space in which we learnt, through practices and initiations, the different roles and tasks expected of us. Our age-group consisted of fifteen members. We went to collect firewood together using donkeys; were often asked by our parents to help one of us whose father was unable to cultivate his fields because of illness; helped build houses and tents in the neighbourhood; shared our meals during religious holidays; and often camped together in one house where we would drink tea and hot milk with bread until the early morning hours.

So, I knew Rouna very well before I met him in Memphis in the summer of 2004. He invited me to his place, a two-bedroom apartment that he shared with four other young Haalpulaar from our home town. The living room was divided into two parts. Right at the entrance was a small place for praying, with two prayer rugs oriented towards the Kaba. Past it were two old sofas surrounding a small television placed on a medium-sized table, under which there were video and DVD cassettes and players. Rouna was wearing Nike jogging pants with a white T-shirt. 'You see where we live!' he said. He continued commenting about their experience as young men living away from their families. 'You see I am cooking, that's because my wife and my mother are far from here. People back home cannot imagine the kind of life we live here.' While Rouna cooked rice and meat, I asked him where he had learnt cooking, to which he replied that he became a really good cook during his stay in France and Belgium. After lunch I asked him to tell me more about his migration experience, which he did enthusiastically. 'You can write a whole book about my experience', he said to me. He repeatedly insisted that migration was a man's job. It proved, according to him, that you are a 'real man', someone who can face adversity and difficult conditions in foreign places without giving up.

Rouna is forty years old. He is married and has left his wife with her mother in Thilogne. He visits once in two years or so, often spending four to six months with his family on each visit. Rouna's itinerary had taken him to various places: Dakar, Ouagadougou, France, Belgium, New York and now Memphis. He left Thilogne for the first time in 1984 at the age of sixteen, to go to Dakar. Rouna never went to school but had attended Quranic school since he was four years old as did many young Toroodo boys of his age. By the time he left Thilogne he had already memorized the Qur'an. Luckily, he had an uncle in Dakar who served in the special police (Gendarmerie) and who welcomed him into his house in Yarakh. Most young men of his age who arrived in Dakar for the first time and did not have relatives to host them, went to live in accommodation rented by young Haalpulaar from their village or neighbouring villages. These places are called *suudu* and are very important in helping newcomers from rural areas to find their way in the city through group solidarity.

For four consecutive years Rouna was engaged in seasonal migration between Thilogne and Dakar. He always left his village after harvesting the fields in the highlands where the Haalpulaar grow millet during the rainy season. In early October he helped his father and his younger brother prepare the Walo fields inundated by the Senegal River. From November to end-June, he worked in Dakar as a national lottery ticket vendor. Every week he got bundles of lottery tickets from his uncle's shop in Sandaga, a market in the heart of Dakar. He arranged the tickets on a long wooden plank and travelled the streets of Dakar plateau in search of customers. He always carried a small bag in which he kept the remaining tickets, his money and the paper sheet containing the winning numbers of the last lottery draws.

At the end of each week he returned to his uncle's place in Sandaga to pay him back his money and take another lot of lottery tickets. He gave part of his profits to his uncle who played the role of banker, since Rouna did not have a bank account. Before returning to Thilogne he would use some of his savings to buy clothes and shoes for himself and presents for his family. He also made sure he had enough cash to distribute to younger age-groups of his neighbourhood, as was common practice among returnees. Boys and girls younger than the returnee would greet him, welcome him back, and ask for their 'cola nuts'. The returnee gave between 250 and 500 CFA to each age-group as their 'cola nuts'. The returnee invited members of his own age-group to share a meal that was usually prepared the morning after his arrival. His female age-group (*fedde rewre*) received generous 'cola nuts', from him usually worth thousands. Each time Rouna went from Dakar to Thilogne, he honoured these socially legitimate expectations.

In 1989, Rouna decided to go to Burkina Faso, where he had an older brother and an uncle. With the savings he had accumulated during the four years of seasonal migration to Dakar, he was able to pay for the train ticket from Dakar to Bamako, the bus ride to Bobo Dioulasso and from there to Ouagadougou. He stayed in Ouagadougou for two years. His brother had a stall in the central market where he sold sunglasses, watches, stereo radios, calculators, wallets, etc. He introduced Rouna to his customers. Four months later, his brother left for Central Africa and Rouna took over the stall. After two years, he got a Swiss visa along with other young Thilognese. They went to Senegal to say goodbye to their families and get the blessings of their parents before commencing on this new leg of their migration experience. From Switzerland they crossed by foot to France. Rouna worked there with Renault for four years before joining his brother (who had travelled from Central Africa to Brussels on a Belgian visa) in Belgium.

Rouna did not have any proper documentation during his stay in Europe, which led to his repatriation from Belgium in 1998 after a police ID control check, in Brussels. He applied for asylum in France and Belgium, but was denied in both countries. Aware of the legal precariousness of his situation, Rouna had saved most of his income during the eight years he spent in Europe. These savings, which were sent to a Senegalese bank account by the intermediary of a cousin living in Dakar, made his repatriation from Belgium less painful because he did not come back to Senegal empty-handed. With the money he had saved, he got married. He was able to use his brother's passport which had expired with one entry on the American visa in it, to apply and obtain an American visa in Ouagadougou (his brother had migrated from Brussels to the US after getting an American visa in Ouagadougou). Rouna arrived in New York in 1998. He spent four months there before joining his brother in Memphis, Tennessee.

Reflecting on his trajectory, Rouna shook his head and said: 'It is really an adventure. I never imagined I would end up here in Memphis.' He went on to comment that when you are a man you have to confront the adversities and hardships of life. This subjective perception of migration as a learning experience for men is held not only by Haalpulaar migrants, but also by the larger African migrant community, as attested to by Janet McGaffey and Remy Bazzenguissa-Ganga (2000) in the case of Congolese migrants in Paris. Migration as an 'adventure' is therefore comparable to an initiation process whereby young boys learn how to become men. Migration is also perceived as a form of '*jihad*' or holy war against poverty and underdevelopment (ibid.).

Samba and Rouna's trajectories, although very common among the Haalpulaar in the United States, do not reflect the shorter itineraries of most newcomers who were students or second-generation Haalpulaar from Africa and Europe. The arrival of an increasing number of Haalpulaar migrants led eventually to the exploration of new destinations within the United States.

Building a Community in Brooklyn

Fulton Street in Brooklyn, New York, has become a Haalpulaar place in less than two decades of Haalpulaar migration. In fact, it has been renamed Futa Street by the Haalpulaar migrants, Futa being the name given to regions predominantly inhabited by the Haalpulaar (Futa Djalon in Guinea Conakry, Futa Macina in Mali, Futa Toro in Senegal and Mauritania, for instance). The groceries, the hair-braiding salons and the restaurants on Fulton Street are owned by Haalpulaar from Senegal, Guinea Conakry, Mali and Mauritania, and have been renamed. Thus there is Futa Grocery Store, Futa Fashion and Halware Hair Braiding Salon. The groceries and restaurants serve primarily ethnic customers. Along the street there are hundreds of apartments rented by Haalpulaar migrants. Prior to 2003, Haalpulaar traders used to set up their stands on the street just in front of their apartment. In 2003, however, the city council issued a ban against occupying the pavement for trading purposes. Now Haalpulaar traders are dispersed across three trading points in New York City: Battery Park, Fifth

Avenue and Canal Street, which is where traders from various African countries put up their stands. But there are still a few Haalpulaar traders who have rented a small commercial space along Fulton Street and some others who have transformed the entrance of their apartment into small shops. Despite the ban, Fulton continues to be an ethnic locality where the Haalpulaar feel at home.

The transformation of Fulton to a home for Haalpulaar migrants took time and tremendous efforts by the pioneers of Haalpulaar migration in America. The first Haalpulaar settlers occupied a two-bedroom apartment and received newcomers to whom they provided shelter, food and inventory to start up trade. Samba recalls:

> Life in New York was very hard in the early 1990s. There were only few Haalpulaar in Brooklyn and we were all living in the same place. 1146 Fulton Street became the home for Haalpulaar migrants and businessmen in transit. Before leaving Senegal or Central Africa Haalpulaar migrants were given the address. It was a place where all Haalpulaar were welcomed even if they didn't have a member of their family or someone from their village among the pioneers who were paying the rent, the utility bills and the food for the newcomers. When I first arrived I stayed for free in this community apartment. I did not have to pay for anything for the first three months. Life was not easy or comfortable in this apartment. It was crowded and there was a lot of tension between people. We had to queue up for everything: taking a shower, eating, going to the bathroom, etc. Sleeping was very difficult because of continuous movement of people going to work or coming back. The mattresses were not enough for the crowd and most of them were in very bad shape.

But life would have been harder, Samba explains to me, without this community arrangement to help newcomers. New York is a big city, and it is difficult to find one's way without any help. This was particularly true for people who could not at that time speak any English. Pioneers like Samba, for the most part, were people who had not been to a western school, although some of them were literate in Arabic by virtue of having attended Quranic schools in their home town.

The migrants followed various itineraries: from their home (in the Senegal River Valley) to Dakar, the capital city of Senegal, and from Dakar to Central Africa. Some travelled to Mali and Burkina Faso, others to Côte d'Ivoire, Togo, Benin, Niger, Ghana and Nigeria. The majority, however, ended up in Gabon, Cameroon, Central African Republic, Congo-Brazzaville, the Democratic Republic of Congo (formerly known as Zaire) and Angola. Routes to Central Africa, as the Haalpulaar migrants describe them, are very frustrating, tiring and difficult. Travelling along these routes is seen therefore as a proof of courage, masculinity and commitment to the idea of social success as it is defined in their home communities. For the youth, travel to Central Africa is a rite of passage, like circumcision or marriage.

The most important occupation of Haalpulaar migrants in New York City until the mid-1990s was petty trade and street-vending. Those who did not find their way into trade were employed in cleaning services and sanitary work. There were some exceptions of highly educated individuals who got well-paid jobs as vendors in big stores. Trading and street-vending are activities that Haalpulaar migrants learnt and honed during their migration itinerary. In the streets of Dakar, one encounters young Haalpulaar migrants selling newspapers, lottery tickets, toys, cola nuts; in Ouagadougou they sell sunglasses and watches; and in Central Africa they control the retail trade in major cities like Libreville, Bangui, Pointe Noire, etc.

All the pioneering Haalpulaar migrants in the US spent many years in different African cities as street vendors and shopkeepers. The most successful were in import businesses, or in mining and trading in diamonds (Bredeloup 2007). They travelled between African capital cities and Asia or Europe. In all major African cities, like Ouagadougou, Libreville, Yaoundé, Brazzaville and Pointe Noire, where an important Haalpulaar community had settled down, ethnic social networks were developed to help newcomers. Diop, in his study of Haalpulaar migrants in Dakar in the 1960s, explains how young Haalpulaar men who did not have families in the city organized themselves in *suudu* or room networks to help each other and other newcomers who had no where to go. Ten to fifteen young men would rent one or two rooms and each would cook in turn. At the end of each month, they would all contribute towards paying for rent and food. Newcomers were integrated and started paying monthly contributions after getting work. Usually people from the same village got together in a *suudu*. But in cases where some small villages were not well-represented, people were integrated into a *suudu* which housed members of a neighbouring village. The *suudu* was an important resource for newcomers not only because they were welcomed, lodged and fed for free, but also because they were helped to find a job, navigate the city and adapt to urban life.

Today, wherever they go, the Haalpulaar reproduce solidarity networks along similar lines. While the names of the systems may vary – *suudu* in Dakar, the *barme* or cooking pot in France – the principles and practices are quite simi-lar. The type of ethnic solidarity found in New York was therefore the reproduc-tion of solidarity mechanisms applied elsewhere in similar circumstances (Manchuelle 1997; Kane 2000).

Moving to Cincinnati
In the middle of the 1990s, Haalpulaar migrants who had arrived in great numbers in New York tried, like other West African migrants, to discover other American states. The traders were the first to move around the sountry, following African-American festivals. Columbus, Ohio, in particular, attracted itinerant traders, some of whom decided to use Columbus as the base for their trade because of its strategic positioning between the north, the south and the midwest. They were later joined by Haalpulaar workers who left New York for two main reasons: its reputation of denying asylum to Haalpulaar Mauritanians; and the harsh competition created by the large numbers of Haalpulaar and other

West African traders in New York. To this day, Columbus, Ohio hosts one of the largest Haalpulaar communities. Later, with the transfer of Haalpulaar employees by Clean Services to Cincinnati, many of the early settlers in Columbus decided to move there.

By 1995, street-vending became saturated with the arrival of hundreds of new Haalpulaar. At the same time, local businesses in New York felt threaded by this crowd of street vendors occupying the sidewalks and the fronts of shops all day long. The city council of New York took drastic measures to dismantle the African market in Harlmen in mid-1990 (Stoller 2002). As a result, some Haalpulaar traders went back to Brooklyn where they started a new market along Fulton Street where most of them had their apartments. But the arrival of a large number of migrants combined with the restrictions on street-vending put in place by the city forced many to go to what they called the 'bush' or *ladde* in Pulaar. The process of switching from trade to wage workers or the other way around is very common among Haalpulaar migrants. Getting a paid job, however, requires getting one's papers in order. Although many of the Haalpulaar were from Mauritania and were offered asylum on the basis of the violence due to ethno-racial conflict between Senegal and Mauritania in 1989, there were also a significant number of Haalpulaar from Senegal who did not get asylum and who were therefore asked to leave the country. Most of them who received a judge's letter asking them to leave the country understood it to mean that they were being asked to leave New York. So a majority went to Columbus and Cincinnati in Ohio, while others moved to Pennsylvania where there is a large Haalpulaar community in Philadelphia.

The first Haalpulaar workers in Cincinnati came to the city because they were brought by their employers in New York, who recruited cheap labour in New York for the central, midwestern and southern states which do not have a large Latino population, unlike the southern and western states sharing a border with Mexico. One of the main employers of Haalpulaar labour migrants, Clean Services, profited from this very cheap labour force, and started sending them to Ohio, Kentucky and Tennessee where many food processing factories were in desperate need of labour. The migrants continued to be employed by Clean Services, but worked in other factories which signed contracts with Clean Services. Clean Services therefore operated as a job placement agency, sending its own employees to work for other companies. They appointed team leaders and supervisors among the Haalpulaar migrants who were responsible for the employees, and to whom the bi-weekly pay cheques for the employees were sent.

The first groups of Haalpulaar arrived in Cincinnati and Memphis in early 1995. Demba, who was one of the first to move to Cincinnati, explains how they ended up in this city.

> I was in New York where it was difficult to find a job if you don't speak any English. There are some people who are lucky to have a salaried job with the city council as sanitation agents and others working for Clean Services. But these

people were in New York at the right moment. The only option left for newcomers like me was selling like everybody in the streets. But people like me are not gifted in selling. I used to sit a whole day without selling anything. I started to be impatient in New York. When I heard that Clean Services was recruiting people to send to Ohio I did not hesitate one moment. I grabbed the opportunity and went with a group of 30 people. Clean Services paid for our hotel rooms for the first two weeks. It was not for free of course. They drew the costs from our pay cheques. After the first two weeks we were able to find four cheap apartments on Montgomery Road. The group split into six groups each occupying one two-bedroom apartment. We all worked for Club Chef which is a vegetable processing factory. Life was cheaper in Cincinnati compared to New York City. We talked to family members and friends whom we had left in New York about our positive experience. Those who did not have anything to do in New York decided to join us. Now [2004], there are more than a thousand Haalpulaar migrants in Cincinnati.

Club Chef, a vegetable processing and packaging firm, employed a large number of the first arrivals in the city. Most of the workers in Club Chef lived in Mulberry Square. The employer provided school buses for the transportation of employees from Mulberry to the factory. The salaries, at $350 a week, were very low. The job was physically very demanding and the workplace very cold for these migrants from hot and dry countries. They accepted both the low pay and the difficult working conditions because most of them are illegal immigrants who have no official/legal papers. People who have a legal status, traders or taxi drivers, rent out their papers to those who do not have a legal status. In many cases the arrangement made is to let the owner of the papers claim tax refunds since the illegal immigrant uses his social security number.

The arrangement between Clean Services and Club Chef lasted just two years. After the termination of the contract, Haalpulaar migrants started to look for jobs with other factories in the border area between Ohio and Kentucky. Many were able to find better paying jobs with Schwans Food. Between 1997 and 2004, the number of Haalpulaar employees (both men and women) in Schwans Food increased exponentially due to the promotion of two young Haalpulaar to the positions of team leader and supervisor. The working conditions, however, were and continue to be quite harsh: the workers are provided little protection against the sub-zero temperature in the chain production room (where they make frozen pizza).

Mulberry Square in Cincinnati has become a small Futa where Haalpulaar migrants have reproduced their cultural and religious practices. More than two hundred apartments in the Mulberry building are occupied exclusively by Haalpulaar migrants. All community activities are held in the building: association meetings, classes in Pulaar and English, religious ceremonies, etc. Living together in a closed environment makes it easier for the community to have social control over its members. Everybody keeps a check on everyone else.

Individual members who deviate from community norms have accusing fingers pointed at them. Mulberry is a good example of what Stoller (2002) calls a vertical village.

Building a Community in Memphis, Tennessee

Memphis, Tennessee has become home to one of the largest Haalpulaar communities in southern United States. The Haalpulaar who first arrived in Memphis were brought by Clean Sevices, the same company that brought Haalpulaar migrants to Cincinnati. Amadou recalls that in 1996 there were less than twenty Haalpulaar in the city. He was the supervisor of the group and had the responsibility of making sure that the employees did their jobs properly. They were all employed as cleaners in casinos along the Mississippi: some were in charge of cleaning the floors, others collected trash. Amadou's work was to make sure the place was tidy both inside and outside. He also handled the bi-weekly cheques of the employees. The casino managers would speak to him if they were unhappy with the work of the Haalpulaar employees. He reported to the head office of Clean Services in New York.

Clean Services continued to control Haalpulaar migrants until 2000, when the casinos refused to renew the contract and decided to directly hire cleaners. Most of the Haalpulaar were able to easily land jobs. In fact Amadou and some of the more educated young Haalpulaar were able to find better paid jobs as cashiers, table supervisors or security agents. The high demand for cheap labour has made the two-jobs option attractive to Haalpulaar migrants. A large majority of them work sixteen hours a day, often in two different casinos. It was the two-job regime that caused many Haalpulaar workers to leave New York and Ohio and come to Memphis. Because of this regime, however, often days go by before migrants living in the same apartment see each other in waking hours. Alioune told me how he sometimes leaves voice-messages on the telephone to communicate with his roommates.

> I don't have another option. When I come from work they are already sleeping and before they wake up, I am already sleeping. We can spend weeks like this if some of us decide to work on Wednesday, which is often the common rest-day for many of us working in the casinos.

The two-job regime combined with the reputation of Tennessee judges being more amenable to accepting asylum cases, led to the rapid growth of the Haalpulaar communities in Memphis. Most of them lived in adjacent apartment complexes along Winchester Road, not far from Memphis airport. They soon started to address the needs of the community such as finding a place to pray and establishing social networks. They rented a two-bedroom apartment in Coventry to serve as a mosque and guest room for visiting Muslim clerics.

In 2004, they bought a warehouse which they transformed into a great mosque where they prayed on Fridays. In 2008, they inaugurated another mosque. They also created a 'corpse repatriation and burial' society that organizes the sending of the corpse of any member who dies in Memphis. In 2004, some of the Haalpulaar migrants created informal (and illegal) transport services to cater to the large number of Haalpulaar workers living around Winchester Road and working in Mississippi. There are several of these red vans connecting Coventry to the casinos. Elimane, one of the drivers, makes make two round trips in the morning, two in the afternoon and two in the evening. It is a lucrative job for him and he has many reliable customers who pay him in advance.

A number of ethnic businesses have opened up with the arrival of women from Africa, to join their husbands. Restaurants, hair-braiding salons, grocery stores and money-transfer agencies have been set up to serve the community and its African American neighbours. Community events such as cultural days, religious celebrations and family ceremonies have become commonplace in Memphis. As Imam Deme stated during the inauguration of the Haalpulaar great mosque, 'now we can say that the Haalpular have arrived at the destination. Before getting a place of worship, we were still strangers. Now, with the construction of the mosque, we have become settlers.'

Conclusion

The Haalpulaar correspond to a large degree to what Manchuelle (1997) called 'willing migrants', who are in a state of continuous motion from place to place to find a living not just for themselves but primarily for the people they have left behind in their villages in the Senegal River Valley. Wherever they go, the patterns of migration are very similar. Enduring several hardships, the pioneers prepare the ground for subsequent migration into the host country. They help newcomers find their way and also help in creating a sense of community among the migrants. Their success in the host country shapes the dreams of their family, friends and other members of their community in Senegal. Meanwhile, all resources and networks are mobilized to help the young Haalpulaar to achieve their dreams.

The path of socio-economic insertion of Haalpulaar migrants varies enormously on the basis of who constitutes the migrant group: pioneers, students or boy-Dakars. The pioneers are traders and self-employed. They are not interested in low-paid jobs because they make a lot of money, even though their livelihood is based on businesses that operate at the margins of the law, to paraphrase McGaffey and Bazinguissa-Ganga. The students come with the advantage of knowing a little bit of English, which they improve upon very rapidly in order to compete for high-paying work in factories. The boy-Dakars and the rural folk are concentrated in unskilled, low-paid jobs.

What this essay demonstrates is the manner in which Haalpulaar labour migrants and traders rely on group solidarity to secure a visa, plane ticket, housing and food, and to find a job or start street-vending. Chain migration mechanisms are how the Haalpulaar extend their geography of migration. Until the mid-1980s it was not common for Haalpulaar labour migrants and traders to go America. Their popular destinations were Central Africa and France. The stories of Haalpulaar diamond dealers in Central Africa who made huge fortunes motivated a mostly uneducated Haalpulaar youth to migrate in the 1970s. After the decline of diamond trade, it was France that captured the imagination of young Haalpulaar migrants, since migrants returning home from France painted it as the ideal place to acquire riches and fame. In the recent past, however, America has replaced France as the popular destination for migrants. The pioneers of Haalpulaar migration to America, like Siley and Samba, brought with them new stories of success; consequently, young Haalpulaar have come to the conclusion that wealth is to be found in America. The successive waves of Haalpulaar migrants to America are a testimony of this change in perception.

The essay also demonstrates that the Haalpulaar have reproduced similar mechanisms of solidarity and community-building, whether in Dakar, Libreville, Gabon, Paris or New York, and it is these mechanisms that have sustained increased migration from the home country and between countries. This process of exploring new destinations, where some settle on a more or less permanent basis, has accelerated the wide dispersal of Haalpulaar migrants across the globe over the past two decades.

References

Babou, Chekh Anta (2002), 'Brotherhood Solidarity, Education and Migration: The role of the Dahira among the Murid community of New York', *African Affairs*, vol. 101, no. 403, pp. 151–70.

Bredeloup, S. (2007), *La Diams'pora du fleuve Sénégal: Sociologie des migrations Africaines*, IRD Editions, Presse Universitaire du Mirail, Toulouse.

Carter, Donal (1997), *States of Grace: Senegalese in Italy and the new European immigration*, University of Minnesota Press, Minneapolis.

Diop, Abdoulaye B. (1965), *Société Toucouleur et Migration*, IFAN, Dakar.

Diop, Momar Coumba, ed. (2008), *Le Senegal des migrations: Mobilité, identité et societes*, Karthala, Paris.

Ferguson, James (1999), *Expectations of Modernity: Myths and meaning of urban life on the Zambian copperbelt*, University of California Press, Berkeley.

Geschiere, P. and B. Meyer, eds. (1999), *Globalization and Identity: Dialectics of flow and closure*, Blackwell, Oxford.

Kane, Abdoulaye (2000), 'Diasporas villageoise et développement local en Afrique: le cas de Thilogne Association Développement', *Hommes et Migrations*, no. 1229, pp. 96–107.

——— (2005), 'Les diasporas africaines et la mondialisation', *Horizons Maghrébins*, no. 53, pp. 54–61.

Levitt, Peggy (2000), *The Transnational Villagers*, University of California Press, Berkeley.

Manchuelle, Fraçois (1997), *Willing Migrants: Soninke labour diasporas, 1848–1960*, Ohio University Press, Ohio.

McGaffey, J. and R. Bazenguissa-Ganga (2000), *Congo–Paris: Transnational traders on the margins of the law*, Indiana University Press, Bloomington.

McLaughlin, Fiona (1995), 'Haalpulaar Identity as a Response to Wolofization', *African Languages and Cultures*, vol. 8, no. 2, pp. 153–68.

Quiminal, Cathérine (1986), *Gens d'ici, gens d'ailleurs*, Christian Bourgeois, Paris.

Stoller, Paul (2002), *Money Has No Smell: The Africanization of New York City*, University of Chicago Press, Chicago.

Timera, Mahamet (1996), *Les Soninké en France: d'une histoire à une autre*, Karthala, Paris.

Labour Conflict

The Uses of Militancy in Regeneration
Negotiating Deindustrialization

Heike Doering

This essay analyses the responses to deindustrialization in two British coalfields of Leicestershire and Kent. In particular, it is concerned with changing labour identities (both individual and collective) in the context of resource mobilization for socio-economic transformation. Deindustrialization has been accepted as a process with varying causes, consequences and time-scales. The same is true for the responses to the process variously described as restructuring, regeneration, or economic and community development. The question of place and local embeddedness of economic, social and cultural responses – 'actually occurring regeneration' (Henderson *et al.* 2007) – however, has rarely been the focus of attention. This essay therefore draws attention to the locally specific trajectories of those involved in restructuring, from miner to local politician, union leader to community representative, in the new social topography of places in transition. These paths are characterized by both national regeneration regimes and local traditions of trade union militancy. Such traditions and their integration in the local social organization influence the way in which cultural and social resources are mobilized in the pursuit of economic resources in the course of restructuring.

This essay engages with Przeworski's ideas on the material basis of consent to examine the impact of traditions of labour militancy in the era of deindustrialization. For the two cases discussed here, this means that the 'embeddedness' of the mining industry in the local economic structure is manifest in the social and political consequences of its decline. Despite similarities in the economic importance of mining in terms of employment for Kent and Leicestershire, the integration of the collieries in the local economy varied considerably. The industry in Leicestershire, though extremely important, was but one element in an urbanized industrial setting. In contrast to this, mining communities were isolated industrial occurrences in Kent, an area dominated by agriculture and services.

The essay will discuss the specific patterns of embeddedness of the mining industry in these two cases, and the resulting patterns of trade union organization and potential for mobilization in the event of mining decline. This means outlining the results of the intersection of particular historical, economic, political and social conditions. The distinctiveness of the mining communities in both

Kent and North West Leicestershire needs to be seen in relation to their location within their region as well as within the British coal mining industry. It is, therefore, necessary to locate these places in the context of what has long been seen as the homogeneous occupational culture of coal mining. Within this narrative, mining communities have been described as unique and homogeneous, both in their heyday (Bulmer 1975) and their decline (Coalfields Task Force [CTF] 1998).[1] Unpacking these assumed similarities requires a short historical outline of developments in the industry in each area, the local political, economic and social structure, as well as an overview of developments since the closure of the collieries.

Theoretical and Methodological Background

The arguments in this essay are based on extensive archival research,[2] semi-structured interviews and a period of observation in the Kent coalfield to examine the process of coalfield regeneration. Data have been investigated and interpreted within a theoretical framework inspired by Burawoy (1985) and Przeworski (1985) concerning the manufacturing of consent of the working class to the maintenance of capitalist structures of accumulation. Both are influenced by Gramsci's writings on the achievement of hegemony. Przeworski's main argument is that workers have powerful reasons for supporting capitalism since it can satisfy their material needs in the form of future wages. The 'satisfaction of these material needs constitutes the basis for class compromise in advanced capitalism' (King and Wickham-Jones 1990: 395). Workers are likely to further capital's interests to secure their own future well-being. They thus consent to the 'perpetuation of profit as an institution' (Przeworski 1985: 180).

While this argument is directed towards understanding the dynamics of wage negotiations, the present essay investigates it in relation to the dynamics of negotiating deindustrialization and regeneration. Przeworski claims that 'capitalists are thus in a unique position in a capitalist system: they represent future universal interests while interests of all other groups appear as particularistic and hence inimical to future developments' (ibid.: 139). This creates constraints for all social groups, as the pursuit of their material interests is linked to the interests of capital and thus the profitability of investment (Przeworski and Wallerstein 1988). The question, then, is how can (ex-)workers' interests be included and actualized in the responses to deindustrialization, and how do traditions of collective organization affect these interests? The forms such organization can take should not be limited to trade union representation. Rather, the case studies presented here aim to show the importance of the interaction of collective representation of workers' interests outside the state as much as inside the state. This is where democracy and therefore the state enter the picture. Democracy is seen

---

[1] The homogeneity argument has been extensively discussed and questioned. See, for instance, Benson (1989), Gilbert (1995) and Ackers (1996).

[2] Research was carried out in the County Record Offices of Kent and Leicestershire, and the Modern Records departments of Leicestershire County Council, North West Leicestershire District Council and Dover District Council.

as a system which organizes conflicts between different groups in a way that 'outcomes are related to the particular combinations of strategies pursued by different groups' (Przeworski 1985: 141). The system thus makes some strategies to win concessions or benefits more likely to be successful for a particular group than others – based on the distribution of economic, ideological and organizational resources.

Militancy is a specific strategy of the mobilization of resources which can, in certain circumstances, achieve optimal outcomes. Przeworski argues, however, that there is an optimal level of militancy. Capitalism will always generate gains from the working class, so concessions can only be achieved in a way that capitalism can still gain these profits. The notion of the optimal level of militancy is used here to argue that traditions of collective action have an influence on the relationship between different social actors beyond the production process in the course of deindustrialization and the different responses formulated and implemented to address its consequences. Such a discussion is interesting in the context of the coal industry, as both during the phase of production and the phase of decline and regeneration, the negotiation of the relationship was characterized by the prominent role of the state. As a nationalized industry, negotiations between the union and the National Coal Board inevitably meant negotiating with the state, or rather, manoeuvring state policies concerning energy, industry and the economy in general. Following widespread pit closures, any regeneration activity was also primarily state-driven. So, once again, those who were affected by the closure of the industry saw themselves reacting to or demanding state activity. In both periods, however, the interests of capital were at stake, as was the creation of conditions for the accumulation of capital. In this context, it makes sense to investigate the processes of mobilization and the development of different local traditions of collective organization – from trade union militancy to its successors in local state institutions as well as community groups – and their involvement in regeneration.

The Case Studies

Mining has been part of the economic structure in North West Leicestershire for centuries. The coalfield here is located to the northwest of the city of Leicester, with Coalville and Ashby-de-la-Zouch as the urban settlements. At the beginning of the Victorian period, the Leicestershire coalfield was one of the older British coalfields producing substantial amounts of coal (Griffin 1981). Migration into the coalfield occurred in two phases: in the Victorian period during the main expansion of the coalfield; and in the early period of major nationwide closure of collieries in the late 1950s and early 1960s. Even though Coalville's growth was based on coal, the increasing importance of the textile and hosiery industries in the wider area resulted in a more heterogeneous industrial, and thus social and political, structure by the early twentieth century. Leicestershire's was a highly profitable coalfield and on the eve of nationalization it was described as 'the district with the highest output per man shift, lowest costs, highest wages and the highest profits in preceding years' (Nationalization Valuation Board in Tookey 2001: 498). Throughout the 1950s, output per man-shift remained the highest in North West Leicestershire in national comparison, as did the amount of profit per tonne. Until the National Power Loading Agreement in 1966, the North West Leicestershire miners were among the highest wage earners in the industry (Park 1999).

Even if it was one of the marginal coalfields in Britain – its six collieries[3] producing around 3 m tonnes of the 108 m tonnes produced nationally in 1981/82 – in terms of employment the coal industry was central for North and West Leicestershire. In 1981, 26.5 per cent of male employment was in the energy and water sector, most of which was situated in the local collieries. In some communities around Coalville, the proportion of men working in the mines was as high as 40 per cent (BSHF 1990). The only sector employing more people in North West Leicestershire was manufacturing (34 per cent). Representative of the county as a whole, the service industry was under-represented in the district and the number of women working was the lowest in Leicestershire (58 per cent economic activity rate).[4]

The Kent coalfield covers an area of 190 square miles which includes coal seams under the sea, with Ramsgate as a boundary in the north and Sturry near Canterbury as a boundary in the west. Its development was first considered in the late nineteenth century with the earliest borings in the 1890s almost a byproduct of early attempts to build a tunnel across the Channel. Only from 1912 did coal mining become commercially viable in the area.[5] The Kent contribution to national coal output did not exceed 1 per cent till the time nationalization was brought about (Supple 1987). Recruitment was one of the major issues in the establishment of the coalfield. The Kent collieries found it difficult to employ local green labour unacquainted with the mines, and imported labour either from established coalfields around the country or from their own older collieries (Pitt 1979). As part of the development process, the collieries also provided accommodation. Consequently, the Kent coalfield is characterized by settlements which were constructed with the sole purpose of serving a colliery, adjacent to but socially separate from affluent farming villages and hamlets, and isolated in a predominantly rural area.

In contrast to North West Leicestershire, in 1981, mining was an isolated occurrence in terms of industrial employment in East Kent. Further, in comparison to the UK as a whole or to North West Leicestershire, mining and manufacturing were under-represented in Dover district. Despite the presence of a

[3] Bagworth, Desford, Ellistown, Snibston, South Leicester, Whitwick.
[4] This refers to the economic activity rate of women between the ages of sixteen and sixty-five based on the Census 1981 data.
[5] Snowdown Colliery was sunk in 1907 by Arthur Burr; it was closed in the early 1920s but reopened by Pearson & Dorman Long Ltd. in 1924. Betteshanger was sunk in the early 1920s by Pearson & Dorman Long. Tilmanstone was operated by Tilmanstone (Kent) Collieries Ltd. and Chislet by Chislet Colliery Ltd.

small number of major manufacturing companies, the dominant industries in East Kent were the ferries and the ports in Dover. The service and transport sectors employed more than half of the working-age population. Figures for the district, however, belie considerable differences within the area. So although for Dover as a whole, male employment in the energy and water sector only stood at 12 per cent for communities such as Aylesham, Elvington and the Mill Hill ward in Deal,[6] the mining industry provided jobs for up to 45 per cent of the male working-age population. Employment in the urban wards was dominated by services, in contrast to the importance of manufacturing in the rural coalfield wards. Similarly, district figures show that employment for women was concentrated in sectors associated with the seaside economy, i.e. transport, distribution and services (tourism). In the rural coalfield wards, however, a considerable proportion (up to 46 per cent in both Aylesham and Eythorne wards) of women worked in manufacturing.

In the coalfields of both Leicestershire and Kent, the political effect of the mining industry can be seen in the traditional preference for the Labour Party. Residents in both areas were faced with the fact that the coalfield wards with a pro-Labour tendency are situated in counties with a preference for the Conservative party. In Kent, this is exacerbated in that although the rural coalfield wards are Labour-dominated, the wider district has always been controlled by Conservatives. In the history of the local council, Labour only controlled the district for a four-year period (1995–99), preceded by a Liberal Democrat–Labour alliance. Similarly, Kent County Council is Conservative-led, with only one term without Conservative control (1993–97) in its 120-year-history. The one term without Conservative control fortuitously coincided with the Labour control of Dover district. Especially since the introduction of the cabinet system in Dover District Council in 2001, which distributes portfolios among the ruling party, coalfield interests have been marginalized in representational terms. In the case of Leicestershire, North West Leicestershire District Council has been traditionally Labour-controlled. The County Council was not ruled by a clear majority for most of the period of interest here. Miners and their union representatives often made their way into the local authority council. This made for a strong representation of miners' interests not only through their collective organization, but also through local state institutions, in a period when the local authority had control over issues of local economic development. This configuration of relations between different actors is of importance for the impact it can have on strategies for extracting concessions.

In summary, the different development trajectories of the two coalfield areas have had a profound effect on the social organization therein.[7] Mining as

---

[6] These were linked to the Snowdown, Tilmanstone and Betteshanger collieries, respectively.

[7] See Beynon and Austrin (1994), Beynon *et al.* (1994), Gilbert (1992), Waller (1983), Barron (2006), for similar accounts in the coalfields or mono-industrial settlements of the North East, South Wales and Nottinghamshire.

an industry grew gradually over the centuries in Leicestershire with the major phase of expansion occurring in the nineteenth century. The industry developed alongside other industries, facilitating the development and growth of a local working class, and a tradition of unionization and collective organization. It also, however, ensured that the experience of miners was not singular but embedded in local industrial culture. So that even though the pervasiveness of an industrial working-class culture facilitated the forging of a cohesive collective identity among miners, Park (1999: 188) argues that 'the geographical contiguity of Leicestershire mining communities such as Ellistown, Hugglescote and Whitwick with the largely non-mining town of Coalville' led to a 'dilution' of the *specific* cultural and class identities of miners.

In Kent, the ad hoc development of the collieries 'in the middle of a pre-industrial society [where] farming, fishing and the holiday trade were the economic mainstay of the area' meant not only the lack of an available work force, but also that the industrial worker was almost unknown, except as 'a day tripper on a seasonal spree in Margate' (Pitt 1979: 22). From the beginning of the operation of the coalfield, the policy of recruiting experienced miners from other coalfields created a gap between the existing population and the newcomers. The resulting 'communities' were relatively closed and isolated from the prior residents of the area. The occurrence of high unionization rates in the mining settlements was in direct contrast to unionization in the surrounding area, like in Thanet (Pickvance 1990), and as such the mining settlements were culturally distinct from the rest of the districts they were located in. This social isolation strengthened the experience of insularity in the communities and also their identification with their own clearly demarcated community (Pitt 1979).

The miners in Kent were not a homogeneous social and political body: they had migrated to the newly operating coalfield from other mining areas and brought with them different mining traditions which needed to be adapted to new working (geological) conditions. This resulted in parochialism if not fragmentation, and a strong commitment to 'place' as a pervasive element of the local culture and the local politics. Divisions occurred not only between the 'indigenous' residents of Kent and the miners, but also within the miners themselves (cf. Waller 1983). The idea of a 'coalfield' as a coherent economic, social and cultural space, then, is not applicable either to Kent or to Leicestershire. Thus there are different mining communities, but there is no community of miners.

Places of Militancy?

Miners have had the image and symbolic function of stormtroops of the proletariat in British history. The militancy record of individual coalfields, however, undermines such a blanket assumption. The Leicestershire coalfield lacked a long history of political activism (Tookey 2001). Rather, it was distinguished by the moderate approach of its unions, a good employment record and high wages. The union in this coalfield was characterized by recurring conflicts of opinion between the rank-and-file and the union officials, as well as by a wavering attitude towards industrial action. The militancy record of the coalfield is somewhat mixed: it was supportive of the national unions in some major strikes and lockouts, e.g., 1912, 1921, 1972 and 1974; but it also had high numbers of working miners during the 1926 lockout. In some cases, solidarity among miners was also facilitated by support from the management and colliery owners, who valued the tradition of good owner–worker relations more than they did a potential long-term conflict.

This mixed attitude towards strikes is related to the 'pecuniary nature of Leicester miners' who were willing to strike on matters of principle rather than a belief in working-class consciousness (Park 1999). This was especially the case in the strikes of the 1970s which were centred on wage demands, but despite low levels of support in area ballots (37 per cent and 61.6 per cent, respectively), no strike-breaking occurred (Griffin 1981). This display of militancy was a direct result of the introduction of the National Power Loading Agreement in 1966, which had had a negative effect on wages in the area even if it meant a single national wage structure for the industry (Park 1999).

The moderacy of the Leicestershire miners was based on good working conditions, high wages and cooperative management. All these ingredients were necessary to maintain a balance of interests and the continued functioning of the industry. In this sense, the Leicestershire miners can be seen to exemplify Przeworski's ideas about the necessity of concessions and compromise as a result of the optimal level of militancy. Nowhere was this more visible than in the 1984–85 strike. The predominant aim of the strike was the prevention of colliery closures. The announcement of local pit closures in North West Leicestershire in 1979, with the accompanying prospect of job security at a new super colliery, made for ambivalent conditions for the Leicestershire miners. The formal run-down of the coalfield based on streamlining had been agreed to between the management and the unions. Mr McSporran of the NUM Power Group explained that union cooperation had been made possible particularly due to 'the early retirement and early redundancy schemes' (North West Leicestershire Area of Mining Decline [NWLAMD] 11 June 1982). This programme was seen as protecting the miners' material interests (redundancy payments) as much as the management's interest in retaining a young and qualified work force (Park 1999). In Przeworski's view, miners' consent to closures while achieving guarantees of job security is rational. These agreements then formed an element in the area's lack of support for the strike, and strengthened ideas of a lack of connection between local and national union agendas. Subsequent successes in recruiting individuals into the new Union of Democratic Mineworkers (UDM) are therefore not surprising.

If the pursuit of high wages was the dominant element in the Leicestershire miners' militancy, this was not the case in Kent. Interestingly, the Kent miners together with the Leicestershire miners were among the highest paid in the coal industry (Ashworth 1986). This, however, resulted from a different set of circumstances. Whereas accounts of the Leicestershire coalfield mention the alienation of its miners from the national union organization, descriptions of the Kent coalfield similarly mention differences between local convictions and national agendas. During the 1950s, the Kent NUM saw campaigns concerning economic and foreign policies to progress towards socialism as their remit, as much as industrial action. The Kent collieries had a reputation of militancy based on the harsh working conditions encountered in the particularly deep and wet pits of the area, as well as stories about the work force being predominantly constituted of (descendants of) blacklisted miners in the 1920s. There does not, however, seem to be a unified (one) Kent coalfield but four Kent collieries rather, with their specific conditions of ownership, labour relations and social relations. Differences between the collieries in terms of militancy were already apparent in the early years of their operation. For instance, a sizeable majority of miners at Snowdown broke the strike of 1926, quite contrary to the militant image of Kent miners (Park 1999). Only in the 1970s was there a shift in the traditionally moderate collieries towards a more radical leadership. Subsequently, Kent miners supported strikes ferociously. There was, however, a small back-to-work movement – most disappointingly for some union representatives – at Betteshanger, led by Peter McGibbon. A number of men had been dismissed during the strike and in contravention of the national executive decision to end the strike on 5 March 1985 and return to work, Kent miners actually continued their strike for another week, picketing and thus exacerbating conflicts which had surfaced during the year. The experience of these twelve months of victimization, defeat as well as the community effort still resonate in the mining communities in Kent, and have become an important part of their collective identity, forming the basis of any understanding of state intervention in the area.

The Tilmanstone and Snowdown closures in 1986 and 1987 were unopposed by the miners, possibly because of the offered redundancy packages (and in all likelihood, the threat of their withdrawal should the work force insist on review procedures). At Betteshanger, there was stronger miners' opposition amid suggestions of worker or management buy-out plans, which did not come to fruition. These closure narratives still provide ground for divisions between the collieries. Research participants, especially former miners, continued to talk about the colliery closures in the context of betrayal and attack, placing the closures in the same interpretative frame as state responses during the strike. Consequently, policy makers or representatives of public agencies often remarked on antagonistic attitudes towards agencies of the state, and the lack of cooperation and trust, to the extent that one interviewee said he felt that the miners were fighting the strike of 1984 all over again (local politician, 30 May 2007).

In Leicestershire, then, moderate unionism was coupled with a similarly consensual local political situation under the hegemony of the Labour-controlled local council. The sense of being locally embedded for the Leicestershire miners, however, manifested itself in a distinct feeling of being outsiders in the national union and mining as marginal to the local collective industrial self. On the other hand, the experience of marginalization within their local economy and culture for the Kent miners was counteracted by their central position in the national union. The Kent miners were central to the union and thus the union was central to their local collective identity. Their militant unionism in a predominantly Conservative district and county created a tension that was absent in the Leicestershire coalfield. These were thus the starting points for coalfield regeneration, or rather, the struggles over the mobilization of economic, social and symbolic resources in the reorganization of socio-economic relations.

The Aftermath of Deindustrialization

Recent economic indicators for East Kent and North West Leicestershire present a positive view of the response of both areas to economic restructuring (DCLG 2007). Both areas show employment adjustment, in the sense that the employment rate is higher than the national average at 77 per cent for East Kent and 80 per cent for North West Leicestershire. Changes in the labour markets, in both cases, occurred along similar and, in particular, gendered lines. The general picture is one of employment in mining for men being replaced by other sectors (manufacturing, transport or distribution). At the same time, despite rising female economic activity rates, women's employment opportunities shifted from manufacturing to services. The changes in North West Leicestershire and East Kent are then, to a certain degree, exemplary of wider changes in the economy of the United Kingdom. In both cases, labour market adjustment did not result in a long-term increase in unemployment but showed an increase in economic activity. This has been reported for all coalfields (Fieldhouse and Hollywood 1999; Beatty and Fothergill 1996, 2005). In North West Leicestershire 25 per cent of the male population of the fifty-five to fifty-nine age group, amounting to about 2,000 men, withdrew from the labour market. Similarly, male economic activity fell in Dover district (13 per cent in the fifty-five to fifty-nine age group, and 17 per cent in the sixty to sixty-five age group). Early retirement had been one of the favoured options for the reduction of unemployment in North West Leicestershire by all actors concerned: the NCB, the unions and the local authorities. Evidence from the 2001 Census also suggests that this development was only temporary and can be linked to the colliery closures.

The socio-economic transformation of these areas occurred in the context of shifting relations of power between workers, residents, the central and local state, and capital. In Przeworski's (1985: 142) words, the 'prior probabilities [which had been attached] to the realization of interests of particular groups' had shifted. The Leicestershire mining unions had accepted the closure of the coalfield by 1982, and at the same time were eagerly awaiting the opening of the local super pit. There was no concerted industrial action; only negotiation of redundancy, early retirement and potential transfer terms. A reaction to the potential employment issues of such structural economic change, however, did come from the local authorities. Following the announcement of the closure of the coalfield in 1979, representatives of the Leicestershire County Council (LCC), North West Leicestershire District Council (NWLDC) and Hinckley and Bosworth

Borough Council (HBBC) formed a committee to deal with the problems poten-tially arising from the expected colliery closures by the end of the decade.[8] Pro-posals for action were drawn up, and comprised (in the order suggested) the attraction of manufacturing and service industries, the provision of industrial land, the improvement of the road network, encouraging labour mobility, the need for external assistance, and the reclamation of derelict land. Labour mobi-lity explicitly meant striving for occupational mobility through the acquisition of skills, rather than geographical mobility. Commuting was described as anything but a partial solution to the county's problems:

> It reduces and dissipates the 'community', particularly resulting in the loss of younger people and fails to help maintain a lifestyle built around local employ-ment; it relies on uncertain economic prospects elsewhere; . . . and it may even-tually result in increased out-migration from the area. *It is a solution resulting often from an inability or unwillingness to intervene in economic development.* (NWLDC, Planning and Development Committee, 23 April 1980; author's emphasis)

Here, a policy of local authority intervention rather than a reliance on market mechanisms was promoted. In its emphasis on preemptive measures, the approach of the LCC differed from the approach followed nationally even if the gist of the suggested policies, e.g., the promotion of the area and the provision of land for business, were fairly 'traditional' (Turner 1993). From 1982 onwards, the local authorities in North West Leicestershire had come to the conclusion that not all jobs lost through the colliery closures were likely to be replaced by jobs in the manufacturing sector. The growth of existing industries as well as the growth of service sector industries, especially tourism, was necessary and encouraged (NWLAMD, 20 January 1982). Further, by the late 1980s, British Coal had decided that the jobs at the new colliery would be offered to miners displaced by the closure of collieries in Nottinghamshire – a strategy to ensure the presence and dominance of the more 'cooperative' Union of Democratic Mineworkers. In addition to a number of small-scale projects aimed at creating tourist attractions and managed work spaces, the main attention in North West Leicestershire was geared towards providing industrial estates. The success of the reindustrialization strategy depended not only on the nature of the provided sites, but also on their accessibility. Thus, the decision to develop the road network around Coalville as well as the regional road network, i.e. the A42/M42 link between the East and the West Midlands, was instrumental in (re)locating Coalville and North West Leicestershire on the industrial map and central to the distribution industry, with warehouses springing up on industrial estates planned and developed during the 1980s and 1990s. It thus also gained in attractiveness as a base for professionals commuting to nearby cities.

---

[8] This was the North West Leicestershire Area of Mining Decline Joint Committee. Documents relating to the meetings of the Committee are abbreviated in the text as NWLAMD.

The early pre-closure development of a strategy which combined district (local) as well as regional (county) interests allowed for a coalition of interests which included local authority members across parties as well as local authority officers. This was built on a history of integrating miners' and industrial interests into local political agendas, enabling a 'flexible', 'business-like' approach which took advantage of funding opportunities on regional, national and European scales. According to local authority officers and members, the biggest success in the repositioning of North West Leicestershire was the designation of the area as 'National Forest'. This designation was instrumental in shaping the regeneration strategy in the area towards a 'ruralization' strategy with the creation of a working forest which would facilitate the transformation of North West Leicestershire from a place of production to one of consumption.

The early intervention of the local state and its continuing efforts to maintain this impetus have had a significant effect on the regeneration trajectory. At the same time, however, these efforts were secured by the rising number of economic development professionals rather than local politicians. So, even if the initial trigger came from the miners' representatives in the local state, the actual implementation saw them marginalized and without input, as economic development professionals moved their agenda more and more towards market concerns. The initial 'concessions' won through an effective representation in the state quickly dissipated to make way for the interests of capital.

In North West Leicestershire, economic development of the 'Area of Mining Decline' had been a central concern of the local authorities at a time when they were able and encouraged to act. Thus, site reclamation had preceded the advent of national initiatives such as the National Coalfields Programme and the Coalfields Task Force under the Labour government from 1997 onwards. The Kent sites, in contrast, were only included into English Partnership's National Coalfields Programme in 1999 after persistent lobbying from the Coalfields Communities Campaign. At the same time, the major economic development function for the region was delegated to the Regional Development Agency in 1999. Consequently, the Kent mining communities 'felt isolated and ignored in the national context' (ODPM 2003: Ev 74), and a 'legacy of mistrust and a tendency for the Kent communities to conclude that their views are often misrepresented by those administering the National Programme' developed.

Tilmanstone, Chislet and Betteshanger colliery sites have all been redeveloped into industrial estates. The site of Snowdown Colliery was privately owned and its lease remained with the Coal Authority until its transfer to the National Coalfields Programme in 1999. It has since remained derelict till April 2010. There was also a proposal for the expansion of Aylesham in the policy context of providing affordable housing in the southeast: the addition of at least 1,000 new homes was planned. The expansion of the village has been repeatedly suggested since the late 1980s, but has been similarly repeatedly put on hold due to the fluctuating housing market. The most successful and most welcomed projects in Aylesham comprised the development of new workshop facilities providing incubation space for start-up businesses, and the conversion of the former secondary school into Aylesham and Community Workshop Trust which offers training and conference facilities. This was conceived by a former miner and local councillor who took advantage of national funding and local council support during the phase of Labour control. Each of the sites, then, exemplifies a problem of regeneration in the area as well as general trends, such as companies relocating rather than being formed anew (cf. Turner 1993; Hudson 2000), economic success not necessarily meaning community involvement or interest (ODPM 2003; SQW 2007), and questions of material as much as symbolic ownership leading to conflict between different interest groups and thus determining the success of regeneration initiatives.

In the context of a national policy agenda which increasingly favoured collaborative governance arrangements in the delivery of regeneration services, the Regional Development Agency reacted to a prior lack of community consultation. Community liaison forums were established 2000 onwards. These have become the forum for (ex-) miners' representatives to negotiate the terms of the symbolic (rather than economic) regeneration of the area. This, however, has been beset by issues of traditional antagonisms, and, in the view of local politicians and activists, has come to resemble a continuation of old conflicts between labour, capital and the state. Reproducing existing interpretations of the specificity of miners and their interests, the local authority argued that 'the trustees of the miners' welfare who seek to gain control of the project are willing to let the project fail rather than yield control of their establishment' (ODPM 2003: Ev 128). This configuration of the local political field, with diminished influence of local institutions, has had a profound influence on the capacity of individuals and collectives to act (cf. Gissendanner 2004). Economic development struggles at the political level, therefore, are mainly fought through the planning system, which is the District Council's main (if not only) opportunity to intervene in the economic fortunes of the area. Given the lack of representation at a local state level, the interests of particular mining communities have been voiced through institutions and campaigns outside of the state, and as a continuation of the strong traditions of trade unions in the area.

Concluding Remarks

Discussions on mining communities have often emphasized a certain homogeneity that is purported to characterize a particular local social organization dominated by the colliery. A number of studies have undermined this emphasis with regard to questions of geology, productivity, the labour process, social and cultural conditions (e.g., Benson 1980; Greasley 1995; Fine 1990). One aspect which needs more attention, however, is the 'embeddedness' of the mining industry in the local economic structure. Economically speaking, then, although there are similarities in the importance of mining in male employment for Kent and Leicestershire in quantitative terms, the integration of the collieries in the local economy was quite different. In North West Leicestershire, mining, being one element in an overall 'industrial' setting, fostered social and political integration. As an isolated industrial occurrence in an agricultural area in Kent, the social circumstances of mining were characterized by social and political marginalization. The deep, 'doily-like' (Allen *et al.* 1998) penetration of mining industry, culture and politics on a limited geographical scale formed the basis of a particular kind of trade union militancy in the two counties. These 'hot spots' had the capacity to become black spots in a variety of ways in the regeneration process – for local marginality is not always reproduced on a national scale. The experience of marginalization within their local economy and culture for the Kent miners was counteracted by their central position within the national union. This was characterized by strong links to the national union and an awareness of (inter)national working-class consciousness. The militant unionism of the Kent miners in a predominantly Conservative district and county thus created a tension that was absent in the North West Leicestershire coalfield.

In Leicestershire, moderate unionism met a similarly consensual local political situation, under the hegemony of the Labour-controlled local council. The socially and spatially pervasive nature of mining facilitated the political prioritization of the coalfield issues locally. This dimension of marginalization in the local economic, political and social landscape was therefore an important element in the make-up of the regeneration experience. Local integration, however, also fuelled a sense of apartness from national union agendas and strengthened strategies of moderacy. Park (1999: 180) argues that 'Leicestershire's sense of a long history of apartness or otherness resulted in its miners feeling forgotten, or worse, deliberately ignored by their big brothers in areas such as Yorkshire and South Wales.'

The position and make-up of the local authorities in the case study areas are a consequence of different variables. It is not sufficient to take into account the spatial and economic embeddedness of a locality; the position of each locality in the wider (national) social space in relation to different social spheres needs to be considered as well. Differences in political strategies or the formation of political coalitions to tackle economic problems are not only the result of differences in local economic interests, but also a consequence of established or emerging processes of political mobilization and organization which are based on 'prevailing ideologies, party apparatuses and institutions' (Pickvance 1990: 184). This again highlights the necessity of looking at the intersection of the local and the extra-local scales in different social spheres, and in determining any locality's position in the social space and the 'system of representations' (Allen *et al.* 1998: 10). The traditions of labour involvement in local state institutions both hindered and facilitated access to resources in the regeneration process in the cases discussed here. Both areas show the effects of sub-optimal militancy in Przeworski's terms. In North West Leicestershire concessions to management and integration in the local state meant an acceptance of decline as much as a marginalization of miners' representatives in the ultimately 'marketized' process of regeneration. The result is a superficially economically successful region with rising house prices but underlying structural inequalities, an employment struc-ture which is polarized between low-wage, low unionized distribution and ser-vice work, and the arrival of an entrepreneurial middle class visible through an increase in commuting of residents to service industry-based jobs in the Midlands and an increase in self-employment. One of the stories that can be told about North West Leicestershire's regeneration is therefore of how the coalfield became the imagined countryside and thus (selectively) affluent. North West Leicestershire is then not only deindustrialized but reimagined into a classless arcadia.

In Kent, traditions of antagonism between (socially and geographically) marginalized miners and the institutions of the local, regional and national state provided an environment which similarly limited inclusion of their representa-tives in the decision-making stages of regeneration policies. Even recent attempts at consultation and communication were marred by nationally and regionally fixed priorities for the provision of a capital-friendly economic as well as social infrastructure. Being a marginal area in an 'economically dominant' region of the UK marginalized the Kent mining communities even further in relation to other disadvantaged areas in older industrial regions. The area did not exist as a coherent spatial, political, social or economic entity. Attempts at repositioning it therefore remained incoherent and were dogged by the economic performance of the rest of the region. Regeneration in the area has 'suffered from too many loosely connected initiatives' (ODPM 2003: Ev 175). Both trajectories are con-strained by the overarching national regeneration regimes which temporarily both allow for and demand (consenting) local participation, and they thus need to make a hegemonic project out of regeneration. Optimal militancy, then, must not only be fostered at the local level, but also at the national level of policy formation.

References

Ackers, P. (1996), 'Life after Death: Mining history without a coal industry', *Historical Studies in Industrial Relations*, vol. 1, pp. 159–70.

Allen, J., D. Massey, A. Cochrane, J. Charlesworth, G. Court, N. Henry and P. Sarre (1998), *Rethinking the Region*, Routledge, London/New York.

Ashworth, W. (1986), *The History of the British Coal Mining Industry, Volume 5: 1945–1982, The Nationalized Industry*, Clarendon Press, Oxford.

Barron, H. (2006), 'Meanings of Community in the Durham Coalfield during the 1926 Lock-out', unpublished Ph.D. thesis, Trinity College, Oxford.

Beatty, C. and S. Fothergill (1996), 'Labour Market Adjustment in Areas of Chronic Industrial Decline: The case of the UK coalfields', *Regional Studies*, vol. 30, no.7, pp. 637–50.

Beatty, C., S. Fothergill and R. Powell (2005), *Twenty Years On: Has the economy of the coalfields recovered?*, Centre for Regional Economic and Social Research, Sheffield.

Benson, J. ([1980] 1989), *British Coal Miners in the 19th Century: A social history*, Longman, London.

Beynon, H. and T. Austrin (1994), *Masters and Servants*, Rivers Oram, London.

Beynon, H., R. Hudson and D. Sadler (1994), *A Place called Teeside: A locality in a global economy*, Edinburgh University Press, Edinburgh.

Building and Social Housing Foundation (BSHF) (1990), *Regeneration of a Mining Town, Coalville into the 1990s: A future without coal?*, BSHF, Coalville.

Bulmer, M. (1975), 'Sociological Models of the Mining Community', *Sociological Review*, vol. 23, no. 1, pp. 61–92.

Burawoy, Michael (1985), *The Politics of Production: Factory Regimes under Capitalism and Socialism*, Verso, London.

Cloke, P. and M. Goodwin (1992), 'Conceptualizing Countryside Change: From post-Fordism to rural structured coherence', *Transactions of the Institute of British Geographers*, vol. 17, no. 3, pp. 321–36.

Coalfields Task Force (1998), *Making the Difference: A new start for England's coalfield communities*, Department for Environment, Transport and the Regions (DETR): London.

Department for Communities and Local Government (DCLG) (2007), *Regenerating the English Coalfields: Interim evaluation of the coalfield regeneration programmes*, DCLG, London.

Fieldhouse, E. and E. Hollywood (1999), 'Life after Mining: Hidden unemployment and changing patterns of economic activity amongst miners in England and Wales', *Work, Employment and Society*, vol. 13, no. 3, pp. 483–502.

Fine, B. (1990), *The Coal Question: Political economy and industrial change from the nineteenth century to the present day*, Routledge, London/New York.

Gilbert, D. (1992), *Class, Community and Collective Action: Social change in two British coalfields, 1850–1926*, Clarendon Press: Oxford.

—— (1995) 'Imagined Communities and Mining Communities', *Labour History Review*, 60 (2), pp. 47–55.

Gissendanner, S. (2004), 'Mayors, Governance Coalitions, and Strategic Capacity: Drawing lessons from Germany for theories of urban governance', *Urban Affairs Review*, vol. 40, no. 1, pp. 44–77.

Greasley, D. (1995), 'The Coal Industry: Images and realities on the road to nationalization', in R. Millward and J. Singleton, eds., *The Political Economy of Nationalization in Britain 1920–1950*, Cambridge University Press, Cambridge.

Griffin, C. (1981), *The Leicestershire and South Derbyshire Miners, Volume I: 1840–1914*, NUM Leicester Area, Coalville.

—— (1989), *The Leicestershire and South Derbyshire Miners, Volume III: 1945–1988*, NUM Leicester Area, Coalville.

Henderson, S., S. Bowlby and M. Raco (2007), 'Refashioning Local Government and Inner-City Regeneration: The Salford experience', *Urban Studies*, vol. 44, no. 8, pp. 1441–63.

Hudson, R. (2000), *Production, Places and Environment: Changing perspectives in economic geography*, Prentice Hall, Harlow.

King, D.S. and M. Wickham-Jones (1990), 'Social Democracy and Rational Workers', *British Journal of Political Science*, vol. 20, no. 3, pp. 387–413.

Massey, D. (1995), *Spatial Divisions of Labour: Social structures and the geography of production*, Macmillan, Basingstoke.

ODPM (2003), *Coalfield Communities: Written Evidence*, Stationery Office, London.

Park, A. (1999), 'A Comparative Study of Community and Militancy in Two Coalmining Settlements in Britain, Canterbury', unpublished Ph.D. thesis, University of Kent, Canterbury.

Pickvance, C. (1990), 'Council Economic Intervention and Political Conflict in a Declining Resort: The Isle of Thanet', in M. Harloe, C.G. Pickvance and J. Urry, eds., *Place, Policy and Politics: Do Localities Matter?*, Unwin Hyman, London.

Pitt, M. (1979), *The World on Our Backs: The Kent miners and the 1972 miners' strike*, Lawrence & Wishart, London.

Przeworski, A. (1985), *Capitalism and Social Democracy*, Cambridge University Press, Cambridge.

Przeworski, A. and M. Wallerstein (1988), 'Structural Dependence of the State on Capital', *The American Political Science Review*, vol. 82, no. 1, pp. 11–29.

SQW (2007), *Interim Evaluation of the East Kent Coalfield: Final Report to the South East of England Development Agency*, South East of England Development Agency, Chatham.

Supple, B. (1987), *The History of the British Coal Industry, Volume 4: 1913–1946, The Political Economy of Decline*, Clarendon Press, Oxford.

Tookey, M. (2001), 'Three's a Crowd?: Government, owners and workers during the nationalization of the British coalmining industry 1945–47', *Twentieth Century British History*, vol. 12, no. 4, pp. 486–510.

Turner, R. (1993), *Regenerating the Coalfields: Policy and politics in the 1980s and early 1990s*, Avebury, Aldershot.

Waller, R.J. (1983), *The Dukeries Transformed: The social and political development of a twentieth century coalfield*, Clarendon Press, Oxford.

Local Labour Relations
as a Starting Point for Global Perspectives
The Case of Erfurt's Trade Unions, *c.* 1890–1914

Jürgen Schmidt

In its 'classical' meaning the term 'labour relations' describes the relationship between employers and employees, and between management and work force, with their different interests and dependencies in regard to their position in the labour market. In the Marxist sense, it is the difference between capital and work. Labour relations are characterized by the aim to regulate working processes by cooperation, confrontation or conflict. The actors in this arena are employees/workers and their organizations, on the one side, and employers and their institutions, on the other. This Marxist understanding still provides a suitable, clear-cut definition and approach to study labour relations. (For an overview, see Blyton *et al.* 2008; Schubert and Klein 2006; Edwards 2003.)

However, it would fall short to characterize the participants in these labour relations by focussing solely on their interests on the workshop floor, in the company or in an economic branch. To fully understand the actors and their actions in labour relations, it is necessary to use a broader framework. First, labour relations have to be seen in the context of the situation from which they emerge. Historically, the state, the community, politics and culture have all influenced self-regulated mechanisms of labour relations. Second, labour relations at the workshop or factory level alone do not fully explain organizational developments among the working class, on the one hand, and property owners, on the other. A worker's life, especially that of a worker in an organized work force, can by no means be explained solely through his/her position in the market and the labour–wage transaction. Rather, a worker's life must be seen in the framework of human beings who require capabilities (Sen 1999) and citizens' rights (Montgomery 1993; Welskopp 2000).

The aim of this essay is to demonstrate the latter approach with regard to the working class and trade unions (excluding the development of entrepreneurs and their associations) through a case study in the Prussian town of Erfurt in the erstwhile German empire. Trade unions will be analysed using the category of social contacts and communication – that is, constellations and patterns that can (but not necessarily) act as mobilizing and action-guiding factors. This approach surmounts the Marxist-oriented analysis with its theoretical categories of class position, class consciousness and class formation. It acknowledges, how-

ever, that capitalist production and working processes are still the pivotal basics
for trade union actions, even as it does not limit its focus only to these elements
as levels of contact and communication.

This approach raises the following questions with regard to the area and
period under study. What limits and boundaries characterized the development
of trade unions on site? Why were some trade unions more successful than
others? How were possibilities of contact created or impeded in the world of
work? Which communication and contact structures facilitated the work of trade
unions and their organization? What role did strikes play? What additional func-
tions did trade unions perform besides the representation of the labour market
interests of their members? What were the inclusion and exclusion mechanisms
that became visible? In developing this perspective, the organizational history of
trade unions becomes embedded in political, cultural, social and historical contexts, and part of the history of work and work processes.

Starting the study from this local perspective by no means excludes a
global perspective. It simply does the opposite of what Marcel van der Linden
did in his book, *Workers of the World* (2008). He created categories, general
schemes and ideal types that were flexible enough to identify labour unions in
different historical and regional contexts. The approach presented here gives a
somewhat more richly detailed description of the local issues. Should there be
more such analyses, it would be possible to ask what factors are relevant in
different global contexts, and what are the similarities and differences between
them. As Andreas Eckert (2010) puts it: 'The global perspective has the potential
to assign a new significance to local and regional perspectives.'

We start by looking at who acted in what manner at the local level and
then go on to examine global perspectives – research locally and think globally,
to put it another way. This also helps to concretize imprecise, florid visions of a
global 'multitude' (Hardt and Negri 2000).

Work Places as Locations of Communication and Contact:
Limits and Opportunities for Trade Union Work in Erfurt

Structural breaks and transformations characterized the German society
and economy after 1870. Germany in this period was characterized by: an increasing engagement with the global economy; a process of urbanization which introduced new lifestyles in the society; the dominance of the secondary sector; and
the creation of new work processes in various industries as a result of rationaliza-
tion, modernization and mass production (Torp 2005; Conrad 2006). With regard to the organization of workers, post-1870 socialist trade unions in Germany
left the so-called artisanal period behind, transformed into organizations based
to a great extent on skilled factory workers and became mass organizations. To
mention only two figures: in 1892 about 215,000 workers were organized in
socialist trade unions, by 1913 the number had jumped to 2.5 million workers
(Schneider 1989: 495). However, in the years around 1900 trade unions also had
to face the boundaries of their influence.

If we look at Erfurt it becomes obvious how workplace experiences and traditions shaped the trade union orientation of workers and the lasting effects this had. To illustrate, in 1895 only 7 per cent of all male and female tailors in Erfurt were organized in trade unions. Even more striking is the example of Erfurt's horticulture sector. In this agricultural-oriented industry which, in the peak season, gave work to thousands of people, trade union representation came about only in 1904, and then too only forty-five skilled gardeners were organized. In the printing sector, however, the situation was totally different: in 1895, 14 per cent of all printers were already organized in unions.

These differences in union representation across professions remained over the following years. By 1907, while 13.7 per cent of all male and female tailors were organized into unions, in the printing industry the proportion of unionized printers in Erfurt had reached 40 per cent. The union of gardeners, established three years earlier (in 1904), on the other hand, had been able to bind only 5 per cent of all employed gardeners by 1907. The clothing and footwear industries showed marked differences with regard to workers organizing themselves into unions: in 1895, 8.2 per cent of shoe workers were organized into the shoemakers' union, placing them nearly at par with the tailors' organization. Within twelve years, however, nearly every second shoe worker was a union member, as compared to only one in every seven workers in tailoring.

A discussion of the production processes and working conditions that led to these different outcomes in different industries is beyond the scope of this essay. Instead, we explore both the structural obstacles to and advantages for possibilities of contact and communication in the working environment. For instance, a major obstacle to the organization of unions in the tailoring and clothing industries lay in the number of workers who were precariously self-employed and/or working from home. Parallels to problems of trade unions nowadays with regard to telecommuting, fake self-employment and individualized working conditions become apparent. Because of the fragmented nature of the workplace it was possible and easy for female and male workers to keep away from organizational and unionist efforts. They could go their individual ways and adapt their work to the requirements of the market economy. In 1888, at a tailors' conference in Erfurt, a speaker deplored the fact that Erfurt's tailors kept their wage level private: 'Nobody knows what the other earns' (Minutes of the Tailors Conference 1888). Obviously, this hampered the ability to organize. Further, many tailors did not see the need to overcome the problem of isolated workplaces. This job-related poverty of social contacts (due to working from home and the putting-out system that was in place in Erfurt during the forty-seven years of the German empire) proved to be a severe structural obstacle for the expansion of trade unions in Erfurt's clothing industry.

Two further structural barriers to the organization of workers were mobility or physical shifting of and the skilled–unskilled divide, both of which would have to be overcome in order to stimulate contacts and establish solidarity and companionship. Mobility of labour could erode links with and relations within unions. Shifting members stayed for only a short period in the town around a core of permanent members and the local organization. The leadership and members of local unions had to assume that at nearly every assembly they would meet new colleagues. For example, between 1886 and 1890, the members of Erfurt's tailors' trade union grew from twenty-seven to seventy-five. But in 1890 only eight of the original members from 1886 were still in the union. The fluctuations in membership could be even more dramatic during on strikes and changes in business cycles. For instance, in 1908 the local organization of woodworkers registered 328 new members, but in the same year the strength of the union dwindled from 408 to 370 members because many workers left Erfurt due to a failed strike and a degraded labour market. Thus the duration of membership varied considerably in different unions (see Table 1). In 1907, nearly half the members of Erfurt's shoemakers' union had spent less than two years in the union, while the union of printers demonstrated much more continuity. This was true not only with regard to 'short-term' members but also for 'veterans'. More than 25 per cent had been members of the printers' union for more than ten years, compared to 9 per cent among shoemakers.

This difference between stable and fluctuating membership had consequences within associations and unions too. The stable group worked in more secur positions and was more integrated in local society than the fluctuating members; members of the stable group were also older. For example, in 1890 the average age of new members in Erfurt's tailors' union was twenty-four, while the average age of the 'veterans' was thirty-four. In the long run, these differences led to different generational experiences among workers.

Divisions between skilled and unskilled workers also had adverse influences on trade unions. In Erfurt, both these factors – fluctuation and the skilled–unskilled barrier – can be observed with regard to workers in large firms in the horticulture industry. Even skilled gardeners did not stay much longer than six months in one firm (see Table 2). In addition, the biggest firms needed up to a thousand non-skilled workers during the busy season. Personnel for these limited-

TABLE 1 *Membership duration in Erfurt's Shoemakers' and Printers' unions, 1907*

	Shoemakers		Printers	
Membership duration	Number	Per cent	Number	Per cent
Less than a year	198	24.8	30	15.0
1–2 years	183	22.9	24	12.0
2–5 years	210	26.3	53	26.5
5–10 years	133	16.7	38	19.0
10–15 years	42	5.3	29	14.5
15–20 years	21	2.6	14	7.0
More than 20 years	11	1.4	12	6.0
Total	798	100.0	200	100.0

Sources: Jahresbericht Gewerkschaftskartell/Arbeitersekretariat 1907: 32; *Gedenkschrift* 1908: Mitgliederverzeichnis (own calculations).

TABLE 2 *Occupation duration of members of the Gardeners' union in Erfurt and Germany, 1904 and 1910*

	Months			Years					Total
	Up to 3	3–6	7–12	Up to 1½	Up to 2	Up to 5	Up to 10	More than 10	
Erfurt 1904	2	22	13	3	4	2	1	0	47
Germany 1904	247	650	249	109	48	83	22	19	1.427
Erfurt 1910	8	3	4	2	0	5	1	0	23
Germany 1910	440	319	225	73	41	63	13	3	1.177

Sources: Jansson 1905; Holzapfel 1911.

duration jobs were drawn from two sources: (i) people living in and around Erfurt (especially women and teenagers who were thus able to earn an additional income in the months from March to September); (ii) migrant workers from the Polish-speaking territory of Prussia on their way to work in the Ruhr Valley who stopped in Erfurt to take up jobs in the horticulture industry. In 1907 the Social Democratic newspaper *Tribüne* reported in an article that horticultural farms 'very often [displayed] frictions between the numerous representatives of different nationalities'. The fact that these 'guest workers' lived in collective accommodation contributed to further segmentation in the horticulture work force.

Virulent antagonism thus developed on the basis of area (rural and urban), age and gender, which was not conducive to unity in the workplace. As a consequence, gardeners who were local residents separated themselves from unskilled, female, teenage and transmigratory casual workers in exclusive, locally rooted gardener associations. In contrast to the socialist trade unions, they were oriented towards compromise and consensus, and negotiated their working conditions and wages in close cooperation with their employers. In the statutes of the 'Flora' association the members undertook not to criticize the 'domestic and commercial affairs of the horticulture firms' (*Tribüne* 1907). Deep divisions between skilled and unskilled workers, and between professional gardeners and casual workers, as well as a lack of communication and contact among the unskilled casual workers, were decisive factors in the failure of trade union organizations in the horticulture sector of the economy.

The workers of the state gun factory faced an obstacle of another kind. In this modern organized factory, established in Erfurt since the late 1860s and wholly dependent on national armament orders, every form of trade union activism was forbidden (see, in general, van der Linden 2008: 239ff). Since the production of rifles was done in teamwork, skilled permanent workers and semi-skilled temporary staff worked together in close cooperation. The teamwork facilitated proximity at the workplace; communication between workers was disrupted, however, because work processes had to be performed on separately positioned machines, which were noisy, in the factory hall. Another obstacle to communication lay in the different occupational background and experience of semi-skilled workers employed only during the peak season of the armaments business cycle (Gothsche 1904: fo. [11 f.]). Since the offered wages were very high, the state enterprise was able to hire a large number of workers. For example, according to the Annual Report of the Chamber of Commerce, 1890 saw a boom in gun production when many shoemakers switched to working at the gun factory, so much so that the local shoe enterprises complained about a shortage of workers. Without doubt it was possible for these men to find occupational pride in their new work not only because it was well paid, but also because it was in the national interest and the guns they produced were a symbol of power and masculinity. With their entry into the gun factory, however, skilled workers and craftsmen broke from their occupational and organizational traditions. They were also aware that only a very small minority would get a chance to become a part of the permanent work force. What they probably saw as a benefit in gun production was the opportunity to earn a lot of money in a short period. Consequently, they voluntarily subordinated themselves to the regime of the enterprise and abstained from union activism. Therefore, the anti-union policy that was predominant in all Prussian state enterprises and which remained the main hindrance for trade union formation proved very successful in the gun factory, which remained a workplace without trade unions until the First World War.

Finally, differences between female and male workers constituted another structural obstacle that led to communication blockades and hampered the development of trade unions. Since, in this case, shopfloor factors as well as factors from outside the factory came together, I shall return to this aspect later.

There were also some structural factors that were on impetus to the organization of workers, on the other hand. For instance, the big shoemaking factories, with up to a thousand workers and a centralized production process, had stable organizational cores in place from the 1880s. Face-to-face communication at the shopfloor level also took place due to the efforts of individual party and union members. Thus the Annual Report of the Workers' Secretariat and Trade Unions Association for 1910 (*Jahresbericht für 1910*) was enthusiastic about the development of Erfurt's shoemaker union in 1910: 'It was a lust to live! Because in this year not only did we advance, but we also took a great leap forward.' Another impetus occurred in an unexpected manner. According to a newspaper report, the staff in the biggest shoe factory of Erfurt had been 'insulted in an unprecedented manner'. What exactly had happened, unfortunately, is not known; but the incident rallied the workers and through several meetings at the factory, the union won new members. This spontaneous mobilization was strengthened by a structural strategy: a strike. The strike, initiated by an elite work force responsible for cutting leather, spread and turned out to be successful, attracting hundreds of new members to the union. All in all, in 1910, Erfurt's shoemakers' union organized two public meetings, twenty-two member conventions and fifty-seven factory meetings attended by nearly 10,000 male and female shoe workers. According to the Annual Report of the Workers' Secretariat and Trade Unions Association (ibid.), the number of members of the shoemakers' union rose from 945 to 2,204 within a year in 1909–10. The success of the strike in 1910 and some successful smaller strikes in the following years had a pull effect, and in 1913 its membership touched 3,000. This meant an organizational rate of more than 50 per cent in Erfurt's shoe industry. Thus organizational traditions, successful strikes and companies with centralized production processes opened up opportunities for communication and social contacts, and formed the basis for this impressive success.

Trade Unions and Strikes

The correlation between trade union movements and strikes has often been emphasized in historical research: 'Experiences of strike make clear the necessity of permanent pressure-group policies and give the impulse for union building' (Schönhoven 1987: 30). On the other hand, Marcel van der Linden (2008: 225ff) has argued from a global historical perspective that contrary to the widely held opinion that strikes need a trade union, it is possible to organize strikes without unions. Therefore, it is worthwhile to enquire into the role of trade unions in the Erfurt strikes.

What we find is that unions were ambivalent in their attitude towards strikes. On the one hand, it was obvious that successful strikes brought in new members, and unions were the organizations best able to prepare for and conduct a strike. On the other hand, in most cases it needed strong unions to conduct a strike successfully. Therefore, unions were cautious in their use of the strike weapon and, to a certain degree, 'strike-preventing associations', too. For example, employers in Erfurt commended the unions because 'the education of the workers by the unions had at times positive effects' in labour relations (*Tribüne* 1914). Such strike-preventing politics were facilitated by the increasing power of mediation authorities such as the industrial court, called the *Gewerbegericht*, after 1890, which were increasingly accepted by the workers. The mediating role of the unions also sat well with the attitude of the local Social Democratic party. Paul Reißhaus, a leading figure in Erfurt's Social Democratic party and a member of the Reichstag since the late 1890s, said in a speech on 'strikes and social democracy', that 'it is an untrue assertion [that] social democracy calls out for strike. In fact one can prove the opposite: the party warned against the use of this double-edged weapon' (*Tribüne* 1897). This attitude stemmed from a tradition. In 1888, at the founding of the tailors' association, Reißhaus had mentioned that he would 'be definitely against strikes since they would be for the economy the same as war was for the commonwealth of people. . . . If enough colleagues would be enlightened enough, strikes would be unnecessary.' That the task of the labour movement, the party as well as the unions was not limited to strike prevention, does not need to be emphasized. It is evident from the numerous strikes organized by the trade unions (Table 3).

Since the basis index for Erfurt (six strikes in 1900) was much lower than for the whole German empire, the variation was much higher in Erfurt than in the *Reich*; but the trend was the same. As a final result one can attribute to strikes several elements connecting the workers. Strikes produced a 'dichotomous world

TABLE 3   *Number of strikes in Erfurt and in Germany, 1900–14 (based on index 1900=100)*

Jahr	1900	1901	1902	1903	1904	1905	1906	1907	1908	1909	1910	1911	1912	1913	1914
Reich	100	86	100	149	188	257	379	306	223	228	276	336	306	270	160
Erfurt	100	67	—	50	117	167	167	200	67	100	167	433	117	133	83

Sources: *Spezialinventar des Stadtarchiv Erfurts* 1966: S. 16; Reich: *Tenfelde/Volkmann (Hg.),*
Streik 1981: S. 287–313; *Grebing, Arbeiterbewegung* 1987: S. 195. There were 6
strikes in Erfurt in 1900 and up to 806 in Germany. In 1911, 26 strikes occurred in
Erfurt as opposed to 2,707 in Germany.

view' that differentiated between workers and employers. Tendencies of disso-
ciation among those standing outside and homogeneity among strikers were
strengthened by the experience of strikes. Through concrete action, strikes and
conflicts with employers, workers practised solidarity, learned to articulate their
interests and experienced a sense of community (Koller 2010: 66–92).

The basis of communication between ordinary members and functionar-
ies, but also between organized and non-organized workers, both deepened and
widened. Strikes were connected with a 'multiplication of experiences' (Lüdtke
1993: 58) and an obvious learning process. 'The insight of the necessity of organization became second nature to the workers', according to an article in the
Tribüne in July 1896. It noted that the workers and their organizations no longer
saw themselves as a 'weak-willed herd' in front of a superior enemy, but perceived 'moral success' in the fact that they were able to oppose the employers as
a 'purposeful labour organization'.

However, strike movements were by no means trouble-free, smoothly
functioning 'communication machines'. There must have been tremendous differences between workers who were willing to strike and those unwilling to strike.
Despite all the dynamism that strikes threw up, one has to consider that a great
number of workers could not be reached by the strikes. As Paul Reißhaus emphasized at a public meeting of shoemakers after their defeat in the big strike of
1891, 'One is convinced that the workers are not yet aware of the power they
have' (Police Report, 10 March 1891). He added that by the end of the strike,
'only a fraction of really energetic and true men remained'. For Reißhaus, therefore, it was now necessary to 'assemble the dispersed army again'. Further, the
more privileged single working groups, such as book printers, used the strike as
a weapon to gain limited demands for their own purpose, and excluded or even
disparaged (female) unskilled workers, the more voices were raised that saw in
such actions no comprehensive solidarity but only pure group egoism.

Finally, the break between organized and non-organized workers remained a difficult obstacle to overcome. For example, in Erfurt in January 1906,
union-organized bricklayers went on strike for a day refusing to work with non-
organized workers (Police Report 1906). The strikers returned to work only after
the non-organized workers left the workshop. At a meeting of Erfurt's shop stew-
ards, a speaker defined criteria that union members needed to meet as follows:
'Those workers who have made no sacrifice for the organization cannot be sup-

ported during an eventual strike with union funds. If this would be made clearer to the indifferent workers I am convinced that the organization would spread much more' (*Tribüne*, November 1896).

Therefore strikes on the whole remained simmering occasions that churned up the everyday work life of workers. Tendencies towards greater rationality, more success-oriented actions and class formation can be seen to be developing during this period if we look back with hindsight. However, viewed at the time they occurred, the strikes showed a broad variety of behaviour, and, in extreme cases, could lead to communication blockades and contact barriers between different groups of workers.

Communication Blockades and Contact Barriers: Women and Trade Unions

Women workers were not welcome in some trade unions, which were male bastions. To cite an example, the Erfurt book binders' union excluded women until 1891. In the case of Erfurt's tailors' union, there were only 57 women in 1907 compared to about 1,500 unorganized women working in the clothing and tailoring industry. Hence the organizational rate among female workers was about 4 per cent as compared to the rate of organized male workers in the tailors' union which stood at 17.6 per cent.

Multiple factors were responsible for these gender-based barriers. First, the ideal of the housewife responsible for the household and child care without doing wage labour was generally upheld (*Tribüne*, April 1913). A *Tribüne* journalist described the feelings of a married woman who had to go to work: 'She reflects how her wedlock developed in a totally other direction than she had imagined. Yes, if she could stay at home, dedicating herself to the children who require so much the love and care of her mother, then she would be satisfied' (*Tribüne*, October 1907).

Women at the workplace were often seen not as comrades but as rivals, and they were especially blamed as being responsible for wage-dumping. In surroundings associated with male honour and male behaviour – think of the previously mentioned 'true men' participating in strikes – the offers of the unions were neither sufficient, nor suitable for female workers. The male 'pub cultural character' of the unions was an additional factor that needs to be considered (Boll 1992: 419f; van der Linden 2008: 245f). The need and striving for equality of members, expressed from the founding period of the union with its endeavour for respectability, could only be achieved arduously.

The different degrees of success across men and women with regard to organization in trade unions show that contacts at the workplace were affected by gender bias. For instance, there were gender-based differences in where workers took their lunch (Table 4). While nearly 30 per cent of the shoe factory's male work force comprised married men who lived close to the factory and went home for lunch, and another quarter and more used the canteen, the overwhelming majority of female workers stayed on at the workplace. They either did not have time to go home and cook (no spouse would be waiting for them with a prepared

TABLE 4   *Male and female workers during lunch-break at the Lingel Shoe Factory in 1911*

	Male		Female		Underaged	
	Number	%	Number	%	Number	%
Eating at home	279	28.7	32	6.2	22	11.4
Eating outside the factory	70	7.2	15	2.9	36	1.7
Eating in the canteen	265	27.3	36	7.0	85	44.0
Eating at the workplace	358	36.8	431	83.9	50	25.9
Total	972	100.0	514	100.0	193	100.0

Source: *ThSTA Gotha, Gewerbeaufsichtsamt Erfurt* (Labour Inspectorate), Nr. 228.

meal) or they did not want to spend money in the canteen. However, this also meant that these female shoe workers could easily be reached for the above-mentioned factory meetings of 1910. But since these meetings were meant for male workers too, they could not take place during the lunch hour when most of them were at home. The workers were thus obviously divided along gender lines.

Therefore, we have to assume gender-specific communication relations between the workers. It is not surprising that the *Tribüne* (June 1905) appealed to women suggesting that they should agitate to join trade unions: 'a woman's nature [*die Eigenart des Weibes*] is finally understood only by a woman' (also see Canning 1992: 736–68). Trade unions could bridge the gender gap only if they were able to integrate the women's perspective of the working world in their contact and communication strategies. This was the case among Erfurt's female shoe workers in the years before the First World War. Female workers made up a large percentage of the work force and were highly integrated into the working process at different levels of qualifications and skills. The male-dominated unions had to accept this; they knew that these women had to be integrated into the funtioning of trade unions. By raising demands not only for higher wages, but also for improvements in washing facilities and action against cases of sexual assault on young female workers, for example, trade unions were able to inte-grate female-specific interests and needs into their agenda (*Tribüne*, July 1910). These factors, combined with successful strike strategies, made unions attractive for women too. Between 1911 and 1913, the number of female shoe workers who were union members rose from 654 to 797; the proportion of women in the shoe workers' union which had commenced at 34.6 per cent in 1911, rose to 39 per cent in 1912, before falling marginally to 37.5 per cent in 1913. Considering that in 1907 about 1,200 women were working in shoe production, we can assume that after 1910 at least half of all women workers were members of the shoemak-ers' union (*Statistics of the German Empire 1907*: 110).

Contacts beyond the Workplace: Trade Unions as Civil Society Actors

Trade unions offered possibilities of participation to formerly excluded people, with their meetings, conferences, festivals and parties. Members got the opportunity to interact with a larger public, to exchange opinions, to discuss with comrades, to find agreement with other colleagues or employers, or support them in conflicts. From this point of view, meetings of trade unionists after work were not just social gatherings, but places to practise democratic interaction.

Rights of democratic participation were acquired and practised in the association meetings. A process of clarification about organizational, programmatic and life/world issues took place in the associations. The public sphere of the association with its often hour-long debates laid the foundation for internal democratic norms. Furthermore, this internal democracy was carried outside the associations to public meetings and was demonstrated there to the public at large. The people's assembly 'embodied the institutional realization of the claim to direct democracy' (Welskopp 2000: 230–54, 291–300; Welskopp 2010: 55–71). At the same time, trade unions and their meetings served as elementary schools for party and union officials where organizational and rhetoric skills could be learnt – an indispensable precondition for voluntary and professional work within trade unions. Although the working class was disadvantaged with regard to the use of time, money and education – resources central for civil society involvement – a large share of workers could be won for a common cause. These unequal dimensions of resources did not prevent civil society behaviour because the labour movement and trade unions offered a perspective. Self-discipline was a fundamental requirement for this involvement at the individual level; the hope of a little individual advancement along with the labour movement surely also played a part.

In addition, trade unions were a decisive part of the social and moral milieu (Lepsius 1973: 56–80; Rohe 1992) of the Social Democratic Party of Germany, participating in rallies, election campaigns and demonstrations. Despite all the ideological and practical differences between trade unionists and party leaders, they were dependent on each other (van der Linden 2008: 253). Without mobilizing trade union members the Social Democrats would have no chance to win elections; without political support from the party the unions would have less scope in their societal tasks for members. The relationship between trade unions and the party remained strong because both organizations had a common interest: to ensure open access to society for the working classes as free and equal citizens. Furthermore, there were also spatial and personal networks in the urban surroundings. For example, in the northern part of Erfurt, at the turn of the last century, a skilled working-class elite lived in newly-built housing estates and shared not only a relatively privileged housing situation, but also met in pubs, at party and union meets, and knew each other as members of consumer cooperatives. These informal networks strengthened the formal relationship at the shopfloor level. As a result, the Social Democratic Party gained up to 80 per cent of the votes in these quarters in the Reichstag elections (Schmidt 2005: 325). On the flip side, this milieu could easily close ranks against workers not belonging to these social groups (unskilled workers, workers distanced from socialist unions and parties). Thus social networks could also lead to social control.

Finally, trade unionists also played an important part in the public-administrative life of Erfurt, especially after 1900: in industrial courts (*Gewerbe-gericht*), in the local job centre and in the local health insurance fund (*Ortskranken-kasse*). Here, skills acquired in the public sphere of the organization were trans-formed into means of political influence. In these institutions trade unions not only defended the interests of their members, they assumed responsibility for the municipality and society as a whole. Within this trend of political engagement of members of the Social Democratic Party, a new dimension emerged: political work attained the status of a salaried profession and gainful employment.

As a whole, trade unions were part of a system of communication and contacts that exceeded mere representation of labour interests. They enabled members to act as citizens (*citoyen/nne*), and union members (and workers in general) were perceived by non-working class groups as rightful citizens within society. In the Wilhelmine authoritarian state, where working classes were expel-led by middle classes from social participation and excluded by state authorities from access to fundamental rights, trade unions created paths for constructive political work and helped workers to gain respectability and acceptance in socie-ty. These civil society effects have to be emphasized since they are important counter-arguments to the critique that emerged after 1900, that unions tended toward 'over-bureaucratization' and were degenerating into a gathering of 'big-wigs or *verbonzung*' (Michels 1989: 141ff).

Conclusion: History of Trade Unions as Micro History or Global History?

A single town, its economic sectors, firms and workers with different dimensions of contacts and communication, pivotal for the organizational suc-cess or failure of trade unions, have been presented in this essay. A clear ranking cannot be made as to which of these social contacts and communication possi-bilities were most decisive for the success of the unions. It was more the inter-relation and linkage between these different factors that opened up possibilities for trade union action. Even highly cooperative working processes at the shopfloor level, such as those in the gun production factories, could not become relevant for union formation processes because an authoritarian management regime blocked such tendencies. On the other side, the situation in the shoe factories illustrates that a combination of individual commitment, liberal management policy and communication-oriented situations in working processes as well as in everyday life, opened up the potential for mobilization on the shopfloor. The available and fought-for communication possibilities at that level became the anchor of trade union work. Further, the chain of the anchor could be strength-ened by communication sites outside the workplace, for example, in pubs and in the neighbourhood. In these spaces, trade unions not only defended and repre-sented the interests of the workers, but also encouraged and facilitated the par-ticipation of people excluded so far, thereby making an important contribution to the modernization and democratization of society.

This essay also examines the exclusion mechanisms that were involved in these processes, related to gender and different skill levels. Categories of social contact and communication concentrated at the local level highlight these differences and ambivalences within trade union organizations. In addition, what becomes clear is that work, if perceived as a 'commodity' to gain respect, respectability and establish well-being beyond mere subsistence, is a central resource for stable organizational structures. Organized workers wanted to transform and change working conditions and labour relations; they did not feel 'the desire to escape' the factory building and their status as workers. They spoke with Albert O. Hirschman, using the 'voice' and not the 'exit' option. (The 'desire to escape' among South African miners has been described by Patrick Harries [1994: 222] and Hirschman [1970]).

These interpretations are based on a local approach. Another approach is a globally oriented trade union history, which Marcel van der Linden takes in his book, *Workers of the World* (2008). It is an approach strongly connected with models, types and clear-cut definitions, in order to make comparisons possible. The problem with this kind of presentation is that numerous contextual factors are inadequately considered. On the other hand, van der Linden opens up new perspectives on the successful representation of the interests of workers employed in the world beyond the European and North American regions, when he emphasizes the existence of collective action and structures besides those of trade unions.

Finally, it is still difficult to view modes of transfer and engagement in the local actions of workers and their organizations in the nineteenth century. What can be more easily described and analysed is the path towards an organization like the Socialist International Movement that was already being defined in the 1860s. However, the Erfurt example shows that shoe workers and gun workers did not dwell much, if at all, upon the global economy, although in both cases the workers were working on machines built in North America.

A first step, therefore, should be to examine, from a comparative global perspective, the differences and similarities in work and work processes, and the results and influences of these factors on the life, actions and organizations of workers. Forms of self-help, solidarity, mutual agreements, strikes and protests, but also forms of resignation, deadening, isolation and self-interest, can become visible in different cultural and historical contexts. Building structures of contact and communication within the work force of an enterprise or on the shopfloor to defend one's interests and to be respected as an independent human being are factors that can be found across national borders. The same is of course true for the boundaries of building contacts and communication (see Sinha 2009: 280–94, 281, for differences between skilled and unskilled workers). They are, so to speak, 'shared experiences' in different cultures and societies (Eckert 2010: 173). They are not simply anthropological constants of an exploited work force, but are induced by societal and cultural contexts, and the structure of working conditions, working processes and labour relations. For example, we can see similar rhetorical means in different cultural contexts, of preventing ill-considered 'clashes' between workers and employers. This was to a great extent due to tactical considerations in the Erfurt case, based upon the idea of mutuality between labour and capital and non-violence in the discourse of Mahatma Gandhi and some Indian trade union leaders (Sinha 2009: 281; see also the above-mentioned appraisal of Erfurt's employers that unions had a positive effect on the work force). Here local studies make a contribution to global labour history and can indeed be a starting point for global perspectives. However, they have to be linked and analysed carefully and sensitively – and with the awareness that totally different contexts could prevail. (See, for example, the discussion on the influence of epidemic diseases on the work force in Bombay by Kidambi in van der Linden and Mohapatra 2009: 106–27, especially 115ff). This could be the silver bullet of global labour history.

References

Blyton, Paul, Edmund Heery, Nicolas Bacon and Jack Fiorito, eds. (2008), *The Sage Handbook of Industrial Relations*, Sage, Los Angeles.

Boll, Friedhelm (1992), *Arbeitskämpfe und Gewerkschaften in Deutschland, England und Frankreich. Ihre Entwicklung vom 19. bis zum 20. Jahrhundert*, Dietz, Bonn.

Canning, Kathleen (1992), 'Gender and the Politics of Class Formation: Rethinking German labor history', *American Historical Review*, vol. 97, no. 3, June, pp. 736–68.

Conrad, Sebastian (2006), *Globalisierung und Nation im Deutschen Kaiserreich*, Beck, München.

Eckert, Andreas (2010), 'What is Global Labour History Good For?', in Jürgen Kocka, ed., *Work in a Modern Society: The German historical experience in comparative perspective*, Berghahn, New York/Oxford.

Edwards, Paul K., ed. (2003), *Industrial Relations: Theory and practice*, Blackwell, Malden, Mass.

Gedenkschrift zum 25jährigen Bestehen des Ortsvereins Erfurt des Verbandes der Deutschen Buchdrucker 1883–1908 (1908), Erfurt.

Gothsche, Hugo (1904), *Die Königlichen Gewehrfabriken*, Liebel, Berlin.

Grebing, Helga (1987), *Arbeiterbewegung: Sozialer Protest und kollektive Interessenvertretung bis 1914*, dtv, Munich.

Hardt, Michael and Antonio Negri (2000), *Empire*, Harvard University Press, Cambridge, Mass.

Harries, Patrick (1994), *Work, Culture, and Identity: Migrant laborers in Mozambique and South Africa, c. 1860–1910*, Witwatersand University Press, Johannesburg.

Hirschman, Albert O. (1970), *Exit, Voice, and Loyalty: Responses to decline in firms, organizations, and states*, Harvard University Press, Cambridge, Mass.

Holzapfel, Michael (1911), *Zur Lage der Gärtnerei-Arbeitnehmer in Deutschland: Nach statistischen Ermittlungen – aufgenommen im Jahre 1910 – des Allgemeinen Deutschen Gärtner-Vereins*, Berlin.

Jansson, Wilhelm (1905), *Zur Lage der arbeitnehmenden Gärtner in Deutschland: Auf Grund von Erhebungen des Allgemeinen Deutschen Gärtner-Vereins und unter Benutzung älteren Materials im Auftrage des Hauptvorstandes des A d. G. V.*, Berlin.

Jahresbericht für 1910: Arbeiter-Sekretariat und Gewerkschaftskartell (Annual Report for 1910: Workers' Secretariat and Trade Union) (1910), Erfurt.

Kidambi, Prashant (2009), 'Contestation and Conflict: Workers' resistance and the "labour problem" in the Bombay Cotton Mills, c. 1889–1919', in Marcel van der Linden and Prabhu P. Mohapatra, eds., *Labour Matters: Towards global histories*, Tulika Books, New Delhi.

Koller, Christian (2010), 'Es ist zum Heulen: Emotionshistorische Zugänge zur Kulturgeschichte des Streikens', *Geschichte und Gesellschaft*, vol. 36, no. 1, pp. 66–92.

Lepsius, M. Rainer (1973), 'Parteiensystem und Sozialstruktur: zum Problem der Demokratisierung der deutschen Gesellschaft', in Gerhard A. Ritter, ed., *Deutsche Parteien vor 1918*, Kiepenheuer & Witsch, Cologne.

Lüdtke, Alf (1993), *Eigen-Sinn: Fabrikalltag, Arbeitserfahrungen und Politik vom Kaiserreich bis in den Faschismus*, Ergebnisse-Verlag, Hamburg.

Michels, Robert ([1910] 1989), *Zur Soziologie des Parteiwesens in der modernen Demokratie: Untersuchung über die oligarchischen Tendenzen des Gruppenlebens*, 4th edition, Kröner, Stuttgart.

Minutes of tailors' conference at Erfurt (1888), 3/111, 5–7 August, Municipal Archive Erfurt (MAE).

Montgomery, David (1993), *Citizen Worker*, Cambridge University Press, Cambridge.

Police Report (1891), Thuringian State Archive, Gotha (ThSTA Gotha), Regierung zu Erfurt, Nr. 495 (Government of Erfurt).

——— (1906), 22 January, quoted in MAE 5/851–1, Bd. 3.

Reißhaus, Paul (1888), quoted in Police Report of tailors' conference at Erfurt, 5–7 August, MAE 3/111–5, fo. 181f.

Rohe, Karl (1992), *Wahlen und Wählertraditionen in Deutschland*, Suhrkamp, Frankfurt am Main.

Schmidt, Jürgen (2005), *Begrenzte Spielräume. Eine Beziehungsgeschichte von Arbeiterschaft und Bürgertum am Beispiel Erfurts 1870–1914*, Vandenhoek & Ruprecht, Göttingen.

Schneider, Michael (1989), *Kleine Geschichte der Gewerkschaften: Ihre Entwicklung in Deutschland von den Anfängen bis heute*, Dietz, Bonn.

Schönhoven, Klaus (1987), *Die deutschen Gewerkschaften*, Suhrkamp, Frankfurt am Main.

Schubert, Klaus and Martina Klein (2006), *Das Politiklexikon*, 4th edition, Dietz, Bonn.

Sen, Amartya (1999), *Development as Freedom*, Alfred A. Knopf, New York; Oxford University Press, London.

Sinha, Nitin (2009), 'Forms of Workers' Protest amidst Dilemmas of Contesting Mobilizations: The Jamalur strikes of 1919 and 1928', in Marcel van der Linden and Prabhu P. Mohapatra, eds., *Labour Matters: Towards global histories*, Tulika Books, New Delhi.

Spezialinventar des Stadtarchivs Erfurt (1966), Magistrat der Stadt, Erfurt.

Statistik des Deutschen Reiches (Statistics of the German Empire) (1907), Bd. 207.

Tenfelde, Klaus and Heinrich Volkmann, eds. (1981), *Streik: Zur Geschichte des Arbeitskampfes in Deutschland während der Industrialisierung*, Beck, Munich.

Torp, Cornelius (2005), *Die Herausforderung der Globalisierung: Wirtschaft und Politik in Deutschland 1860–1914*, Vandenhoeck & Ruprecht, Göttingen.

Tribüne (1896), Nr. 164, 17 July.

——— (1896) Nr. 262, 7 November.

——— (1897) Nr. 270, 19 November.

——— (1905) Nr. 142, Supplement, 21 June.

——— (1907) Nr. 249, Supplement, 24 October.

——— (1907) Nr. 273, 22, Supplement, November.

——— (1910) Nr. 169, Supplement, 22 July.

——— (1913) Nr. 98, Supplement, 27 April.

——— (1914), Nr. 100, April 30, *Gewerbeinspektor für den Regierungsbezirk Erfurt (1911)* (*Report of the Business Inspector for Erfurt district*, quoted according to Nr. 100, April).

van der Linden, Marcel (2008), *Workers of the World: Essays towards a global labour history*, Brill, Leiden.

van der Linden, Marcel and Prabhu P. Mohapatra (eds) (2009), *Labour Matters: Towards global histories*, Tulika Books, New Delhi.

Welskopp, Thomas (2000), *Das Banner der Bruderlichkeit: Die deutsche Sozialdemokratie vom Vormarz bis zum Sozialistengesetz*, Dietz, Bonn.

——— (2010), 'The Vision(s) of Work in the Nineteenth Century German Labour Movement', in Jürgen Kocka, ed., *Work in a Modern Society: The German historical experience in comparative perspective*, Berghahn, New York/Oxford.

The Inspection Générale du Travail and the Resolution of Labour Conflicts in French West Africa

Omar Gueye

The colonial administrative system was established in French West Africa in the early 1920s. At the time, African workers had little or no rights and were often involved in forced labour. An early attempt made by the colonial state to organize labour in French West Africa was through the decrees of 22 October 1925 and 29 March 1926, which sought to regulate 'indigenous work' in the colonies (ARS K133: 26). These led to a series of legislations on obligatory labour, women's labour and child labour.[1] Three factors, however, necessitated the creation of a body to look specifically into labour relations, and prevent or resolve labour conflicts: first, the advent of wage work and the labour market in French West Africa; second, the success of African workers in garnering support for their demands from political actors as well as the West African population at large, in the turmoil after World War II; and third, the problems arising from the employment of both European and 'indigenous' workers in Senegal. Consequently, the Inspection Générale du Travail came into being in Senegal through a decree issued on 20 January 1932. Following the Brazzaville conference in 1944, the Inspection du Travail was reorganized by the decrees of 1946 and 1952 which extended its jurisdiction to the entire French West Africa. This essay traces the history of the establishment of the Inspection du Travail, its role and the manner of its functioning.

The institution was led by an Inspector who came under the authority of the Governor General in Dakar, Senegal, and its powers were applicable to all colonies of French West Africa (ARS K147: 26).[2] Offices were established in each colony to look into labour questions. The Inspection du Travail functioned in two ways. On the one hand, it sought to find urgent and equitable solutions in situations of conflict that were paralysing the economy. Thus, for instance, Inspectors Masselot and Pelisson were instrumental in resolving the Senegalese general

---

[1] The key texts constituting the base of labour regulation were contained in the decree of 1925 and used repeatedly. Following the recommendations of the International Labour Office, laws on women and child labour were taken from these texts.

[2] This was a circular issued by Governor General Baker to the Lieutenant Governors of each colony. The administrator of the district of Dakar gave the order to create a Factory Inspectorate in each colony.

strike (1946) and the French West African railroad strike (1947–48), two of the largest labour movements in Africa then. On the other hand, the Inspection sought to prevent labour conflicts through consulting and counselling in instances of individual and collective disagreement. It proved successful in this objective, with strikes becoming relatively rare after the first few years of post-war disorder. Thus the Inspection du Travail became the essential mechanism for both regulating and controlling labour in French West Africa, and subsequently, in the post-colonial states.

The Legislation of March 1937

The establishment of the Inspection Générale du Travail preceded the recognition of trade union rights for French West Africans. Partial trade union rights were granted by the Popular Front regime through two decrees issued in March 1937: the Trade Unions and Trade Associations decree (ARS K4: 1; 11 March), and the Conciliation and Collective Agreements decree (20 March). These decrees permitted the creation of professional organizations, and established a conciliation and arbitration process with the goal of preventing individual and collective disagreements. The actions of trade unions, however, were limited by the colonial subtext: strikes were rare and industrial disputes were limited to a few sectors, in particular the railways.[3]

The role of the Inspection Générale du Travail was also limited at the time, due to the desire of the colonial administration to exercise control over the population in general and workers in particular. World War II and changes in the French empire, however, accelerated the process of regulation and enhanced the powers of the Inspection du Travail to fully intervene in the domain of work.

Reorganization of the Inspection du Travail

World War II led to a break in political development in general, and trade union evolution in particular. The Vichy regime passed a decree on 2 May 1939 which suspended political and trade union rights on grounds of requirements of war (ARS 2G41: 19, Dakar and Dépendances[4]) and organization of the 'nation in times of war'.

It was only in 1944, with the Conference of Brazzaville (31 January to 8 February), that new provisions for the organization of labour were created. The integral right to set up trade unions was granted by the decree of 7 August, and promulgated in French West Africa on 16 September 1944. The Inspection Générale du Travail was brought back into force by the decree of 17 August 1944 to overcome the weaknesses of labour legislation, and to create a framework of

---

[3] In September 1938, a strike by railwaymen at Thies ended in firing and bloodshed, accelerating the departure of the Popular Front regime from Senegal. See, for instance, Nicole (1985) and Birame (1972).

[4] Report on the operation of the various services of the district. In 1941 France was occupied by the German army and French African colonies were required to take part in the war efforts against Germany.

dialogue, conciliation and dispute resolution. These decrees put an end to the restrictions on trade union rights for unionists who could read and write French (de Benoist 1982). Two years later, the decrees of 8 April 1946 and 10 June 1946 once again laid out the objectives and terms of application of the Inspection Générale du Travail. The Brazzaville conference thus granted an important place to the labour question in the African colonies, whilst also ensuring reconstitution of the specialized body that was the Inspection du Travail within the Ministry for the Colonies and giving it more prerogatives than it formerly had.

These decisions were a corollary of changes engendered by the French Union replacing the French empire. The new colonial authority sought to redefine the relationship it had with the population in general and with workers in particular. This was necessitated by the psychological and geo-strategic changes which accompanied the war, especially the rising aspirations of the Africans (ibid.: 23). Indeed, political agitation in French West Africa added momentum to trade union agitations towards the end of the war, especially in 1946, 1947 and 1948 (ARS 2G45: 46, Dakar and Dépendances; Annual Report, Inspection Générale du Travail).

The Inspection Générale du Travail played a key role in solving post-war crises in French West Africa. The reinforcement of its powers proved important. Its mission was defined by the general decree of 13 October 1948, which in turn was based on the guidelines issued by the Grand Conseil de l'Afrique Occidentale in January 1948, and the above-mentioned ministerial directives of 1944 and 1946. These supplemented the provisions adopted in 1946 (ARS K357: 26, Inspection Générale du Travail, Note for the Minister, 8 July 1946) and the powers/jurisdiction of the Inspection were now extended to all local services across all territories of French West Africa.

It was thus a rejuvenated Inspection du Travail that was placed at the heart of the system of regulation, control and resolution of labour issues. The organization was aware of its importance, and defined the scope of its role and the ways in which it could intervene effectively to resolve labour conflicts. In the exercise of their mission of counsel and information, the Inspectors no longer had to limit themselves strictly to labour problems; the competencies of the Inspection Générale du Travail could be brought to bear on 'all the political and economic aspects of the great question raised by the strengthening of social peace' (ibid.). With such a broadly defined mission, Inspectors had liberty of action and conducting initiative for their investigations.

With the passing of the decree of 20 March 1937, individual contracts came to be concluded on the basis of regulations contained in collective bargaining agreements, and, in the absence of adequate legislation, these agreements came to govern the life of an employed person. According to a report of the first six-month period of the Inspection Générale du Travail, Dakar and Dépendances (ARS 2G37: 141):

This is a collective bargaining agreement on working conditions concluded on the one hand between the representatives from one or more trade unions or occupational classes of workers, and on the other hand between one or more organizations of employers or any other grouping of employers taken individually.

Collective bargaining agreements were regarded as the mode by which the Inspection du Travail would find solutions to conflicts. As reported by the Inspector General of French West Africa, Pierre Pélisson:

> The Inspection Générale du Travail, almost completely disarmed on the legislative and lawful level, was obviously brought to give a detailed attention to this way of regulating by equal negotiations between employers' organizations and workers.

Territorially these agreements were limited to French West Africa, to which the decree of 20 March 1937 applied, and sectorally they were confined to four professions: agricultural, forestry, industrial and commercial.

Conflicts of the Post-War Period

The Inspection Générale du Travail played an active role in the management of labour issues and the resolution of conflicts in 1946, 1947 and 1948. Two key players during this period were the Inspectors General Masselot and Pélisson.

Inspector General Masselot played a key role in resolving the Senegalese general strike of 1946 (see ARS K325, Inspector to the Governor General; Cooper 1996: 472; Guéye 1990: 124; Suret-Canale 1978: 82–122; de Benoist 1984: 21–28). The gravity of the strike compelled the Minister for the Colonies to call in Masselot, who was considered a 'specialist in industrial disputes'. His strategy consisted in negotiating separately with the strikers. He thus succeeded in breaking the unity of the workers and precipitated the negotiations that ended the crisis.

Inspector General Pélisson was called in to end the railway strike of 1947–48 in Dakar-Niger. His approach was based on conciliation and arbitration, as stipulated by the decrees of March 1937: 'the inspector must be called to contribute to the solution of any disagreement'. He succeeded in bringing together the delegation of workers led by Ibrahima Sarr and the railroad management represented by its Federal Director, Cunéo. He benefited a lot from the support of the High Commissioner, Paul-Bechard. (See ARS K457: 179; Sène 1987; Suret-Canale 1978: 82–122; de Benoist 1984: 21–28.)

The Inspection Générale du Travail thus followed the path of negotiation which led to agreements, which were essentially results of the deliberations of the committees for arbitration. With regard to the protocol on which the future of the workers depended, Inspector Baup was elected to intervene to supervise the agreements (ARS K458: 179, note on the application of the protocol on the resolution of conflict, and the creation of a free trade union for railway men, 1947–49). For the Inspection du Travail, it was a question of taking special care to ensure that the problems that caused the strike might not once again become causes for conflict.

The Inspection Générale du Travail also filled the vacuum caused by the absence of a Labour Code, a result of the law promulgated on 7 May 1946 that abolished the 'Code for Indigenous Workers'. With its withdrawal, the 'indigenous' worker, now a 'citizen', was effectively deprived of the only recourse available to him for redressal. Meanwhile, the abolition of forced labour in overseas territories by the law of 11 April 1946 unlocked a new future for labour regulation in the colonies (see Fall 1993). These factors led to the increasingly important role of the Inspection du Travail, assigned as it was with the tasks of preventing and regulating collective and individual conflicts (ARS 2G 48: 1, Inspection Générale du Travail to the Minister for the Colonies, 4 June 1949).

Inspection Générale du Travail: The Golden Age

The year 1948 saw the end of the greatest conflict of the post-war period in French West Africa, the strike of the railway men of Dakar-Niger. This strike was the culmination of a series of confrontations that began in 1945. There was an urgent need to enforce measures for a lasting peace. The Inspection Générale du Travail played a key role in resolving this dispute. In the absence of a Labour Code, its efforts were based on the provisions of the decrees of March 1937, in particular those relating to conciliation and arbitration (ibid.).

It also contributed to the conclusion of many collective agreements in various sectors (ibid.). The effort to give French West Africa an 'ensemble of collective agreements which constitutes a true subsidiary labour regulation while waiting for the code' began in 1946, and was accomplished in 1947–48 (ibid.). A significant number of collective agreements were concluded, 52 in 1948 alone, reflecting intense activity on the part of the Inspection du Travail. The number of agreements, however, varied widely according to the degree of evolution of economic activity and the complexity of the structure of the labour market in the

TABLE 1   *Collective agreements in French West Africa in 1948 (%)*

	Valid collective agreements in 1946	*Collective agreements reached in 1947*	*Collective agreements reached in 1948*
Total French West Africa	44	55	53
Senegal	24	37	26
Dahomey	–	–	4
Mauritania	1	5	–
Guinea	10	3	6
Sudan	3	5	9
Ivory Coast	7	4	4
Upper Volta	–	–	4
Niger	–	–	–

French colonies. Thus the highest number of agreements between 1946–48 were reached in Senegal, which was the most advanced territory in these respects: 86 out of 152, i.e. 56 per cent of the total number of agreements (Table 1). Thus 1948 was a golden age for the Inspection Générale du Travail.

Resolution and Prevention of Conflicts

The question of wages constituted the principal issue faced by the Inspection Générale du Travail. In order to bring workers and employers closer on this issue, it relied on collective agreements as well as Advisory and Joint Committees of Labour, which played a decisive role in determining the outcomes of disputes. The Inspection also actively worked on prevention of disputes. Not only did it work toward eliminating the causes of conflict, being familiar with the evolution of trade unions, their manpower, organization and concerns, it also encouraged a constant process of education and training. Even though its means and prerogatives were limited in the face of inherent contradictions and difficulties in the world of labour, it achieved remarkable results in the years 1948–52, the period during which a Labour Code was in the process of adoption.

Advisory Committees of Labour were instituted by the general decree of 5 July 1946 in each local Inspection Générale; in Senegal, the Committee was made official by the decree of 29 March 1947. Each Committee was led by an Inspector and contained equal numbers of representatives of employers and workers (ARS K357: 26, note for the Minister, 8 July 1946).[5] The creation of the Advisory Committees contributed to the application of labour regulations and also equipped the local Inspectors to fulfil their mission. They could be consulted on all questions relating to the organization of labour and the condition of workers.

The Inspection du Travail made a decisive contribution to the resolution of many individual and collective disagreements especially in the period before the voting in of the Labour Code. Since employers and workers did not have recourse to any other fast and inexpensive legal procedure to resolve their disagreements, it became quite natural for them to approach the offices of the Inspection Générale du Travail in order to reach a fair agreement (ARS 2G51: 24, pertaining to industrial disputes). This considerably increased the conciliation efforts undertaken by the Inspection du Travail from 1948 to 1952, many of which led to a resolution of conflicts, both individual and collective. Hence, except for the general strike of African railwaymen of 1947–48, there were no major labour strikes in French West Africa and almost all disagreements were concluded peacefully.

Individual Disagreements at Work

The Inspection Générale du Travail resolved disputes between employers and individual employees through the use of reconciliation procedures (ARS

---

[5] The decree noted: 'the Inspection du Travail can invite to take part in the work of the advisory committee whose debates are led by the inspector . . . an equal number representatives of the employers and representatives of the workers'.

2G48: 1, pertaining to work-related disagreements). The number of such disagreements resolved through reconciliation increased from 3,345 cases in 1948 to 15,154 in 1951, an increase of more than 453 per cent. This considerably reduced the number of cases transferred to the courts: 91 in 1948 and 196 in 1951. 'Written or verbal consultations' were added to the official reconciliation procedures undertaken by the Inspectors (10,600 in 1948), which helped to keep situations from escalating. The territory of Senegal accounted for more than 63 per cent of the total number of reconciliations in 1951 (up from 46 per cent in 1948). This fact is explained by the higher density of paid workers in this territory as compared to other parts of French West Africa.

The majority of the disagreements (78 per cent in 1948) arose from problems of wages, leave, compensation and breach of contract (ARS 2G48: 1, pertaining to labour disagreements). Among these, wages were the main source of conflict (42 per cent), reflecting the prevailing socio-economic stresses after the war.

Most of the cases that reached the courts concerned European workers; it can be imputed, therefore, that disagreements involving African workers were dealt with through reconciliation. Indeed:

> during the discussion of a disagreement between African worker and employer, the employee and the Inspector himself, are fatally in a position of inferiority . . . for lack of a friendly solution, there will no possible recourse for the employee, since he does not have pecuniary means necessary to bring and maintain a case in front of the court. (ARS 2G51: 24, pertaining to industrial disputes)

In the event of failure of a 'negotiated' solution brought about by the intervention of the Inspection du Travail, the situation could become frustrating for the Afri-

TABLE 2 *Individual disagreements, by mode of resolution*

Territories	Conflicts settled through reconciliation		Conflicts transferred to the legal courts	
	1948	*1951*	*1948*	*1951*
French West Africa	3,345	15,154	91	196
Senegal-Mauritania	1,541	9,553	1	15

Source: Inspection Générale du Travail reports, 1948 and 1952.

TABLE 3 *Causes of individual disagreements*

Wages	42%
Notices	13.5%
Paid leave	8.9%
Professional classification	7.8%
Breach of contract, severance pay	5.6%
Miscellaneous	2.2%

can worker and the Inspector, both of whom were deprived of other means of recourse. Thus, irrespective of the competence of the Inspection du Travail and the results of its actions, it was necessary to outline a proper framework for the resolution of labour conflicts, including the creation of other specialized agencies such as labour courts, and also to ensure simplification of the procedures.

Collective Conflicts

With the exception of the railwaymen's strike in 1947–48, there were no significant collective conflicts till 1952. This was essentially because the Inspectors found solutions very quickly and did not allow the functioning of the colonies to be disrupted, as had happened with the railwaymen's strike. This established fact showed the effectiveness of the Inspection Générale du Travail and its 'prevention is better than cure' attitude:

> The Inspection stuck in this field to follow very closely the evolution of the social climate in order to prevent as far as possible, the possible causes of open disagreements. When some broke out, it immediately intervened to hasten the solution of it. (ARS 2G48: 1, labour disagreements)

The intervention of the Inspection thus allowed reduction or resolution of conflicts and led to a fall in the number of collective disagreements after 1947.

The colony of Senegal-Mauritania was a centre of turbulence and agitation, and was where the Inspection du Travail was most active. This territory witnessed 77 collective conflicts in 1947, of which twelve were regulated by preventive conciliation, six led to strikes and one resulted in a lockout. The number of conflicts dropped to nineteen in 1948. Table 5 notes the reduction in the number of collective conflicts after 1948: only 43 such conflicts took place in 1951.

Like in the case of individual disagreements, the issue of wages was primarily responsible for collective disagreements as well, with at least two-thirds of all cases involving this factor as the cause of dispute. Evidently, wages were at the heart of the concerns of workers, and, therefore, of the Inspection du Travail. Nevertheless, wage-related collective disagreements affected some industries more than others. Thus, while 71 per cent of all collective disagreements in 1948 stemmed from the issue of salaries or perquisites, 44 per cent of these hit the industrial sector and 27 per cent were in the commercial sector.

Suspending work as a means of protest was a violation of the provisions of the decree of 20 March 1937 which related to reconciliation and arbitration. In fact spontaneous strikes, though they did not observe the normal procedure, were not of major importance since they did not affect more than one establishment. Because of their spontaneity, usually neither the employers nor the union representatives were informed in advance (ARS 2G51: 24, pertaining to industrial disputes). The Inspection du Travail did not pay great importance to them:

> The concerted suspensions of work decided by the personnel were generally brutal demonstrations of an external dissatisfaction, and the lockout itself

TABLE 4   *Collective disagreements in 1947–48 in French West Africa*[6]

Territories	Conflicts 1947	Conflicts 1948	Conciliation	Strikes (duration)	Lockout
Senegal	77	19	12	6 (3 days)	1
Mauritania	38	3	3	–	–
Guinea	6	13	13	–	–
Sudan	40	8	–	8 (6 days)	–
Ivory Coast	–	3	–	3 (6 days)	–
Upper Volta	3	9	6	3 (6 days)	
Dahomey-Niger					
Total	164	55	34	–	1

TABLE 5   *Collective disagreements in French West Africa in 1951*

Collective conflicts	43
Suspension of work	30 (29 strikes and 1 lockout)
Reconciliation	8
Arbitration	5

Source: ARS 2G51: 24, pertaining to industrial disputes.

TABLE 6   *Causes of collective disagreements in French West Africa in 1948*

Salaries or perquisites	71%
Breaches of contract, dismissal	13%
Application of collective agreements	5%
Repatriation, vacation	1%
Professional classification	3%
Various causes	7%

much more one act of externalization of the employer's bad mood, than the exercise of a means of pressure on his employees. It was thus preferable to try to reconcile the conflict as soon as possible and put an end to the strike quickly, rather than to take the route of sanctions (ibid.).

The Inspection du Travail thus always worked on the principle of prevention and reconciliation.

Strikes in Dakar: 25–31 January 1951

A series of strikes hit Dakar during 25–31 January 1951. These were distinguished by their wide-ranging nature and the resolve of the striking work-

[6] The table recapitulates the downward trend of the conflicts and the recourse to reconciliation described above. While 164 collective disagreements occurred in 1947, only 55 were recorded in 1948, of which 34 were regulated by preventive reconciliation (61 per cent). Twenty strikes and one lockout occurred with suspension of work, of which the longest lasted six days.

ers to confront the employers. On 23 January, the Secretary-General of the Confederated Trade Unions of Dakar, Abbas Guèye, presented to the management of each principal company of the city, 'a motion requesting the attribution of a premium of 15 per cent for all personnel, to allow them to face the rise in the cost of living while waiting for the fixing of the new wages.' If this demand was not met, a series of strikes of warning would begin at the times specified in the motion (ibid.).

Non-responsiveness of the companies to this demand of the trade unions led to the commencement of the strikes on 25 January, had been scheduled. The Advisory Committee of Labour met to discuss the minimum wage and the rate was fixed by a decree on 29 January. Immediately Abbas Guèye was informed that the demonstration organized under his leadership was illegal and that he was open to legal proceedings. The strikes ceased the following day, on 30 January (ibid.).

This series of strikes held lessons for the legality of strikes and the use of reconciliation procedures. In each case, the Inspectors mentioned the appropriateness of the lawful procedure of arbitration, drawing attention to the possible dangers 'of unwise actions'. Indeed, such actions were likely to lead to mass suspensions, and would have been difficult to end without loss of prestige for the leaders and the constituents.

The position of the Inspection Générale du Travail was reinforced by this call to wisdom, i.e. recourse to the arbitration and conciliation procedure. The Inspection used this procedure like an absolute weapon to avoid frustrations caused by conflicts. Thus all collective disagreements from 1949 to 1951 between employers and workers were invariably addressed by means of arbitration. Employers' federations, however, objected to the liberal use of arbitration in situations that to them appeared normal. This point of view was officially stated in a letter from the SCIMPEX to the Inspection Générale du Travail on 21 April 1950: 'We allow ourselves to draw your attention to this tendency to resort to arbitrations and to regard as collective conflicts, likely to be prejudicial with the law and order, the even unwise claims expressed by the trade unions or other groupings of workers' (ibid.).

The presence of employers led the administrative staff to adopt an indifferent stance towards workers. Had they been given cause to be afraid of the Inspection du Travail as well, it could have led to actions adverse to general interest, law and order. It was necessary to avoid such a situation. An attitude of precaution thus prevailed over all other considerations.

The use of arbitration and conciliation procedures by the Inspection Générale du Travail made a considerable contribution to the resolution of individual and collective disagreements, despite the objections raised by employers' federations. Conflicts with some of the mature trade union organizations were solved or at least diminished.

In a general sense, the political development of Africans was determined by and dependent on the awakening of workers to their role in economic and social development. This is why particular attention was paid to the employees' social conditions. The Inspection's general approach to the labour question was to focus on social relationships, especially relating to the material and moral well-being of workers. It played a key role in balancing socio-political issues by the resolution or prevention of disputes, despite limitations. The political awareness of Africans in general, and workers in particular, showed a progressive awakening which proved to be decisive for the future of the territories of French West Africa and the French Union.

Conclusion

Faced with so many important opportunities for conflict resolution and the socialization of work relationships, the Inspection Générale du Travail played an essential role as an institutional organization in the African work life cycle: initially because of the relevance of its responsibilities, then due to the importance of the sectors in which it intervened, and finally on account of the historical context in which it acted. Its considerable achievements preceded the benefits that followed the adoption of the Labour Code of 1952, which resulted in political visibility for workers as well as Africans at large.

From the evidence put forth in this essay, it becomes evident that going beyond an institution that was established with the objective of providing a 'technical' perspective for a work life cycle, the Inspection Générale du Travail essentially played the role of a peacemaker and an instrument of economic and socio-political regulation under colonial rule.

References

Ba, Alioune (1993), *L'évolution de la législation du travail au Sénégal: de la loi sur la journée de huit heures, (1991) à l'adoption du code du travail d'outre-mer (1952)*, Mémoire de maîtrise, UCAD, FLSH, Dakar.

Bernard-Duquenet, Nicole (1985), *Le Sénégal et le Front Populaire*, l'Harmattan, Paris.

Cooper, Frederick (1991), 'Le mouvement ouvrier et le nationalisme: La grève générale de 1946 et la grève des cheminots de 1947–1948', *Historiens–Géographes*, no. 2e semestre, pp. 32–42.

—— (1996), *Decolonization and African society: The labour question in French and British Africa*, Cambridge University Press, Cambridge.

—— (2004), *Décolonisation et travail en Afrique (Afrique britannique et Afrique francophone 1935–1960)*, Karthala, Paris.

Coquery-Vidrovitch, Catherine (1985), *Afrique Noire, Permanences et Ruptures*, Payot, Paris.

de Benoist, Joseph Roger (1982), *L'Afrique Occidentale Françaises de 1944 à 1960*, NEA, Dakar.

—— (1984), 'La bataille des cheminots', *Afrique Histoire*, no. 4, pp. 21–28.

Dewitte, Philippe (1981), 'La CGT et les syndicats d'AOF (1945–1957)', *Le mouvement social*.

Fall, Babacar (1993), *Le Travail Forcé en AOF 1900–1949*, Karthala, Paris.

Fall, Mar (1989), *L'Etat et la question syndicale*, l'Harmattan, Paris.

Guèye, Omar (1990), *La grève générale de 1946 au Sénégal*, Mémoire de maîtrise, UCAD, FLSH, Dakar.

—— (2000), *L'évolution du mouvement syndical au Sénégal de la veille de la deuxième guerre mondiale au vote du code du travail en 1952*, thèse de Doctorat, 3e cycle, UCAD, FLSH, Dakar.

Lakroum, Monique (1983), *Le travail inégal: paysans et salariés face à la crise des années trente*, l'Harmattan, Paris.

Lô, Magatte (1988), *Sénégal: Syndicalisme et participation responsable*, l'Harmattan, Paris.

Martens, Georges (1983), 'Révolution ou participation: syndicats et partis politiques au Sénégal', *le Mois en Afrique*, nos. 205–206, février–mars.

Naville, Pierre (1952), 'Notes sur le syndicalisme en Afrique Noire', in *Présence Africaine*, Seuil, Paris.

N'Dour, Birame (1991), 'Luttes labourieuses en "situation coloniale", cheminots du Dakar–Niger, 1919–1951', *Historiens–Géographes du Sénégal*, no. 6, 2e trimestre, pp. 43–53.

November, Andreas (1965), *L'évolution du mouvement syndical en AOF*, La Haye, Mouton, Paris.

Sarraut, Albert (1923), *La mise en valeur des colonies françaises*, Payot, Paris.

Sène, Mor (1987), *La grève des chemins de fer Dakar Niger: 1947–1948*, Mémoire de maîtrise, UCAD, FLSH, Dakar.

Suret-Canale, Jean (1971), *Afrique Noire: 1900–1945*, Editions Sociales, Paris.

—— (1978), 'La grève des cheminots Africains d'AOF (1947–1948)', *Cahiers d'histoire de l'institut Maurice THOREZ*, no. 28, pp. 82–122.

Thiam, Iba Der (1972), *La grève des cheminots de septembre 1938*, 2 vols, Mémoire de maîtrise, UCAD, FLSH, Dakar.

—— (1983), 'L'évolution politique et syndicale du Sénégal colonial de 1840 à 1936', Thèse de Doctorat d'Etat, Université Paris I Sorbonne.

Archives Nationales du Sénégal: Fonds AOF
Sous-série 2G: Rapports périodiques

2G33–8, *Rapport annuel de l'inspection du travail de l'AOF sur l'application de la réglementation du travail indigène*, 1933.

2G346151, *Rapport annuel sur le travail 'indigène'*, 7 juin 1934.

2G35–25, *Rapport annuel de l'inspection du travail sur l'emploi et la main-d'œuvre indigène*, 1935.

2G36–26, *Rapport annuel sur l'emploi et la main-d'œuvre indigène*, 1936.

2G37–141, *Rapport du premier semestre de l'inspection du travail de Dakar et Dépendances*, 1937.

2G39–28, *Rapport annuel de l'inspection du travail de la Circonscription de Dakar et Dépendances*, 1939.

2G39–29, *Rapport annuel sur le travail et la main-d'œuvre au Sénégal*, 1939.

2G40–136, *Rapport annuel sur le travail et la main-d'œuvre au Sénégal*, 1940.

2G41–19, *Rapport annuel sur le fonctionnement des différents services de la Circonscription de Dakar et Dépendances*, 1941.

2G43–22, *Rapport annuel de l'inspection du travail de Dakar et Dépendances*, 1943.

2G44–19, *Rapport annuel du Gouverneur des colonies Administrateur de la Circonscription de Dakar et Dépendances*, 1944.

2G44–26, *Rapport annuel de l'inspection du travail de Dakar et Dépendances*, 1944.

2G45–20, *Rapport annuel sur le travail et la main-d'oeuvre*, 1945.

2G46–3, *Rapport annuel de l'inspection générale du travail de l'AOF*, 1946.

2G47–3, *Rapport annuel de l'inspection générale du travail de l'AOF*, 1947.

2G48–1, *Rapport annuel de l'inspection générale du travail de l'AOF* 1948

2G50–60, *Rapport semestriel de l'inspection du travail*, 1950.

2G50–66, *Rapport annuel de l'inspection régionale du travail de Kaolack*, 1950.

2G51–67, *Rapport annuel de l'inspection territoriale du Sénégal et le Mauritanie*, 1951.

2G52–71, *Rapport annuel de l'inspection régionale du Sud Sénégal*, 1952.

2G52–160, *Rapport annuel de la Direction des Affaires Politiques*, 1952.

2G52–198, *Rapport de synthèse sur le mouvement syndical*, 1952.

2G53–108, *Rapport annuel sur l'activité des services*, 1953.

2G54–59, *Rapport annuel de l'inspection régionale du Sud Sénégal*, 1954.

2G56–53, *Rapport annuel de l'inspection territoriale du travail du Sénégal-Mauritanie*, 1956.

2G57–2, *Rapport annuel de l'inspection du travail et des lois sociales du Sénégal*, 1957.

2G57-36, *Rapport annuel de l'inspection du travail et des lois sociales du Sénégal*, 1957.

2G57-39, *Rapport annuel de l'inspection du travail et des lois sociales du Sénégal*, 1957.

2G58-14, *Rapport annuel de l'inspection du travail et des lois sociales du Sénégal*, 1958.

Sous-série 17G: Affaires politiques (1895–1920), Fonds ancien

17G130 (17), Conférence de Brazzaville, 1944.

Sous-série 18G: Affaires administratives en AOF

18G48 (17), Documents et Correspondances générales, 1948.

18G250 (160), Inspection générale des affaires administratives, 1948–1960.

18G167 (165), Inspection du travail et des lois sociales, 1958.

Série K: Travail, Main-d'œuvre et esclavage (1807–1958), Fonds AOF

K18 (1), Rapport sur les conflits du travail, sur les fonctionnaires et les syndicats, et sur les menaces de grève (1936–1938).

K21 (1), Textes organiques et principes: notes et rapports sur les projets de règlementant le travail et l'emploi de la main-d'œuvre indigène (1937–1940).

K22 (1), Inspection du travail: logement, bureau et personnel (1950).

K24 (1), Document sur la Conférence internationale du travail de Philadelphie, grève à Dakar et Dépendances, 1944.

K34 (1), Organisation des inspections générales du travail: logement, 1950.

K50 (2), Organisation et Fonctionnement de l'inspection du travail en AOF (1944–1950).

K82 (26), Préparation de la réglementation du travail 'indigène' libre et l'établissement du décret du 22 octobre 1925 (1924–1925).

K84 (26), Législation du travail indigène: étude des contrats (1922–1932).

K122 (26), Création de l'inspection du travail en AOF: Documentation et Principes applicables dans les territoires de la fédération (1931–1943).

K124 (26), Conseils d'arbitrage (1931–1944).

K133 (26), Refonte du décret du décret de 1925 sur la réglementation du travail indigène : observation portant sur l'ensemble (1932–1937).

K147 (26), Main-d'œuvre indigène: Documentation relative à la fourniture de pièces périodiques, Rapport des inspecteurs du travail, plan de campagne, tableaux, correspondances (1928–1944).

K217 (26), Problèmes de main-d'oeuvre, rapport de tournée du gouverneur-inspecteur du travail à travers l'AOF (1937).

K220 (26), Rapport de tournée des inspections du travail (1937–1940).

K229 (26), Conflits du travail au Sénégal (1937–1940).

K317 (26), Conférence de Brazzaville: Documentation générale (1944).

K378 526), Différends collectif entre la Régie des chemins de fer et son personnel africain (1947–1948).

K402 (132), Direction des Affaires politiques (inspection du travail): organisation de l'inspection du travail (1944).

K419 (144), Travail: organisation, grèves à Dakar et Dépendances, rapport annuel de l'inspection du travail (1948).

K430 (179), Inspection générale et territorial du travail: organisation et fonctionnement.

K431 (179), Relation de l'inspection du travail et les services du gouvernement général (1947–1952).